The Five Rules for Successful Stock Investing

Morningstar's Guide to Building Wealth and Winning in the Market

Pat Dorsey
Director of Stock Analysis

WILEY

John Wiley & Sons, Inc.

Published by John Wiley & Sons, Inc., Hoboken, New Jersey
Published simultaneously in Canada

For general information about our other products and services, please contact our Customer Care Department within the United States at 800-762-2974, outside the United States at 317-572-3993 or fax 317-572-4002.

Wiley also publishes its books in a variety of electronic formats. Some content that appears in print may not be available in electronic books. For more information about Wiley products, visit our web site at www.wiley.com.

Library of Congress Cataloging-in-Publication Data:

Dorsey, Pat.
    Five rules for successful stock investing : Morningstar's guide to building wealth and winning in the market / Pat Dorsey.
        p.   cm.
    ISBN 0-471-26965-4 (CLOTH)
    ISBN 0-471-68617-4 (PAPER)
    1. Investments.   2. Stocks.   I. Morningstar, Inc.   II. Title.
    HG4521.D646   2004
    332.63′22—dc22

                                        2003018287

Printed in the United States of America
10   9   8   7

Contents

Foreword

BECAUSE I'M THE founder of Morningstar, you might think I invest most of my personal assets in mutual funds. The truth is I own few mutual funds. Nearly all of my assets are in stocks. Although I love funds, I have an even greater passion for stocks. Funds are great for those who don't want to spend a lot of time doing research. But if you enjoy analyzing companies— and I think it's a tremendous amount of fun—you can do perfectly well investing in equities yourself.

My interest in equity analysis began in business school at the University of Chicago. There I learned about efficient markets and how collectively security analysts add little or no value. That did little to excite me about stock investing. Why, after all, spend time studying companies if a market basket of stocks will do just as well? After graduation, though, I stumbled across *The Money Masters* by John Train and read about Warren Buffett.

Now that was exciting. Buffett used an approach I could readily grasp and inspired me by showing how much fun and intellectually challenging investing could be. Moreover, Buffett's track record—and the record of others who shared his philosophy—was stellar. I went back and read all the Berkshire Hathaway annual reports. My life changed course as a result.

I went to work as a stock analyst at Harris Associates in Chicago. I chose Harris because I admired its value-oriented, Buffett-like approach, and I liked the people. It was a great job, and I worked with some terrific financial minds—Clyde MacGregor, Chuck McQuaid, Bill Nygren, Ralph Wanger, Sherwin Zuckerman, to name a few. They all practiced a rigorous, bottoms-up investment style that involved looking for companies selling at a discount to their true worth. I spent my days reading annual reports, talking to company managers, and learning from my peers. And I got paid to do it.

The idea for Morningstar came from trying to teach myself equity analysis. I called regularly to get the mutual fund reports from managers I admired—people such as Kurt Lindner (Lindner Funds), George Michaelis (Source Capital), Michael Price (Mutual Shares), Bill Ruane (Sequoia Fund), John Templeton (Templeton Funds), and Ralph Wanger (Acorn). I examined their holdings to see what stocks they were buying and tried to figure out why they were buying them.

One day, when I had all these shareholder reports scattered across my dining room table, I thought it would be useful if someone compiled all that valuable information into a book. The proverbial light bulb clicked. I started to research the mutual fund industry. I could see that it was growing nicely and that there were few sources to help investors make intelligent decisions about funds. Thus, Morningstar was born.

I left my stock analyst job at Harris, cleared out the living room of my apartment, bought several PCs, and got started. I wrote to all the funds to get their materials, entered everything into a database, and six months later a 400-page *Mutual Fund Sourcebook* was sitting on my desk. In 1984, this in-depth fund information was very hard to get—and certainly not available for $32.50. The *Sourcebook,* for example, provided complete portfolio holdings. It took five pages just to list the 800 stocks in Peter Lynch's Magellan Fund. I sold 700 copies of that first publication, and Morningstar was on its way.

By bringing a stock perspective to the mutual fund world, we began to define the Morningstar approach to fund investing. It's hard to believe now, but back then investors purchased mutual funds based on recent returns and not much else. Morningstar brought rigorous, fundamental analysis to the industry. We realized that by looking carefully at the stocks a fund owned, we could understand the manager's strategy more clearly. So we developed our equity expertise as a way of doing better fund analysis.

While Morningstar began by serving fund investors, over time, we broadened our mission to help all investors. And that meant stock investors, too. This wasn't soulless corporate expansion, but logical growth based on a passion for equity analysis. And the more we looked at information available for stock investors, the more we realized that we had something innovative, useful, and unique to offer. There was little new in equity research, and many existing products seemed dated and not particularly helpful. We thought we could do better.

Our approach to equity analysis builds on the Ben Graham and Warren Buffett school of investing. It would be hard to find two better mentors—and we're grateful and indebted to them for all that they have done for investors. You'll find some of their key lessons embedded in our advice—concepts such as *margin of safety* and *economic moats*. We add value by systemizing, broadening, and explaining their approach so you can do it yourself. The result is a robust framework that should serve you well in making your own investment decisions.

But we haven't cornered the market on advice. We've included a reading list, and I urge you to use it as a guide. There aren't many great books on investing, so you should be able to master most of them. If you aren't doing so now, I suggest you begin reading the major business magazines regularly— *Barron's, BusinessWeek, Forbes, Fortune,*—as well as *The Wall Street Journal* daily. You'd be surprised how many investors neglect to do these basic things. Among our own publications, you'll find Morningstar.com and *Morningstar StockInvestor,* our monthly newsletter, helpful. I also recommend all the Berkshire Hathaway annual reports and *Outstanding Investor Digest* for its lengthy interviews with leading money managers.

You need to read widely to build a "latticework of mental models," as Berkshire Hathaway's Charlie Munger says. By looking closely at many companies, you'll see common themes that drive their success or failure. And you'll begin to form models that you can apply to situations you want to analyze. Then you must ask some questions. How is the world changing? How will those changes affect this company's prospects? You can begin to see the challenge and the fun of investing.

The Five Rules for Successful Stock Investing: Morningstar's Guide to Building Wealth and Winning in the Market is the effort of Pat Dorsey, the head of equity research at Morningstar. Among his many talents, Pat can communicate in a clear and engaging way, and he has the rare ability to distill complex questions to a form so that the answer appears obvious. Pat works closely with Haywood Kelly, Morningstar's chief of securities analysis and editor-in-chief of Morningstar.com, and Catherine Gillis Odelbo, president of securities analysis and head of our retail business, to guide our equity effort. We're indebted to all three for what they've created at Morningstar and for defining the investment philosophy that is the framework for this book.

A common quality of successful investors is the steadfast ability to think independently. Don't be swayed by what the "experts" say—even us. Graham and Buffett often point out that if your reasoning is right, that's all you need to worry about. I hope you read this book with a questioning mind. I hope you challenge our thinking. Above all, I hope you learn guiding principles that will shape your personal investment philosophy. Although no one can guarantee success, if you apply the precepts in this book and think for yourself, you'll be well on your way.

JOE MANSUETO

Acknowledgments

ALTHOUGH ONLY ONE name appears on the cover, this book was very much a team effort. Erica Moor kept the project on track and ably orchestrated text, graphics, deadlines, and schedules to produce a finished manuscript, while Amy Arnott worked tirelessly to tighten the initial muddled prose into something worthy of publication. Both deserve a great deal of credit. Dave Pugh at John Wiley & Sons also contributed valuable edits and a fresh perspective on the material. Morningstar designer Jason Ackley transformed complicated concepts into lucid graphics, while analyst Sanjay Ayer collected the data that underpin the tables and charts.

I have the great fortune to work with a group of very talented and dedicated analysts, and a round of applause is due to the entire Equity Analyst team at Morningstar. They contributed the lion's share of this book's second half. This book could not have been written without their accumulated industry expertise. I'm also indebted to Mark Sellers for helping develop Morningstar's investment philosophy; and to Mike Porter, Jason Stipp, and Rich McCaffery for valuable editorial feedback. Mike also deserves credit for shouldering many of my duties while I completed the book. Special thanks go to Haywood Kelly for being not only the world's most patient boss, but a great editor, mentor, and friend. Thanks also to Catherine Odelbo, president of securities analysis and our retail business, for her ongoing support of this project and our equity research efforts at Morningstar, and to founder Joe Mansueto for having the vision to take a risk and build Morningstar. Joe's unwavering commitment to independence and objectivity sets the example for the whole firm.

On a more personal note, my late grandfather, E. V. Patrick, deserves credit for introducing me to investing at a relatively young age, while my parents, Herb and Carol, have given me enormous support throughout my career. None, however, are more deserving of gratitude than my wife Katherine, whose good humor and unflagging patience are my most valuable assets. This book could not have been written without her support.

P. D.

Introduction: Picking Great Stocks Is Tough

SUCCESSFUL INVESTING IS simple, but it's not easy.

One of the big myths of the bull market of the 1990s was that the stock market was essentially a savings account that returned 15 percent per year. You picked up a copy of *Fortune*, you watched a little CNBC, you opened an online account, and you were on the road to riches. Unfortunately, as many investors discovered when the bubble popped, things that look too good to be true usually are.

Picking individual stocks requires hard work, discipline, and an investment of time (as well as money). Expecting to make a large amount of money with only a little effort is like expecting to shoot a great round of golf the first time you pick up a set of clubs. There's no magic formula, and there's no guarantee of success.

That's the bad news. The good news is that the basic principles of successful stock-picking aren't difficult to understand, and the tools for finding great stocks are available to everyone at a very low cost—you don't need expensive software or high-priced advice to do well in the stock market. All you need are patience, an understanding of accounting and competitive strategy, and a healthy dose of skepticism. None of these is out of the average person's grasp.

The basic investment process is simple: Analyze the company and value the stock. If you avoid the mistake of confusing a great company with a great investment—and the two can be *very* different—you'll already be ahead of many of your investing peers. (Think of Cisco at 100 times earnings in 2000. It was a great company, but it was a terrible stock.)

Remember that buying a stock means becoming part owner in a business. By treating your stocks as businesses, you'll find yourself focusing more on the things that matter—such as free cash flow—and less on the things that don't—such as whether the stock went up or down on a given day.

Your goal as an investor should be to find wonderful businesses and purchase them at reasonable prices. Great companies create wealth, and as the value of the business grows, so should the stock price in time. In the short term, the market can be a capricious thing—wonderful businesses can sell at fire-sale prices, while money-losing ventures can be valued as if they had the rosiest of futures—but over the long haul, stock prices tend to track the value of the business.

It's the Business that Matters

In this book, I want to show you how to focus on a company's fundamental financial performance. Analyst upgrades and chart patterns may be fine tools for traders who treat Wall Street like a casino, but they're of little use to investors who truly want to build wealth in the stock market. You have to get your hands dirty and understand the businesses of the stocks you own if you hope to be a successful long-term investor.

When firms do well, so do their shares, and when business suffers, the stock will as well.

Wal-Mart, for example, hit a speed bump in the mid-1990s when its growth rate slowed down a bit—and its share price was essentially flat during the same period. On the other hand, Colgate-Palmolive posted great results during the late 1990s as it cut fat from its supply chain and launched an innovative toothpaste that stole market share—and the company's stock saw dramatic gains at the same time. The message is clear: Company fundamentals have a direct effect on share prices.

This principle applies only over a long time period—in the short term, stock prices can (and do) move around for a whole host of reasons that have nothing whatsoever to do with the underlying value of the company. We firmly advocate focusing on the long-term performance of businesses because the short-term price movement of a stock is completely unpredictable.

Think back to the Internet mania of the late 1990s. Wonderful (but boring) businesses such as insurance companies, banks, and real estate stocks traded at incredibly low valuations, even though the intrinsic worth of these businesses hadn't really changed. At the same time, companies that had not a prayer of turning a profit were being accorded billion-dollar valuations.

The Long-Term Approach

Given the proclivity of Mr. Market to plead temporary insanity at the drop of a hat, we strongly believe that it's not worth devoting any time to predicting its actions. We're not alone in this. After talking to literally thousands of money managers over the past 15 years or so, we've discovered that none of the truly exceptional managers spend any time at all thinking about what the market will do in the short term. Instead, they all focus on finding undervalued stocks that can be held for an extended time.

There are good reasons for this. Betting on short-term price movements means doing a large amount of trading, which drives up taxes and transaction costs. The tax on short-term capital gains can be almost double the rate of long-term capital gains, and constant trading means paying commissions more frequently. As we'll discuss in Chapter 1, costs such as these can be a huge drag on your portfolio, and minimizing them is the single most important thing you can do to enhance your long-term investment returns.

We've seen this borne out in long-term studies of mutual fund returns: Funds with higher turnover—ones that trade more—generally post lower results than their more deliberate peers, to the tune of about 1.5 percentage points per year over 10 years. This may not sound like much, but the difference between a 10 percent annual return and an 11.5 percent annual return on a $10,000 investment is almost $3,800 after 10 years. That's the price of impatience.[1]

Having the Courage of Your Convictions

Finally, successful stock-picking means having the courage to take a stance that's different from the crowd. There will always be conflicting opinions about the merits of any company, and it's often the companies with the most conflict surrounding them that make the best investments. Thus, as an investor, you have to be able to develop your own opinion about the value of a stock, and you should change that value only if the facts warrant doing so—not because you read a negative news article or because some pundit mouths off on TV. Investment success depends on personal discipline, not on whether the crowd agrees or disagrees with you.

Let's Get Started

My goal in this book is to show you how to think for yourself, ignore the day-to-day noise, and make profitable long-term investment decisions. Here's our road map.

First, you need to develop an investment philosophy, which I'll discuss in Chapter 1. Successful investing is built on five core principles:

1. Doing your homework
2. Finding companies with strong competitive advantages (or economic moats)
3. Having a margin of safety
4. Holding for the long term
5. Knowing when to sell

Building a solid stock portfolio should be centered on these five ideas; once you know them, you'll be ready to start learning how to look at companies.

Second, I'll take a step back and review what *not* to do—because avoiding mistakes is the most profitable strategy of all. In Chapter 2, I'll go over the

---

[1]Alice Lowenstein, "The Low-Turnover Advantage," *Morningstar Mutual Funds,* 30 (August 15, 1997): S1–S2.

most common mistakes that investors make. If you steer clear of these, you'll start out ahead of the pack.

In Chapter 3, I'll show you how to separate great companies from mediocre ones by analyzing competitive advantages, which we call *economic moats*. I'll explain how economic moats are what help great companies keep their top-tier status and why they're a big part of what separates long-run winners from flashes in the pan. Understanding the sources of a firm's economic moat is critical to thoroughly analyzing a company.

Chapters 4 through 7 show you how to analyze companies by reading their financial statements. First, I'll describe how financial statements work—what the line items mean and how the different statements fit together. Once you know how to read balance sheets and income statements, I'll show you a five-step process for putting all the numbers in context and finding out just how solid a company really is. I'll also show you how to evaluate management.

In Chapter 8, we'll look at how you can detect aggressive accounting, and I'll tell you what red flags to watch out for so you can minimize the odds of a big blowup in your portfolio.

In Chapters 9 and 10, I'll show you how to value stocks. You'll learn the underlying theory of investment value, when ratios such as price-to-earnings are (and aren't) useful, and how to figure out whether a stock is trading for more or less than its intrinsic value. The cheapest stock isn't always the best investment, and what looks expensive may actually be cheap when viewed from another angle.

Chapter 11 provides two case studies. I'll apply the tools presented in the previous chapters to two real-world companies, so you can see for yourself how the process of fundamental analysis works in practice.

In Chapter 12, I'll explain the 10-Minute Test, a quick-and-dirty checklist that can help you separate firms that are unlikely to be worth your time from the ones that deserve a thorough, in-depth examination.

In Chapters 13 through 26, I'll lean on Morningstar's team of equity analysts to give you tips for analyzing different sectors of the stock market. From semiconductors to drugs to banks, we'll tell you exactly what you need to know to analyze companies from every corner of the market. You'll learn what industry-specific characteristics separate the great firms from the also-rans, what industry jargon means, and which industries are more (and less) likely to offer fertile hunting ground for great investment ideas.

Finally, we'll wrap up with some recommended readings for those who want to learn more.

The structure of the book is the same as the basic investment process that we advocate: Develop a set of investing principles, understand the company's competitive environment, analyze the company, and value the stock. If you can follow this process while avoiding most big mistakes, you'll do just fine as an investor.

The Five Rules for Successful Stock Investing

IT ALWAYS AMAZES me how few investors—and sometimes, fund managers—can articulate their investment philosophy. Without an investing framework, a way of thinking about the world, you're going to have a very tough time doing well in the market.

I realized this some years ago while attending the annual meeting of Berkshire Hathaway, the firm run by billionaire superinvestor Warren Buffett. I overheard another attendee complain that he wouldn't be attending another Berkshire meeting because "Buffett says the same thing every year." To me, that's the whole point of having an investment philosophy and sticking to it. If you do your homework, stay patient, and insulate yourself from popular opinion, you're likely to do well. It's when you get frustrated, move outside your circle of competence, and start deviating from your personal investment philosophy that you're likely to get into trouble.

Here are the five rules that we recommend:

1. Do your homework.
2. Find economic moats.
3. Have a margin of safety.
4. Hold for the long haul.
5. Know when to sell.

Do Your Homework

This sounds obvious, but perhaps the most common mistake that investors make is failing to thoroughly investigate the stocks they purchase. Unless you know the business inside and out, you shouldn't buy the stock.

This means that you need to develop an understanding of accounting so that you can decide for yourself what kind of financial shape a company is in. For one thing, you're putting your own money at risk, so you should know what you're buying. More important, investing has many gray areas, so you can't just take someone else's word that a company is an attractive investment. You have to be able to decide for yourself because one person's hot growth stock is another's disaster waiting to happen. In Chapters 4 through 7, I'll show you what you need to know about accounting and how to boil the analysis process down to a manageable level.

Once you have the tools, you need to take time to put them to use. That means sitting down and reading the annual report cover to cover, checking out industry competitors, and going through past financial statements. This can be tough to do, especially if you're pressed for time, but taking the time to thoroughly investigate a company will help you avoid many poor investments.

Think of the time you spend on research as a cooling-off period. It's always tempting when you hear about a great investment idea to think you have to act now, before the stock starts moving—but discretion is almost always the better part of valor. After all, your research process might very well uncover facts that make the investment seem less attractive. But if it is a winner and if you're truly a long-term investor, missing out on the first couple of points of upside won't make a big difference in the overall performance of your portfolio, especially since the cooling-off period will probably lead you to avoid some investments that would have turned out poorly.

Find Economic Moats

What separates a bad company from a good one? Or a good company from a great one?

In large part, it's the size of the economic moat a company builds around itself. The term *economic moat* is used to describe a firm's competitive advantage—in the same way that a moat kept invaders of medieval castles at bay, an economic moat keeps competitors from attacking a firm's profits.

In any competitive economy, capital invariably seeks the areas of highest expected return. As a result, the most profitable firms find themselves beset by competitors, which is why profits for most companies have a strong tendency over time to *regress to the mean.* This means that most highly profitable companies tend to become less profitable as other firms compete with them.

Economic moats allow a relatively small number of companies to retain above-average levels of profitability for many years, and these companies are often the most superior long-term investments. Longer periods of excess profitability lead, on average, to better long-term stock performance.

Identifying economic moats is such a critical part of the investing process that we'll devote an entire chapter—Chapter 3—to learning how to analyze them. Here's a quick preview. The key to identifying wide economic moats can be found in the answer to a deceptively simple question: How does a company manage to keep competitors at bay and earn consistently fat profits? If you can answer this, you've found the source of the firm's economic moat.

Have a Margin of Safety

Finding great companies is only half of the investment process—the other half is assessing what the company is worth. You can't just go out and pay whatever the market is asking for the stock because the market might be demanding too high a price. And if the price you pay is too high, your investment returns will likely be disappointing.

The goal of any investor should be to buy stocks for less than they're really worth. Unfortunately, it's easy for estimates of a stock's value to be too optimistic—the future has a nasty way of turning out worse than expected. We can compensate for this all-too-human tendency by buying stocks only when they're trading for substantially less than our estimate of what they're worth. This difference between the market's price and our estimate of value is the margin of safety.

Take Coke, for example. There's no question that Coke had a solid competitive position in the late 1990s, and you can make a strong argument that it still does. But folks who paid 50 times earnings for Coke's shares have had a tough time seeing a decent return on their investment because they ignored a critical part of the stock-picking process: having a margin of safety. Not only was Coke's stock expensive, but even if you thought Coke was worth 50 times earnings, it didn't make sense to pay full price—after all, the assumptions that led you to think Coke was worth such a high price might have been too optimistic. Better to have incorporated a margin of safety by paying, for example, only 40 times earnings in case things went awry.

Always include a margin of safety into the price you're willing to pay for a stock. If you later realize you overestimated the company's prospects, you'll have a built-in cushion that will mitigate your investment losses. The size of your margin of safety should be larger for shakier firms with uncertain futures and smaller for solid firms with reasonably predictable earnings. For example, a 20 percent margin of safety would be appropriate for a stable firm such as Wal-Mart, but you'd want a substantially larger one for a firm such as Abercrombie & Fitch, which is driven by the whims of teen fashion.

Sticking to a valuation discipline is tough for many people because they're worried that if they don't buy today, they might miss the boat forever on the stock. That's certainly a possibility—but it's also a possibility that the company will hit a financial speed bump and send the shares tumbling. The future is an uncertain place, after all, and if you wait long enough, most stocks will sell at a decent discount to their fair value at one time or another. As for the few that just keep going straight up year after year—well, let's just say that *not making* money is a lot less painful than *losing* money you already have. For every Wal-Mart, there's a Woolworth's.

One simple way to get a feel for a stock's valuation is to look at its historical price/earnings ratio—a measure of how much you're paying for every dollar of the firm's earnings—over the past 10 years or more. (We have 10 years' worth of valuation data available free on Morningstar.com, and other research services have this information as well.) If a stock is currently selling at a price/earnings ratio of 30 and its range over the past 10 years has been between 15 and 33, you're obviously buying in at the high end of historical norms.

To justify paying today's price, you have to be plenty confident that the company's outlook is better today than it was over the past 10 years. Occasionally, this is the case, but most of the time when a company's valuation is significantly higher now than in the past, watch out. The market is probably overestimating growth prospects, and you'll likely be left with a stock that underperforms the market over the coming years.

We'll talk more about valuation in Chapters 9 and 10, so don't worry if you're still wondering how to value a stock. The key thing to remember for now is simply that if you don't use discipline and conservatism in figuring out the prices you're willing to pay for stocks, you'll regret it eventually. Valuation is a crucial part of the investment process.

Hold for the Long Haul

Never forget that buying a stock is a major purchase and should be treated like one. You wouldn't buy and sell your car, your refrigerator, or your DVD player 50 times a year. Investing should be a long-term commitment because short-term trading means that you're playing a loser's game. The costs really begin to add up—both the taxes and the brokerage costs—and create an almost insurmountable hurdle to good performance.

If you trade frequently, you'll rack up commissions and other expenses that, over time, could have compounded. Every $1 you spend on commissions today could have been turned into $5.60 if you had invested that dollar at 9 percent for 20 years. Spend $500 today and you could be giving up more than $2,800 20 years hence.

But that's just the beginning of the story because frequent trading also dramatically increases the taxes you pay. And whatever amount you pay in taxes each year is money that can't compound for you next year.

Let's look at two hypothetical investors to see what commissions, trading, and taxes can do to a portfolio. Long-Term Lucy is one of those old-fashioned fuddy-duddies who like to buy just a few stocks and hang on to them for a long time, and Trader Tim is a gunslinger who likes to get out of stocks as soon as he's made a few bucks (see Figure 1.1).

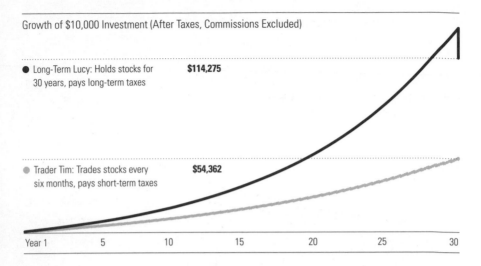

Growth of $10,000 Investment (After Taxes, Commissions Excluded)

● Long-Term Lucy: Holds stocks for   **$114,275**
   30 years, pays long-term taxes

● Trader Tim: Trades stocks every   **$54,362**
   six months, pays short-term taxes

| Year 1 | 5 | 10 | 15 | 20 | 25 | 30 |

Figure 1.1   Tim turns over his portfolio every six months, incurring a 35% short-term capital gains tax. Lucy's gains are taxed at only 15% thanks to her buy-and-hold strategy, and more of her money compounds over a longer time. *Source:* Morningstar, Inc.

Lucy invests $10,000 in five stocks for 30 years at a 9 percent rate of return and then sells the investment and pays long-term capital gains of 15 percent. Tim, meanwhile, invests the same amount of money at the same rate of return but trades the entire portfolio twice per year, paying 35 percent short-term capital gains taxes on his profits and reinvesting what's left. We'll give them both a break and not charge them any commissions for now.

After 30 years, Lucy has about $114,000, while Tim has less than half that amount—only about $54,000. As you can see, letting your money compound without paying Uncle Sam every year makes a huge difference, even ignoring brokerage fees.

And since holding a single stock for 30 years may not be realistic, let's consider what happens if Lucy sells her entire portfolio every five years, reinvesting the proceeds each time. In this case, she winds up with about $96,000—which is not much less than $114,000 and is still much more than Tim's $54,000 (see Figure 1.2).

These examples look at just the tax impact of frequent trading—things look even worse for the traders once we factor in commissions. If we assume that Tim and Lucy pay $15 per trade, Tim nets only about $31,000 after 30

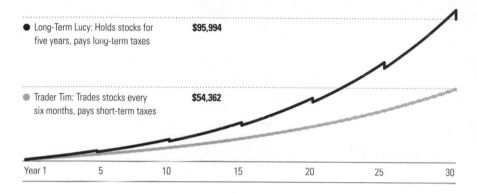

Growth of $10,000 Investment (After Taxes, Commissions Excluded)

● Long-Term Lucy: Holds stocks for   **$95,994**
five years, pays long-term taxes

● Trader Tim: Trades stocks every   **$54,362**
six months, pays short-term taxes

Year 1   5   10   15   20   25   30

Figure 1.2   Lucy decreases her holding period to 5 years from 30 years, but the benefit of lower taxes and a longer compounding period still nets her significantly more than Tim. *Source:* Morningstar, Inc.

years and Lucy nets $93,000, again assuming she holds her stocks for five years (see Figure 1.3).

The real-world costs of taxes and commissions can take a big bite out of your portfolio. Extending your average holding period from six months to five years yields about $62,000 in extra investment returns. Lucy gets a lavish reward for her patience, don't you think?

One final thought: To match Lucy's $93,000 portfolio value, Tim would need to generate returns of around 14 percent each year instead of 9 percent. That's the true cost of frequent trading in this example—about five percentage points per year. So, if you really think that churning your portfolio will get you five extra percentage points of performance each year, then trade away. If, like the rest of us, you were taught some humility by the bear market, be patient—it'll pay off.

Know When to Sell

Ideally, we'd all hold our investments forever, but the reality is that few companies are worth holding for decades at a stretch—and few investors are savvy enough to buy only those companies. Knowing when it's appropriate to bail

Growth of $10,000 Investment (After Taxes, Commissions Included)

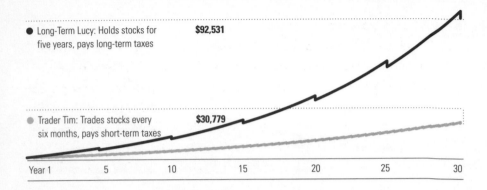

● Long-Term Lucy: Holds stocks for   **$92,531**
  five years, pays long-term taxes

● Trader Tim: Trades stocks every   **$30,779**
  six months, pays short-term taxes

Year 1   5   10   15   20   25   30

Figure 1.3   When commissions are taken into account, Tim's returns suffer far more than Lucy's. *Source:* Morningstar, Inc.

out of a stock is at least as important as knowing when to buy one, yet we often sell our winners too early and hang on to our losers for too long.

The key is to constantly monitor the *companies* you own, rather than the *stocks* you own. It's far better to spend some time keeping up on the news surrounding your companies and the industries in which they function than it is to look at the stock price 20 times a day.

Before I discuss when you *should* sell a stock, I ought to point out when you *shouldn't* sell.

The Stock Has Dropped

By themselves, share-price movements convey no useful information, especially because prices can move in all sorts of directions in the short term for completely unfathomable reasons. The long-run performance of stocks is largely based on the expected future cash flows of the companies attached to them—it has very little to do with what the stock did over the past week or month.

Always keep in mind that it doesn't matter what a stock has done since you bought it. There's nothing you can do to change the past, and the market cares not one whit whether you've made or lost money on the stock. Other market participants—the folks setting the price of the stock—are looking to the future, and that's exactly what you should do when you're deciding whether to sell a stock.

The Stock Has Skyrocketed

Again, it matters little how those stocks have done in the past—what's important is how you expect the company to do in the future. There's not *a priori* reason for stocks that are up substantially to drop, just as there's no reason for stocks that have tanked to "have to come back eventually." Most of us would be better investors if we could just block out all those graphs of past stock performance because they convey no useful information about the future.

So when should you sell? Run through these five questions whenever you think about selling a stock, and you'll be in good shape.

Did You Make a Mistake?

Did you miss something when you first evaluated the company? Perhaps you thought management would be able to pull off a turnaround, but the task turned out to be bigger than you (and they) thought. Or maybe you underestimated the strength of a company's competition or overestimated its ability to find new growth opportunities. No matter what the flub, it's rarely worth holding on to a stock that you bought for a reason that's no longer valid. If your initial analysis was wrong, cut your losses, take the tax break, and move on.

Have the Fundamentals Deteriorated?

After several years of success, that raging growth company you bought has started to slow down. Cash is piling up as the company has a tougher time finding profitable, new investment opportunities, and competition is eating away at the company's margins. Sounds like it's time to reassess the company's future prospects. If they're substantially worse than they used to be, it's time to sell.

Has the Stock Risen Too Far above Its Intrinsic Value?

Let's face it: The market sometimes wakes up in an awfully good mood and offers to pay you a price far in excess of what your investment is really worth.

There's no reason not to take advantage of other investors' good nature. Ask yourself how much more the market is willing to pay you than your estimate of the value of the stock and how likely it is that your estimate of its value could go up over time. You don't want to sell wonderful companies just because they get a little pricey—you'd incur capital gains and wouldn't be taking advantage of compounding. But even the greatest companies should be sold when their shares sell at egregious values.

Is There Something Better You Can Do with the Money?

As an investor, you should always be seeking to allocate your money to the assets that are likely to generate the highest return relative to their risk. There's no shame in selling a somewhat undervalued investment—even one on which you've lost money—to free up funds to buy a stock with better prospects.

I did this myself in early 2003 when I noticed that Home Depot was looking awfully cheap. The stock had been sliding for almost three years, and I thought it was worth about 50 percent more than the market price at the time. I didn't have much cash in my account, so I had to sell something if I wanted to buy Home Depot. After reviewing the stocks I owned, I sold some shares of Citigroup, even though they were trading for about 15 percent less than what I paid for them. Why? Because my initial assessment of Citigroup's value had been too optimistic, and I didn't think the shares were much of a bargain any more. So, I sold a fairly valued stock to purchase one that I thought was very undervalued.

What about my small loss on the Citi stock? That was water under the bridge and couldn't be changed. What mattered was that I had the opportunity to move funds from an investment with a very modest expected return to one with a fairly high expected return—and that was a solid reason to sell.

Do You Have Too Much Money in One Stock?

This is the best reason of all to sell because it means you did something right and picked a winner. The key is to not let greed get in the way of smart portfolio management. If an investment is more than 10 percent to 15 percent of your portfolio, it's time to think long and hard about trimming it down no matter how solid the company's prospects may be. (These percentages are a rough guide—you might be comfortable with more money in a single stock, or you might want to be more diversified.) It simply doesn't make sense to have too many of your eggs in one basket.

Investor's Checklist: The Five Rules for Successful Stock Investing

▶ Successful investing depends on personal discipline, not on whether the crowd agrees or disagrees with you. That's why it's crucial to have a solid, well-grounded investment philosophy.

▶ Don't buy a stock unless you understand the business inside and out. Taking the time to investigate a company before you buy the shares will help you avoid the biggest mistakes.

▶ Focus on companies with wide economic moats that can help them fend off competitors. If you can identify why a company keeps competitors at bay and consistently generates above-average profits, you've identified the source of its economic moat.

▶ Don't buy a stock without a margin of safety. Sticking to a strict valuation discipline will help you avoid blowups and improve your investment performance.

▶ The costs of frequent trading can be a huge drag on performance over time. Treat your stock buys like major purchases, and hold on to them for the long term.

▶ Know when to sell. Don't sell just because the price has gone up or down, but give it some serious thought if one of the following things has happened: You made a mistake buying it in the first place, the fundamentals have deteriorated, the stock has risen well above its intrinsic value, you can find better opportunities, or it takes up too much space in your portfolio.

Seven Mistakes to Avoid

IN A LOT of ways investing is like tennis. In tennis, having a killer serve and a great backhand will win you a lot of points, but any advantage that these skills confer can be quickly wiped out with a string of double faults or unforced errors. At the end of a five-set match, it's often the player with the least mistakes who wins. Just being able to consistently get the ball back over the net—no matter what your opponent throws at you—counts for a great deal.

Investing is pretty similar. Unless you know how to avoid the most common mistakes of investing, your portfolio's returns won't be anything to get excited about. You'll find that it takes many great stock picks to make up for just a few big errors.

So, before we dive into the company analysis process, I want to introduce you to seven easily avoidable mistakes that many investors frequently make. Resisting these temptations is the first step to reaching your financial goals:

1. Swinging for the fences
2. Believing that it's different this time
3. Falling in love with products
4. Panicking when the market is down

5. Trying to time the market
6. Ignoring valuation
7. Relying on earnings for the whole story

Swinging for the Fences

This ties back to the importance of buying great companies with strong economic moats. Loading up your portfolio with risky, all-or-nothing stocks—in other words, swinging for the fences on every pitch—is a sure route to investment disaster. For one thing, the insidious math of investing means that making up large losses is a very difficult proposition—a stock that drops 50 percent needs to double just to break even.

For another, finding the next Microsoft when it's still a tiny start-up is really, really difficult. You're much more likely to wind up with a company that fizzles than a truly world-changing company, because it's extremely difficult to discern which is which when the firm is just starting out.

In fact, small growth stocks are the worst-returning equity category over the long haul. Why? First, the numbers: According to Professor Kenneth French at Dartmouth,[1] small growth stocks have posted an average annual return of 9.3 percent since 1927, which is a good deal lower than the 10.7 percent return of the S&P 500 over the same time period. Lest you sneeze at that 1.4 percent difference between the two returns, let me point out that it has an absolutely enormous effect on long-run asset returns—over 30 years, a 9.3 percent return on $1,000 would yield about $14,000, but a 10.7 percent return would yield more than $21,000.

Moreover, many smaller firms never do anything but muddle along as small firms—assuming they don't go belly up, which many do. For example, between 1997 and 2002, 8 percent of the firms on the Nasdaq were delisted each year. That's about 2,200 firms whose shareholders likely suffered huge losses before the stocks were kicked off the Nasdaq.

Believing that It's Different This Time

The four most expensive words on Wall Street are "It's different this time." History does repeat itself, bubbles do burst, and not knowing market history is a major handicap.

---

[1] Kenneth French, http://mba.tuck.dartmouth.edu/pages/faculty/ken.french/data_library.html.

In the spring of 2000, for example, the financial press started writing that semiconductor stocks were no longer cyclical. That turned out to be pretty close to the top in chip shares. A year later, energy stocks were all the rage, and many analysts were projecting their earnings to grow at 20 percent for the next several years. Then, the economy slowed, hurting the demand for power, and new plants came online, driving up the supply. As a result, energy stocks such as Mirant and Calpine tanked 50 percent to 60 percent even before the Enron debacle sealed their fate.

The point here is very simple: You have to be a student of the market's history to understand its future. Any time you hear someone say, "It really is different this time," turn off the TV and go for a walk.

Falling in Love with Products

This is one of the easiest investment traps to fall into. Who wouldn't have thought that Palm was a great investment after buying a Palm Pilot when they were first introduced a few years ago? It seems entirely logical, but the reality is that great products do not necessarily translate into great profits. For example, Palm was the first company to invent a handheld organizer that was relatively easy to use and affordable, but consumer electronics is simply not an attractive business. Margins are thin, competition is intense, and it's very tough to make a consistent profit.

Although great products and innovative technologies do matter when you're assessing companies, neither matters nearly as much as economics. Sure, Palm made a great device that millions of people purchased, and the firm even acquired one of its chief competitors, but the industry's dismal economics still caught up with the firm in the end—Palm lost hundreds of millions of dollars in 2001 and 2002, and as of mid-2003, the firm's shares had plunged more than 98 percent since they started trading in early 2000.

When you look at a stock, ask yourself, "Is this an attractive business? Would I buy the whole company if I could?" If the answer is no, give the stock a pass—no matter how much you might like the firm's products.

Panicking When the Market Is Down

Stocks are generally more attractive when no one else wants to buy them, not when barbers are giving stock tips. It's very tempting to look for *validation*— or other people doing the same thing—when you're investing, but history has shown repeatedly that assets are cheap when everyone else is avoiding them. (In the words of Sir John Templeton, one of the first investors to systematically scour foreign markets for bargains, "The time of maximum pessimism is the best time to buy.")

The most famous example of this is a *BusinessWeek* cover story from the 1979 that asked the question, "The Death of Equities?" not long before the start of an 18-year bull market in stocks.[2] More recently, *Barron's* featured Warren Buffett on its cover in late 1999, asking, "What's Wrong, Warren?" and bemoaning Buffett's aversion to technology stocks.[3] Over the next three years, the Nasdaq tanked more than 60 percent, and Berkshire Hathaway shares appreciated 40 percent.

We also see empirical—rather than anecdotal—evidence of this in a study that Morningstar has conducted every year for the past several years, in which we look at the performance of unpopular funds. After looking at which fund categories attracted the most money and which categories experienced the strongest outflows, we found something very interesting. The asset classes that everyone hated outperformed the ones that everyone loved in all but one rolling three-year period over the past dozen years.

The difference can be striking. For example, investors who went where others feared to tread and bought the three least-popular fund categories at the beginning of 2000 would have had roughly flat investment returns over the subsequent three years. That was much better than the market's average annual loss of about 15 percent over the same time period and miles ahead of the performance of the popular fund categories, which declined an average of 26 percent per year during the three-year period.

Going against the grain takes courage, but that courage pays off. You'll do better as an investor if you think for yourself and seek out bargains in parts of the market that everyone else has forsaken, rather than buying the flavor of the month in the financial press.

---

[2] "For better or for worse, then, the U.S. economy probably has to regard the death of equities as near-permanent condition—reversible some day, but not soon" from "The Death of Equities," *BusinessWeek,* p. 54 (August 13, 1979).

[3] Andrew Bary, "What's Wrong, Warren? Berkshire's Down for the Year, but Don't Count It Out," *Barron's,* p. 16 (December 27, 1999).

Trying to Time the Market

Market timing is one of the all-time great myths of investing. There is no strategy that consistently tells you when to be in the market and when to be out of it, and anyone who says otherwise usually has a market-timing service to sell you.

Consider an interesting study in the February 2001 issue of *Financial Analysts Journal,* which looked at the difference between buy-and-hold and market-timing strategies from 1926 through 1999 using a very elegant method. The authors essentially mapped all of the possible market-timing variations between 1926 and 1999 with different switching frequencies.[4]

They assumed that for any given month, an investor could be either in T-bills or in stocks and then calculated the returns that would have resulted from all of the possible combinations of those switches. (For the curious, there are 2^{12}—or 4,096—possible combinations between two assets over 12 months.) Then they compared the results of a buy-and-hold strategy with all of the possible market-timing strategies to see what percentage of the timing combinations produced a return greater than simply buying and holding.

The answer? About one-third of the possible monthly market-timing combinations beat the buy-and-hold strategy. You may be thinking, "I have a 33 percent chance of beating the market if I try to time it. I'll take those odds!" But before you run out and subscribe to some timing service, consider three issues:

1. The results in the paper cited previously *overstate* the benefits of timing because they looked at each year as a discrete period—which means they ignore the benefits of compounding (as long as you assume that the market will generally rise over long periods of time, that is).
2. Stock market returns are highly skewed—that is, the bulk of the returns (positive and negative) from any given year comes from relatively few days in that year. This means that the risk of *not* being in the market is high for anyone looking to build wealth over a long period of time.

---

[4] Richard J. Bauer Jr. and Julie R. Dahlquist, "Market Timing and Roulette Wheels," *Financial Analysts Journal,* 57(1), pp. 28–40.

3. Not a single one of the thousands of funds Morningstar has tracked over the past two decades has been able to consistently time the market. Sure, some funds have made the occasional great call, but none have posted any kind of superior track record by jumping frequently in and out of the market based on the signals generated by a quantitative model.

That's pretty powerful evidence that market timing is not a viable strategy because running a mutual fund is a very profitable business—if someone had figured out a way to reliably time the market, you can bet your life they'd have started a fund to do so.

Ignoring Valuation

This one came back to haunt many people over the past few years. Although it's certainly possible that another investor will pay you 50 times earnings down the road for the company you just bought for 30 times earnings, that's a very risky bet to make. Sure, you could have made a ton of money in CMGI or Yahoo! during the Internet bubble, but only if you had gotten out in time. Can you honestly say to yourself that you would have?

The only reason you should *ever* buy a stock is that you think the business is worth more than it's selling for—not because you think a greater fool will pay more for the shares a few months down the road.

We'll talk a lot more about the concept of intrinsic value and valuation more in Chapters 9 and 10. For now, just remember that the best way to mitigate your investing risk is to pay careful attention to valuation. If the market's expectations are low, there's a much greater chance that the company you purchase will exceed them. Buying a stock on the expectation of *positive news flow* or *strong relative strength* is asking for trouble.

Relying on Earnings for the Whole Story

At the end of the day, cash flow is what matters, not earnings. For a host of reasons, accounting-based earnings per share can be made to say just about whatever a company's management wants them to, but cash flow is much harder to fiddle with. The statement of cash flows can yield a ton of insight into the true health of a business, and you can spot a lot of blowups before they happen by simply watching the trend of operating cash flow relative to earnings. One hint: If operating cash flows stagnate or shrink even as earnings grow, it's likely that something is rotten.

We'll talk more about the importance of analyzing cash flow in Chapters 5 and 6 and I'll show you how to use it to detect potential accounting problems in Chapter 8.

If you can avoid these common mistakes, you'll be miles ahead of the average investor. Now, let's move from what you shouldn't do to what you should do. In the next chapter, I'll show you how to separate great companies from average ones by analyzing economic moats.

Investor's Checklist: Seven Mistakes to Avoid

▸ Don't try to shoot for big gains by finding the next Microsoft. Instead, focus on finding solid companies with shares selling at low valuations.

▸ Understanding the market's history can help you avoid repeated pitfalls. If people try to convince you that "it really is different this time," ignore them.

▸ Don't fall into the all-too-frequent trap of assuming that a great product translates into a high-quality company. Before you get swept away by exciting new technology or a nifty product, make sure you've checked out the company's business model.

▸ Don't be afraid to use fear to your advantage. The best time to buy is when everyone else is running away from a given asset class.

▸ Attempting to time the market is a fool's game. There's ample evidence that the market can't be timed.

▸ The best way to reduce your investment risk is to pay careful attention to valuation. Don't make the mistake of hoping that other investors will keep paying higher prices, even if you're buying shares in a great company.

▸ Cash flow is the true measure of a company's financial performance, not reported earnings per share.

3

Economic Moats

INVESTORS OFTEN JUDGE companies by looking at which ones have increased profits the most and assuming the trend will persist in the future. But more often than not, the firms that look great in the rearview mirror wind up performing poorly in the future, simply because success attracts competition as surely as night follows day. And the bigger the profits, the stronger the competition. That's the basic nature of any (reasonably) free market—capital always seeks the areas of highest expected return. Therefore, most highly profitable firms tend to become less profitable over time as competitors chip away at their franchises.

You can see this every day in the headlines. Why do generic drug firms employ armies of lawyers to look for patent loopholes? Because large pharmaceutical firms such as Pfizer and Merck are immensely profitable, and even one successful patent challenge will pay off in spades. Why were venture capitalists throwing money at every start-up firm in the networking industry during the late 1990s? Because Cisco was growing at 40 percent per year with operating margins of 25 percent. If a firm is generating big profits, it will surely attract competition.

The concept of economic moats is crucial to the way Morningstar analyzes stocks because a moat is the characteristic that helps great-performing companies to stay that way.

We've learned much about the subject by studying investment great Warren Buffett and Harvard professor Michael Porter, who first set down many of the main principles for analyzing competitive strategy and economic moats.

To analyze a company's economic moat, follow these four steps:

1. Evaluate the firm's historical profitability. Has the firm been able to generate a solid return on its assets and on shareholders' equity? This is the true litmus test of whether a firm has built an economic moat around itself.
2. If the firm has solid returns on capital and consistent profitability, assess the sources of the firm's profits. Why is the company able to keep competitors at bay? What keeps competitors from stealing its profits?
3. Estimate how long a firm will be able to hold off competitors, which is the company's *competitive advantage period.* Some firms can fend off competitors for just a few years, and some firms may be able to do it for decades.
4. Analyze the industry's competitive structure. How do firms in this industry compete with one another? Is it an attractive industry with many profitable firms or a hypercompetitive one in which participants struggle just to stay afloat?

Analyzing economic moats is complicated because there are a nearly infinite number of solutions to the problem of consistently making a buck when your competition wants to take it away, but the process is interesting for precisely the same reason.

Evaluating Profitability

The first thing we need to do is look for hard evidence that a firm has an economic moat by examining its financial results. (Figuring out whether a company might have a moat in the *future* is much tougher, but we'll give it a shot at the end of this chapter.)

What we're looking for are firms that can earn profits in excess of their cost of capital—companies that can generate substantial cash relative to the amount of investments they make. One easy way to do this is by using the metrics in the following questions. Although none of these measures are perfect by themselves—they're really a series of shortcuts—they generally do a good job of identifying which firms have economic moats and which ones don't when they're used together. If you're confused by the financial measures in this section, don't worry: I'll discuss them in detail in the next few chapters.

Does the Firm Generate Free Cash Flow? If So, How Much?

First, look at free cash flow—which is simply cash flow from operations minus capital expenditures. (We'll go over free cash flow more in Chapter 5. For now, just go to a firm's statement of cash flows, which you can find in its quarterly and annual financial filings, look for the line item labeled "cash flow from operations," and subtract the line labeled "capital expenditures.") Firms that generate free cash flow essentially have money left over after reinvesting whatever they need to keep their businesses humming along. In a sense, free cash flow is money that could be extracted from the firm every year without damaging the core business.

Next, divide free cash flow by sales (or revenues), which tells you what proportion of each dollar in revenue the firm is able to convert into excess profits. If a firm's free cash flow as a percentage of sales is around 5 percent or better, you've found a cash machine—as of mid-2003, only one-half of the S&P 500 pass this test. Strong free cash flow is an excellent sign that a firm has an economic moat.

What Are the Firm's Net Margins?

Just as free cash flow measures excess profitability from one perspective, net margins look at profitability from another angle. Net margin is simply net income as a percentage of sales, and it tells you how much profit the firm generates per dollar of sales. (You can find sales and net income on a firm's income statement, which should also be in each of its regular financial filings.) In general, firms that can post net margins above 15 percent are doing something right.

What Are Returns on Equity?

Return on equity (ROE) is net income as a percentage of shareholders' equity, and it measures profits per dollar of the capital shareholders have invested in a company. Although ROE does have some flaws—which we discuss in

Chapter 6—it still works well as one tool for assessing overall profitability. As a rule of thumb, firms that are able to consistently post ROEs above 15 percent are generating solid returns on shareholders' money, which means they're likely to have economic moats. We'll go over ROE in more detail in Chapter 6.

What Are Returns on Assets?

Return on assets (ROA) is net income as a percentage of a firm's assets, and it measures how efficient a firm is at translating its assets into profits. Use 6 percent to 7 percent as a rough benchmark—if a firm is able to consistently post ROAs above these rates, it may have some competitive advantage over its peers.

When you're looking at all four of these metrics, look at more than just one year. A firm that has consistently cranked out solid ROEs, good free cash flow, and decent margins over a number of years is much more likely to truly have an economic moat than a firm with more erratic results. Consistency is important when evaluating companies, because it's the ability to keep competitors at bay for an extended period of time—not just for a year or two—that really makes a firm valuable. Five years is the absolute minimum time period for evaluation, and I'd strongly encourage you to go back 10 years if you can.

In addition, these benchmarks are rules of thumb, not hard-and-fast cutoffs. Comparing firms with industry averages is always a good idea, as is examining the trend in profitability metrics—are they getting higher or lower?

There's also a more sophisticated way of measuring a firm's profitability that involves calculating return on invested capital (ROIC), estimating a weighted average cost of capital (WACC), and then looking at the difference between the two. We'll talk more in Chapter 6, but don't worry if it seems too complicated for you. Using a combination of free cash flow, ROE, ROA, and net margins will steer you in the right direction.

Building an Economic Moat

Next, we need to determine why a firm has done such a great job of holding on to its profits and keeping the competition at arm's length. Although being in an attractive industry can certainly help, the strategy pursued at the company level is even more important. The mere fact that there are excellent companies in fundamentally unattractive industries (e.g., Southwest Airlines) tells us intuitively that this must be the case. Academic research suggests that a firm's strategy is roughly twice as important as a firm's industry when it's trying to build an economic moat.[1]

When you're examining the sources of a firm's economic moat, the key thing is to never stop asking, "Why?" Why aren't competitors stealing the firm's customers? Why can't a competitor charge a lower price for a similar product or service? Why do customers accept annual price increases?

When possible, look at the situation from the customer's perspective. What value does the product or service bring to the customer? How does it help them run their own business better? Why do they use one firm's product or service instead of a competitor's? If you can answer these questions, odds are good that you'll have found the source of the company's economic moat.

In general, there are five ways that an individual firm can build sustainable competitive advantage:

1. Creating *real product differentiation* through superior technology or features
2. Creating *perceived product differentiation* through a trusted brand or reputation
3. *Driving costs down* and offering a similar product or service at a lower price
4. *Locking in customers* by creating high switching costs
5. *Locking out competitors* by creating high barriers to entry or high barriers to success

Real Product Differentiation

This is certainly the most obvious type of economic moat—after all, wouldn't customers always pay more for a better product or service? Unfortunately, simply having better technology or more features is usually not a sustainable strategy because there are always competitors hoping to build a better mousetrap. And because having the best product or service usually means charging a premium price, firms pursuing this strategy often limit the size of their

---

[1] Anita McGahan and Michael E. Porter, "How Much Does Industry Matter, Really?" *Strategic Management Journal, 18,* p. 15 (1997).

potential market. Many customers will be satisfied with a slightly inferior product at a significantly lower price.

More important, it's just plain difficult to constantly stay one step ahead of competitors by adding features or improving a product, which is why few firms are able to use this strategy to create long-term excess profits. This is especially the case in many parts of the technology sector and in the consumer electronics industry—today's vendor of the latest and greatest server, storage system, or DVD player is likely not going to be tomorrow's leading player. Finally, constant innovation generally sucks up a large amount of capital in the form of research and development expenses, which can make a product-differentiation strategy very expensive.

Data-storage manufacturer EMC is a good example. In the mid-1990s, the firm had leapfrogged IBM in this fast-growing area of the technology sector and was winning new customers because its products had features that IBM's lacked. For several years, EMC raked in enormous profits by charging customers substantially higher prices than the competition for its technologically superior products. (In fact, EMC's prices were so high that customers nicknamed the firm "excess margin corporation.")

However, IBM and other competitors didn't give up. Eventually, IBM rolled out products that came pretty close to matching EMC's, and IBM priced them much lower in an effort to win customers back. As a result, IBM began regaining market share, and EMC's business suffered.

The lesson here is that although firms can occasionally generate enormous excess profits—and enormous stock returns—by staying one step ahead of the technological curve, these profits are usually short-lived. Unless you are familiar enough with the inner workings of an industry to know when a firm's products are being supplanted by better ones, be wary of firms that rely solely on innovation to sustain their competitive advantage.

Perceived Product Differentiation

Very often, however, a firm with consistently better products or services creates a brand for itself, and a strong brand can constitute a very wide economic moat. The wonderful thing about a brand is that as long as customers *perceive* your product or service as better than everyone else's, it makes relatively little difference whether it actually is different.

Tiffany is a fabulous example of the power of a brand to create excess economic returns. The simple fact that a piece of jewelry is packaged inside the famous little blue box allows Tiffany to charge a significant premium for its products. This example is fascinating because jewelry has so many objective standards—karats of gold, clarity of diamonds—that measure the quality of an individual piece. The fact that consumers will pay more for a virtually identical diamond ring from Tiffany than from a local jeweler is what defines a truly valuable brand: It increases a consumer's willingness to pay.

Thinking about brands and reputations in this way—whether consumers of a product or service are truly willing to pay more to buy the good from one firm instead of another—helps separate more valuable brands from less valuable ones. What matters is not the existence of the brand, but rather how the brand is used to create excess profits. In fact, brands aren't useful at all in some industries.

Think about companies such as Sony or Ford, both of which have well-known brands. But both firms have struggled to generate solid returns on capital over the past few years because they sell goods that are simply not very amenable to brand-driven price differentiation. Consumers are unlikely to pay much more for a Sony stereo relative to a product from Panasonic with similar features, and they're also unlikely to pay more for a Ford truck just because it has the Ford nameplate.

On the flip side, Abercrombie & Fitch has managed to convince legions of teenagers to pay $25 for a T-shirt just because it has "Abercrombie" on the front. How long this brand will remain strong is tough to predict, but there's no question that it's enabled Abercrombie to charge more for its products over the past several years. In fact, the durability of a brand is a critical component of any brand-based economic moat. Some brands—for example, Coke or Disney—last for generations, but some are much more fleeting.

When you're evaluating whether a strong brand really does create an economic moat, it's not enough to look at whether consumers trust the product or have an emotional connection to the brand. The brand has to justify the cost of creating it by actually making money for the firm, and sustaining a powerful brand usually requires a lot of expensive advertising. Therefore, unless the brand actually increases consumers' willingness to pay and those looser wallets translate into consistently positive returns on capital, the brand may not be worth as much as you'd thought.

Driving Costs Down

Offering a similar product or service at a lower cost can be an extremely powerful source of competitive advantage. It costs Southwest 25 percent less to fly one passenger one mile than the leanest of the major airlines, and it's that advantage that propelled the firm from a Texas upstart to a big-league player in 25 years. Low costs have fattened Dell's profit margins to such an extent that the firm has been able to expand its share of the PC market from around 6 percent in 1997 to more than 15 percent by year-end 2002—a big move in just six years.

Airlines and PCs are known as *commodity* industries, in which products are tough to differentiate. Low-cost strategies work especially well in these types of markets. Even in noncommodity markets, lower costs can bring large advantages as long as the cost advantage is sustainable and not temporary. However, it's not enough to just look at a firm's profit margins and say that such-and-such firm has lower costs than its competitors—you need to identify the sources of those cost savings, which can come in a variety of flavors.

In general, firms can create cost advantages by either inventing a better process or achieving a larger scale. Dell is the classic example of a firm with a process-based advantage. Building PCs only after they're ordered allows the firm to take advantage of the swift price erosion of PC components—parts don't sit in inventory losing value while the firm waits for orders to come in. Over time, Dell has continued to squeeze costs from its supply chain to the point where you could argue that Dell is no longer a technology firm, but rather a manufacturing one.

Process advantages can also be subtler. In the asset-management industry, you might think that Vanguard's size is what allows it to underprice its services—but there are other firms of comparable size with much higher fees. The key is that Vanguard is structured as a mutual organization that's collectively owned by fundholders, rather than a profit-maximizing corporation owned by shareholders. Because of this structure, Vanguard can plow back excess profits into cost-reducing activities, whereas traditionally structured asset management firms will either distribute excess profits to their managers in the form of fat bonuses or allow the cash to pile up on the balance sheet. In Vanguard's case, higher profits allow the firm to push costs down, which attracts more assets, which generates more profits, and so forth. This relatively unique structure means that it will likely be very difficult for any non-mutual asset-management firm to ever match Vanguard's low costs.

Scale advantages are often very difficult for competitors to match because they tend to build on themselves: The largest firms continue to drive down costs and prices, and smaller ones have an increasingly difficult time catching up. The most basic form of a scale advantage comes from simply leveraging fixed costs—in other words, spreading the cost of an asset such as a factory across an ever-larger sales base. Intel, for example, produces far more microprocessors in any given year than archrival AMD, which means its per-chip production cost is a great deal lower than AMD's.

Fixed costs don't have to be factories. For example, the trucks that make up the distribution network of package-delivery service UPS represent an enormous fixed cost that allows the firm to deliver to more locations at a lower cost than almost any other competitor. Although replicating a delivery network that serves only large metropolitan centers might not be too daunting a task for a potential competitor, replicating a network that can deliver to virtually any address in the United States would be another thing altogether. Because it costs UPS very little extra money to put an additional couple of packages on a truck that's already serving a particular delivery route, its profit on those extra couple of packages is high.

Locking In Customers

Customer lock-in, or creating high customer switching costs, is possibly the subtlest type of competitive advantage. Uncovering it requires a deep understanding of a firm's operations. Cost advantages, brands, and better products are all relatively easy to spot from the outside, but knowing exactly what makes it tough for a customer to switch from one firm to another can be difficult to find out. However, it can also be very powerful, which is why firms with high customer switching costs often have wide economic moats.

If you can make it difficult—in terms of either money or time—for a customer to switch to a competing product, you can charge your customers more and make more money—simple in theory, but difficult in practice.

Remember, a switching cost does not have to be monetary—in fact, it rarely is. Much more frequently, what deters customers from dropping a product or service in favor of a competing product or service is time. Often, learning how to use a product or service can require a significant investment of time, which means the benefits of a competing product have to be very large to induce a switch. A consumer might switch brands of tomato sauce because one tastes just a little better than the other, but a word-processing program would have to carry huge advantages over an incumbent program to induce a consumer to throw away the accumulated knowledge and spend time learning the new program.

Medical device firms such as Stryker and Zimmer are perfect examples of how firms can create high switching costs that help ensure customer retention. Both of these firms manufacture artificial joints such as hips and knees, and surgeons have to be trained on how to implant their products—a Stryker hip is different enough from a Zimmer hip that a surgeon can't just choose one or the other based on which is on sale that week. This training process is time-consuming for surgeons, which means surgeons tend to develop preferences for a particular company's products and stick with them. Therefore, Stryker, Zimmer, and their competitors tend to have relatively stable shares of the joint-replacement market—a firm would have to introduce a measurably better product to induce surgeons to incur the retraining costs needed to use the new product.

When you're looking for evidence of high customer switching costs, these questions should help:

- ▶ Does the firm's product require a significant amount of client training? If so, customers will be reluctant to switch and incur lost productivity during the training period.
- ▶ Is the firm's product or service tightly integrated into customers' businesses? Firms don't change vendors of mission-critical products often because the costs of a botched switch may far outweigh the benefits of using the new product or service.
- ▶ Is the firm's product or service an industry standard? Customers may feel pressure from their own clients—or their peers—to continue using a well-known and well-respected product or service.

► Is the benefit to be gained from switching small relative to the cost of switching? Bank customers, for example, often endure slightly higher fees because the lower fees they might get from moving to a competing bank are of less value than the potential hassle of moving their account.

► Does the firm tend to sign long-term contracts with clients? This is often a sign that the client does not want to frequently switch vendors.

Locking Out Competitors

Locking out competitors is the fifth strategy that firms can use to generate lasting competitive advantages. If done well, this can result in years of strong profits. If done *too* well, it can invite the scrutiny of the federal government on antitrust grounds—as Microsoft (and other firms) have discovered.

The most obvious way to lock out competitors is to acquire some kind of regulatory exclusivity, as many casinos do from state governments. Licenses and such are powerful deterrents to competitors but because governments make the rules, they can also change them without warning. U.S. state governments have been known to raise the tax rates on the casinos they license after the casino facilities are in place and generating profits. Although the casinos were still protected from competitors, state governments were able to tax away a larger portion of their excess profits than the casinos initially expected.

Patents fall into the regulatory category as well because a patent holder is legally protected from direct competition for a set period of time. And as large pharmaceutical companies have demonstrated, patents can lead to years of extremely high profit margins. But although patents may deter competition, they tend to attract litigation, which can severely hamper the patent-holder's ability to earn excess returns.

A great example is Pfizer, which holds patents on some of the top-selling drugs in the world. These patents allow the company to charge high prices for new drugs for years after they hit the market. Competition during the life of the patent is usually limited, so profits and cash flows are huge. That's one reason Pfizer's average return on equity over the past decade has been greater than 30 percent and its net profit margins are currently north of 25 percent (compared with around 6 percent for the average S&P 500 company). That's also why it's been a great stock to own over the long haul. In fact, many of the major pharmaceutical players have outperformed the market over the past 10 years because of the economic moats inherent in this industry.

However, although patents and licenses can do a great job of keeping competitors at bay and maintaining high profit margins, they can also be ephemeral. If you're investigating a firm whose economic moat depends solely on a single patent or other regulatory approval, don't forget to investigate the likelihood of that approval disappearing unexpectedly. This will likely involve a detailed reading of the legal proceedings section of the firm's 10-K filing. (You can find financial filings through most firms' Web sites, as well as directly from the SEC's Web site.)

A much more durable strategy for locking out competitors is to take advantage of the *network effect.* A strong network becomes more valuable as the number of users increases—much like a telephone network, which wouldn't be worth much if you could call only a dozen people, but which has immense value given the enormous number of users. Companies that have a network protecting their competitive positions often have very wide economic moats.

In general, markets tend to have strong network effects—the more buyers and sellers that transact in a particular market, the greater the value of that market to participants. As a publicly listed auction market, eBay is the purest example of this idea: The firm has held its own against much larger companies, and it seems unlikely that another competitor will emerge soon.

It should be easy to see why eBay has a near-monopoly in online auctions in most of the world. Because eBay was the first major firm to connect individual buyers and sellers over the Internet in an auction format, the number of buyers and sellers grew very quickly. As more rare baseball cards and vintage posters came up for auction on eBay, more buyers were attracted to the site to bid on those items. Those extra bidders attracted still more sellers— the sellers wanted to go where the buyers were, and the buyers wanted to go where the sellers were.

By the time competitors such as Yahoo! and Amazon.com tried to get into the auction game, it was too late. There were already too many bidders on eBay for sellers to want to switch to a new, smaller auction service—they'd probably get a lower price for their wares because there were fewer bidders on each item. Meanwhile, the bidders weren't interested in going anywhere either because eBay had by far the most items for sale. Thus, eBay gained critical mass and, today, a near-monopoly position in the online-auction market.

Another great example is money-transfer concern Western Union, which is owned by First Data. With more than 170,000 locations worldwide, odds are pretty good that Western Union can get your money wherever you need it to go, and the value of the firm's agent network only grows larger as it adds locations. The central characteristic of a classic network effect is a virtuous circle—more users attract more users.

How Long Will It Last?

Our next topic is assessing the longevity of an economic moat, so we know how long a firm is likely to keep its competitors at bay.

Think about an economic moat in two dimensions. There's depth—how much money the firm can make—and there's width—how long the firm can sustain above-average profits. Technology firms often have very deep but very narrow moats, so they're incredibly profitable for a relatively short period of time until a competitor builds a better product. A niche firm such as WD-40 is just the opposite. It's never going to make an enormous amount of money in any one year by selling cans of household lubricant, but it has such a solid franchise that its excess returns are likely to persist for quite some time.

Estimating how long a moat will last is tough stuff, but you need to at least give it some thought, even if you can't come up with a precise answer. Just being able to separate firms into three buckets—a few years, several years, and many years—is very useful.

In general, any competitive advantage based on technological superiority— real product differentiation—is likely to be fairly short. Successful software firms, for example, can generate huge excess returns because they have high profit margins and they don't need to spend much money on fixed costs such as machinery. However, the duration of those returns is typically very short because of the rapid pace of technological change. In other words, today's leader can quickly become tomorrow's loser because the barriers to entry are so low and the potential rewards so high.

Cost leadership, brands (perceived product differentiation), customer lock-ins, and competitor lockouts can each confer competitive advantage periods of varying lengths—there's no good rule of thumb, unfortunately. To give you some guidance in what separates a wide moat from a narrow moat and what kinds of companies have no moat at all, I've listed 27 well-known large-cap companies in Figures 3.1, 3.2, and 3.3 and included an explanation as to why each firm's moat is wide, narrow, or does not exist. Having these examples will, I hope, help you analyze economic moats when doing your own

Dell	Classic low-cost producer: lean operating structure and direct Internet-based sales allow the company to run circles around its rivals.
eBay	Network effect: The more buyers and sellers the network has, the more attractive it becomes to prospective users and the tougher it becomes for competitors to contend with.
PepsiCo	By far the market share leader in salty snacks and sports drinks, the diversified food company boasts a stable full of strong brands, innovative new products, and an impressive distribution network.
Comcast	Controls roughly one-third of cable households in the U.S. This gives it unparalleled leverage with content providers and equipment suppliers.
Intel	Chipmaker's dominant position gives it significant economies of scale. Brand name and patents are also significant intangible assets.
H&R Block	Dominates the U.S. tax preparation market. One in every seven tax returns filed is prepared by Block.
Wal-Mart	Largest retail company in the world is also the preeminent low-cost provider. The firm flexes its muscles with suppliers in negotiating prices and passes the savings down to consumers.
United Technologies	Operates in a selection of concentrated industries. Buyers of elevators, cooling systems, and helicopters don't switch brands often.
Adobe	High customer switching costs: graphic designers are trained early in their careers to use the company's software and can't do their job without it.
Paychex	Vast sales network provides access to new accounts and scale gives it a cost advantage. Plus, it has pricing power over its diverse and unorganized client base.

Figure 3.1 Some examples of companies with wide economic moats. *Source:* Morningstar, Inc.

Federal Express	Sure, it practically invented overnight delivery, but behind the scenes, FedEx is a cargo airline, and airline margins are thin.
Nokia	Although the Nokia brand is strong, cell phones are becoming commodities.
Kraft	Despite a portfolio of familiar consumer brands, there isn't much breathing space between Kraft and its competitors, which has made it difficult for the firm to exert any pricing power.
Waste Management	Network of 300 landfills creates a wide-moat disposal business, but lack of brand loyalty in its collection business—where customers flock to the lowest price—earns this company a narrow moat.
Disney	Owns some of the most valuable intellectual property in the world, but increasing competition and an absence of creativity have eroded some of the brand's appeal.
ExxonMobil	Enjoys enormous economies of scale, but still operates in a commodity industry.
Target	"Cheap chic" strategy has helped it carve out a moat and differentiate itself from Wal-Mart. However, Target's strategy depends partially on accurately guessing fashion trends, which is more difficult than merely being the low-cost provider of everyday items.
Best Buy	Dominates home-electronics and entertainment-software retailing, but operates in a very economically sensitive industry.
AOL Time Warner	Still has some great media properties, but bungled attempts at formulating a successful broadband strategy have left the AOL business vulnerable.
SBC Communications	Former monopoly over local phone service is facing competition from wireless carriers, cable companies, and long-distance firms that can buy access to its local network.

Figure 3.2   Some examples of companies with narrow economic moats. *Source:* Morningstar, Inc.

General Motors	Operates in deeply cyclical industry. Legacy costs and reputation for mediocre quality puts it at a competitive disadvantage relative to most peers.
Micron	Memory chips are essentially commodities, which leads to product price volatility and lots of competition.
Circuit City	Main competitor Best Buy has higher profit margins, better inventory turnover, and twice the per-store sales numbers.
Staples	A saturated industry, lack of product differentiation, and intense price sensitivity prevent this company from digging a moat.
Maytag	Low-cost Asian producers have forced the company to focus on the premium appliance market, where competition is fierce and product differentiation is difficult to achieve.
Delta	Not the low-cost provider and doesn't offer a differentiated product. In a commodity industry where competition revolves largely around price, its business model is unsustainable.

Figure 3.3   Some examples of companies with no economic moats. *Source:* Morningstar, Inc.

research. I've also included at the end of the book a list of all the companies Morningstar follows that we consider to have wide economic moats.

Industry Analysis

Our last step is to investigate the industry in which the firm operates. Let's face it: It's just plain easier to make money in some industries than it is in others. (Ask the CEO of any airline company.) Although the attractiveness of an industry doesn't tell the whole story—after all, Southwest Airlines has made plenty of money for shareholders—it's important to have a feel for the competitive landscape.

First, get a rough sense of the industry so you can classify it. Are sales for firms in the industry generally increasing or shrinking? Are firms consistently profitable or does the industry go through periodic cycles when most firms lose money? Is the industry dominated by a few large players, or is it full of firms that are roughly the same size? How profitable is the average firm—are operating margins fairly high (more than 25 percent) or fairly low (less than

15 percent)? (An *operating margin* is income from operations as a percentage of sales. I discuss such financial ratios in more detail in Chapter 6.)

You can answer some of these questions by looking at aggregate statistics—average growth rates, average margins, and so on. However, averages can't tell you everything, so be sure that you examine a number of individual companies. An easy way to do this is to look at a list of companies in the industry you're researching sorted by sales or market cap, and examine a dozen or so to get a feel for the industry.

You don't need to do detailed analysis at this point—just glance over sales and earnings growth rates and margins. The most important thing is to look at a variety of firms over a reasonably long time frame—at least 5 years and, preferably, 10.

Investor's Checklist: Economic Moats

▶ Because success attracts competition as surely as night follows day, the most highly profitable companies tend to become less profitable over time. That's why economic moats are so important: They help great companies stay that way.

▶ For concrete evidence of an economic moat, look for firms that consistently earn high profits. Focus on free cash flow, net margins, return on equity, and return on assets.

▶ After you've looked at these specific measures, try to identify the source of the company's economic moat. Companies generally build sustainable competitive advantages through product differentiation (real or perceived), driving costs down, locking in customers with high switching costs, or locking out competitors through high barriers to entry.

▶ Think about economic moats in two dimensions: depth (how much money the company can make) and width (how long it can sustain above-average profits). In general, any economic moat based on technological innovation is likely to be short-lived.

▶ Although the attractiveness of an industry doesn't tell the whole story, it's important to get a feel for the competitive landscape. Some industries are just easier to make money in than others.

4

The Language of Investing

IN THE NEXT three chapters, my goal is to help you understand how financial statements fit together and how you can use them to identify solid companies. First, we'll look at how the three main financial statements fit together by describing what's in them and by following a dollar through a business. Then, we'll build a hot dog stand to see how the operations of a very simple business are represented in financial statements.

In Chapter 5, we'll tour all three statements in detail by looking at the books of a real, complicated company. (Note to readers with some accounting background: You can skip to Chapter 6—Analyzing a Company—unless you want a review of the basics.) In Chapter 11, we'll apply our newfound accounting knowledge to the analytical process by looking at two real-world companies.

The Basics

As an investor, you're mainly going to be interested in the balance sheet, the income statement, and the statement of cash flows. These three tables are your windows into corporate performance, and they're the place to start when you're analyzing a company.

All three of these statements can be found in the three major types of financial filings: an annual report, a 10-K filing, and a 10-Q filing. You're probably familiar with annual reports—those glossy booklets with smiling employees that firms mail out every year—but to really understand a firm, you'll need to look up 10-Ks and 10-Qs. These are dense, detailed sets of financial information that companies file with the Securities and Exchange Commission (SEC) every year (the 10-K) and every quarter (the 10-Q). You can access these reports at http://www.sec.gov/edgar.shtml or http://www.freeedgar.com. The latter is a bit easier to use.

Think of the three statements like this: The balance sheet is like a company's credit report because it tells you how much the company owns (assets) relative to what it owes (liabilities) at a specific point in time. It tells you how strong the framework and foundation of the business is.

The income statement, meanwhile, tells how much the company made or lost in accounting profits during a year or a quarter. Unlike the balance sheet, which is a snapshot of the company's financial health at a precise moment, the income statement records revenues and expenses over a set period, such as a fiscal year.

Finally, there's the statement of cash flows, which records all the cash that comes into a company and all of the cash that goes out. The statement of cash flows ties the income statement and balance sheet together.

Right now, you're probably wondering why we need an income statement and a cash flow statement—after all, if a company makes money, it makes money, right? The difference lies in a confusing concept called *accrual accounting*. Here's how it works. Companies record sales (or revenue) when a service or a good is provided to the buyer, regardless of when the buyer pays. As long as the company is reasonably certain that the buyer will eventually pay the bill, the company can post the sale to its income statement.

The cash flow statement, on the other hand, is concerned only with when cash is received and when it goes out the door. I'll go over the cash flow statement in detail later in this chapter, but here's a quick example.

Let's say that Colgate sells a few cases of toothpaste to Joe's Corner Store for $1,000 on February 15 but gives Joe 60 days to pay because he's a regular customer and has a good track record of paying his bills on time. March 31 rolls around, Joe hasn't paid yet, and Colgate closes its books for the quarter.

Colgate shows $1,000 in sales on its income statement because it shipped the toothpaste to Joe—according to the income statement, the sale is complete, regardless of whether Colgate has received payment. But because Joe hasn't ponied up the grand yet, Colgate will post an entry on its balance sheet to show that Joe owes Colgate $1,000. (The entry goes into the accounts receivable line—more on this later in the chapter.)

As you can see, a company can show rip-roaring sales growth without receiving a cent of cash. In fact, if Colgate produces and sells toothpaste faster than its customers pay for the toothpaste, sales growth would look fantastic even though cash is flowing out the door—which is why we need a statement of cash flows.

Where the Money Goes

Figure 4.1 illustrates how money moves from investors, through the company, to consumers, and back to the company.

This isn't nearly as bad as it looks. Let's follow some money through the company to show you what I mean.

A group of investors and bondholders (1) provide capital to a firm, either by buying shares in the company (stockholders) or by buying the company's bonds (bondholders). The company takes the money and buys fixed assets (2) such as machinery and buildings—and uses those assets to produce inventory (3). Some of the inventory is sold for cash (4), and some is sold on credit (5).

The credit sales are posted to "accounts receivable"—a fancy name for IOU—until the customer pays the firm (6). Once the firm has cash in hand, it can spend it in all sorts of ways. Some of it goes back into production (7), which means buying replacement raw materials to create more inventory, and some of it goes into investment (8), which means buying more machinery or building another factory. (In accounting lingo, you'll usually see any investment that purchases a tangible long-term asset such as a building or factory called "capital expenditure," or simply "capex.")

Another chunk of cash goes to Uncle Sam as taxes (9), and some may flow out as dividends to stockholders if the firm pays a dividend or as interest to bondholders (10) if the firm has debt.

That's really all there is to it. Cash flows in, and (you hope) cash flows out. Let's walk through a simplified company—Mike's Hot Dog Stand—to

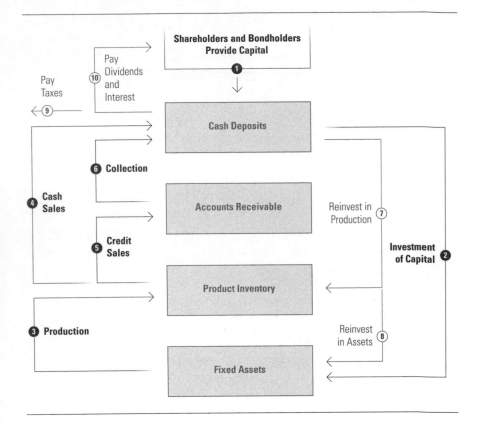

Figure 4.1   How money flows through a company. *Source:* Morningstar, Inc.

illustrate how all of this comes together. We'll use Mike's to introduce many of the specific line items in financial statements that tell us how well a company is doing its core job, which is investing shareholders' money to generate a solid return.

Practical Financials—The Statements in Use

It's the Fourth of July, and Mike thinks he can make a few bucks by setting up a hot dog stand near the parade route. Mike has $100 to start his hot dog–selling operation, with the money provided by the First National Bank of Mom.

I. Borrows $100 from First National Bank of Mom

ASSETS	Before	Change	After
Cash	0	+100	100

LIABILITIES	Before	Change	After
Long-term debt	0	+100	100

Mike spends $70 for lumber, nails, and paint to assemble the stand as well as tongs for turning the dogs on the grill. (He's borrowing Dad's grill to cook the dogs.) Then he buys $20 worth of hot dogs, buns, ketchup, and mustard, and some charcoal and lighter fluid for the grill. He keeps the remaining $10 for making change and such.

II. Buys property, plant, and equipment (PP&E) and inventory

ASSETS	Before	Change	After
Cash	100	−90	10
Inventory	0	+20	20
PP&E	0	+70	70

He's spent $90 ($70 for the stand and $20 for ingredients), but that money hasn't disappeared—it's turned into assets and inventory. As shown in the chart, the $70 he spent on the hot dog stand and the tongs is "property, plant, and equipment," while the $20 in buns and such has become "inventory," and the $10 in cash is just that. Look at the simplified balance sheet in Figure 4.2 to see how this would look if Mike had to file an annual report. (Don't worry if you see an unfamiliar line item—we'll cover it later in the chapter.)

Mike opens for business while the crowd is gathering for the parade and sells 30 hot dogs at $1 apiece. By noon, half the hot dogs, buns, condiments, and charcoal are gone, so Mike's "cost of goods sold" is $10, or half of the $20 he spent to buy supplies. Seven people didn't have any cash on them, so Mike let them buy their dogs on credit—which means we need to record $7 in accounts receivable, which is the money that folks owe to Mike.

Assets	
Cash	10
+ Accounts receivable	0
+ Inventory	20
+ Net PP&E	70
= **Total Assets**	**100**

Liabilities	
Accounts payable	0
Long-term debt	100

Equity	
Retained earnings	0
Depreciation expense	0
Total Liabilities & Equity	**100**

Figure 4.2   Simple balance sheet for Mike's hot dog stand. *Source:* Morningstar, Inc.

III. Sells 30 hot dogs at $1 piece ($10 worth of inventory), with $7 worth being sold on credit (cash not received yet)

ASSETS	Before	Change	After
Cash	10	+23	33
Accounts receivable	0	+7	7
Inventory	20	−10	10

In the middle of the day, Mike runs out of buns, so he has to run over to the corner grocery store to buy more. But when he arrives, he realizes he left his money back at the stand, so he promises the grocer he'll come back with the money on Monday when the hot dog biz slows down. We post $5 to accounts payable, which is money that Mike owes to the grocery store for the buns. (Think of accounts payable like your credit card. If you buy a shirt or a stereo on your Visa, you can use it right away—but you still owe the credit card issuer some cash.)

IV. Buys $5 worth of buns on credit

ASSETS	Before	Change	After
Cash	33	0	33
Inventory	10	+5	15
LIABILITIES			
Accounts payable	0	+5	5

At the end of the second day, Mike realizes that his tongs aren't working as well as they used to, and it's taking him longer to grill each hot dog. The accounting name for this wear-and-tear is *depreciation,* which lets us record the fact that Mike's equipment isn't as productive as it used to be. (In the real world, depreciation isn't recorded at the moment something starts wearing out. It's actually a regular charge that assumes that an asset wears out over a set time period—as long as forty years for a building, and as short as three years for a computer.) Depreciation is a cost of doing business, just like buying hot dogs and buns, because Mike will eventually have to buy another set of tongs if he wants to stay in business. Because all costs have to be recorded—accounting is funny that way—we post $1 to depreciation.

V. Records wear and tear on tongs

ASSETS	Before	Change	After
Net PP&E	70	−1	69

After a long day of serving up delicious dogs to parade-goers, Mike's income statement is shown in Figure 4.3.

And his balance sheet is shown in Figure 4.4.

The eagle-eyed reader will notice that although Mike's net profit was $19, his cash account went up by $23—from $10 to $33—on his personal balance sheet. Why the difference? Let's find out by developing a statement of cash flows from the income statement and balance sheet information that we have available. By following this example, you'll see into the heart and soul of accounting.

To understand how much *cash* Mike's little business generated, we start with his $19 in net profits, which is the difference between what he paid for

Sales		30
− Cost of goods sold		10
− Depreciation		1
= Net Profit		**19**

Figure 4.3   Simple income statement for Mike's hot dog stand. *Source:* Morningstar, Inc.

the hot dogs, buns, and condiments, and what he received in payment for the hot dogs. But to arrive at the cash profits, we first need to add back the $1 in depreciation. You see, although we need to keep track of the expense that Mike incurred by partially wearing out his grilling tongs—remember, accounting is all about keeping score—Mike didn't have to pay out $1 in cash to cover the wear and tear. He'll have to replace the tongs eventually, but as yet, he still has his slightly worn-out pair, and he hasn't laid out any green to fix it.

This is *the* critical difference between accounting profits and cash profits— accounting profits match revenues (hot dogs sold) with expenses (a worn-out

Assets	Original	Final
Cash	10	33
+ Accounts receivable	0	7
+ Inventory	20	15
+ Net PP&E	70	69
= Total Assets	**100**	**124**

Liabilities	Original	Final
Accounts payable	0	5
Long-term debt	100	100

Equity	Original	Final
Retained earnings	0	20
Depreciation expense	0	-1
Total Liabilities & Equity	**100**	**124**

Figure 4.4   Balance sheet for Mike's hot dog stand. *Source:* Morningstar, Inc.

set of grilling tongs) as closely as possible, whereas cash profits measure only the actual dollar bills flowing into and out of a business.

Next, we need to take into account the fact that Mike used up half his original inventory of hot dogs and buns, as well as the fact that he went out and bought an additional $5 worth of buns. His inventory went from $20, to $10, and back to $15. This net decrease in inventory from $20 to $15 is a *source* of cash. In other words, Mike had $20 of capital tied up in inventory at the start of the weekend, but now he has only $15 of capital invested in inventory. As a result, he converted $5 in inventory to $5 in cash.

However, Mike also is owed $7 by hot dog eaters who haven't paid him yet. Because Mike had to pay to produce the dogs they ate and they haven't yet given him any cash, he's used up some money by letting those folks nosh on his tasty dogs on credit. In other words, Mike paid out cash to get the ingredients he needed to make the hot dogs, but he hasn't yet received any cash in return, so his decision to extend credit *used up* $7 in cash.

Finally, let's not forget that Mike himself is the beneficiary of credit because he still owes the grocer $5 for those extra buns he bought. Because Mike received something without paying out cash for it, his cash account *increases* by $5.

We can follow the trail from Mike's $19 in net profits to his $23 in cash flow with this simple table:

Net profits = $19
+ $1 depreciation
+ $10 inventory (hot dogs sold)
− $5 inventory (extra buns purchased)
− $7 accounts receivable (money owed *to* Mike)
+ $5 accounts payable (money owed *by* Mike)
= $23 in operating cash flow

As you can see, the $23 in operating cash flow differs from the $19 in net income because of the choices Mike made in running his little business. For example, if Mike hadn't let anyone buy on credit, but had the same amount of sales, his cash flow would have been $30 ($23 plus $7). Conversely, if the grocer had forced Mike to pay cash for those extra buns, Mike's cash flow would have been $18 ($23 minus $5.) In both cases, however, Mike's net profits would have remained $19.

The key takeaway here is that the income statement and cash flow statement can tell different stories about a business because they're constructed using different sets of rules. The income statement strives to match revenues and expenses as closely as possible—that's why we had to deduct the $1 in depreciation from Mike's profits, and that's why Mike gets to record the $7 in sales that he made on credit. But the cash flow statement cares only about the dollar bills that go in and out the door, regardless of the timing of the actions that generated those dollar bills.

If you look only at the income statement without checking to see how much cash a company is creating, you won't be getting the whole story by a long shot. This simple concept—the difference between accounting profits and cash profits—is the key to understanding almost everything there is to know about how a business works, as well as how to separate great businesses from poor ones. In subsequent chapters, we'll move from our simple hot dog stand to real-world companies to learn how to analyze all three of the financial statements in detail.

Investor's Checklist: The Language of Investing

- ▶ The balance sheet is like a company's credit report because it tells you how much the company owns (assets) relative to what it owes (liabilities).
- ▶ The income statement shows how much the company made or lost in accounting profits during a year or a quarter. Unlike the balance sheet, which is a snapshot of the company's financial health at a precise moment, the income statement records revenues and expenses during a set period, such as a fiscal year.
- ▶ The third key financial statement—the statement of cash flows—records all the cash that comes into a company and all of the cash that goes out.
- ▶ Accrual accounting is a key concept for understanding financial statements. The income statement matches sales with the corresponding expenses when a service or a good is provided to the buyer, but the cash flow statement is concerned only with when cash is received and when it goes out the door.
- ▶ The income statement and cash flow statement can tell different stories about a business because they're constructed using different sets of rules. To get the most complete picture, be sure to look at both.

5

Financial Statements Explained

NOW THAT YOU have a good idea of how businesses generate cash and how profits are recorded on financial statements, let's look at each of the three main financial statements in detail. Unfortunately, not all businesses are as simple as a hot dog stand, so we need to introduce some additional complexity if we want to analyze real companies. But fear not—as we walk through the balance sheet, income statement, and cash flow statement, we'll look at a few real-world companies to see what their financial statements can tell us about how their businesses are functioning.

Wherever possible, I'll refer to excerpts from the financial statements of Dell and Hewlett-Packard (H-P), taken from the two firms' 10-K filings with the SEC. (The Dell excerpts contain data through January 31, 2003, and the H-P excerpts contain data through October 31, 2002.) We'll start with the balance sheet, move on to the income statement, and finish with the statement of cash flows. At the start of each section, you'll see a financial statement from the originally named (and fictitious) "Acme Corporation" that will show you how each statement is organized.

Warning: This chapter may be tough going in parts, but it's possibly the most important chapter of the entire book, since reading financial statements is the foundation for analyzing companies. If you find yourself confused about a concept or getting tired, put down the book and take a break. There's no rush—it'll be here when you get back!

The Balance Sheet

The balance sheet (see Figure 5.1)—sometimes called a "statement of financial position"—tells you how much a company owns (its assets), how much it owes (its liabilities), and the difference between the two (its equity). Equity represents the value of the money that shareholders have invested in the firm, and if that sounds odd, think of it just like your mortgage—your equity in your home is the home's value minus the mortgage. Stockholders' equity in a firm is the value of the firm's assets minus its liabilities.

ACME Corporation: Balance Sheet

(In millions)	2002	2001
Assets		
Current assets:		
Cash and cash equivalents	$284	$205
Accounts receivable	842	827
Inventories	644	697
Other current assets	328	369
Total current assets	$2,098	$2,099
Investments	79	92
Property, plant, and equipment—net	1,874	1,872
Goodwill	633	337
Intangible assets	90	79
Other assets	415	390
Total assets	$5,188	$4,869

Figure 5.1   A balance sheet for the fictitious ACME Corporation. *Source:* Morningstar, Inc.

Liabilities and stockholders' equity		
Current liabilities:		
Short-term debt	412	458
Accounts payable	315	251
Payroll	137	180
Income taxes	173	199
Other current liabilities	449	416
Total current liabilities	$1,486	$1,503
Long-term debt	$ 713	$ 507
Other liabilities	913	830
Total liabilities	$3,112	$2,840
Stockholders' equity:		
Common stock	$ 2	$ 2
Additional paid-in capital	97	97
Retained earnings	4,249	3,971
Treasury stock	-1,589	-1,544
Accumulated other comprehensive income (loss)	-683	-497
Total stockholders' equity	$2,076	$2,029
Total liabilities and stockholders' equity	$5,188	$4,869

Figure 5.1 *(Continued)*.

The basic equation underlying a balance sheet is:

$$\text{Assets} - \text{Liabilities} = \text{Equity}$$

which can also be expressed as:

$$\text{Assets} = \text{Liabilities} + \text{Equity}$$

The key thing to understand about a balance sheet is simply that it must *balance* at all times, hence the name. An increase in liabilities—issuing a bond, for example—causes an increase in assets—the cash received from the sale of the bond. If a firm generates huge profits that drive an increase in assets, equity also increases. This makes sense because the value of shareholders' investment in the firm rises if that firm starts making a ton of money. Let's go through the balance sheet bit by bit to get a better grasp on how it's put together.

Asset Accounts: Current Assets

The accounting gods define *current assets* as those likely to be used up or converted into cash within one business cycle, usually defined as one year. The major portions of this category are cash and equivalents, short-term investments, accounts receivable, and inventories.

Cash and Equivalents and Short-Term Investments: These line items don't necessarily refer to actual greenbacks sitting around in a vault but to money in low-risk, fairly liquid investments. "Cash and equivalents" usually contains money market funds or anything that can be liquidated quickly and with minimal price risk, whereas "short-term investments" is similar to cash—usually, bonds that have less than a year to maturity and earn a higher rate of return than cash but would take a bit of effort to sell. In most cases, you can mentally lump this in with cash when considering how much a firm has on hand to meet an immediate need.

Accounts Receivable: As we saw in the hot dog example, accounts receivable are bills that the company hasn't yet collected but for which it expects to receive payment soon. Watch how this account changes relative to the company's sales—if accounts receivable are rising much faster than sales, the firm is booking a large amount of revenue for which it has not yet received payment. This can be a sign of trouble because it may mean that the firm is offering looser credit terms to increase sales—remember, a firm can record a sale as soon as it has shipped the product—but has less likelihood of ever receiving the cash it's owed.

In Figure 5.2, Dell looks like it was in fine shape on this front. Dell's accounts receivable rose about 14 percent, but sales increased by the same amount, as we'll see later when we look at the company's income statement.

However, H-P's accounts receivable (see Figure 5.3) took a huge jump from $4.488 billion to $8.456 billion, which was a 90 percent increase, whereas sales

Dell Computer Corporation: Partial Balance Sheet		
Assets (millions)	2003	2002
Current assets		
Cash and cash equivalents	$4,232	$3,641
Short-term investments	406	273
Accounts receivable—net	2,586	2,269
Inventories	306	278
Other	1,394	1,416
Total current assets	$8,924	$7,877

Figure 5.2   Dell's current assets. *Source:* Dell SEC filings.

rose only about 25 percent. (Remember, comparing the growth rate of accounts receivable with the growth rate of sales is a good way to judge whether a company is doing a good job collecting the money that it's owed by customers.) Although H-P's results were somewhat distorted by its acquisition of Compaq during this time period, that's still a big discrepancy. At the time, H-P investors would have wanted to keep an eye on accounts receivable to make sure that the firm collected the cash that it was owed by customers.

You'll often see an "allowance for doubtful accounts" just after accounts receivable on the balance sheet. This is the company's estimate of how much money it's owed by deadbeat customers, and which it's consequently unlikely to collect. For example, on H-P's balance sheet, you can see that the firm was assuming that it wouldn't collect $495 million of the money that customers owed it as of October 2002.

Inventories: There are several types of inventories, including raw materials that have not yet been made into a finished product, partially finished products, and finished products that have not yet been sold. Inventories are especially important to watch in manufacturing and retail firms, and their value on the balance sheet should be taken with a grain of salt. Because of the way inventories are accounted for, their liquidation value may very well be a far cry from their value on the balance sheet. Use your common sense when

Hewlett-Packard Company and Subsidiaries: Partial Balance Sheet		
Assets (millions)	2002	2001
Current assets		
Cash and cash equivalents	$11,192	$4,197
Short-term investments	237	139
Accounts receivable, net of allowance for doubtful accounts of $495 and $275 as of October 31, 2002 and 2001, respectively	8,456	4,488
Financing receivables, net of allowance for doubtful accounts of $184 and $68 as of October 31, 2002 and 2001, respectively	3,453	2,183
Inventory	5,797	5,204
Other current assets	6,940	5,094
Total current assets	$36,075	$21,305

Figure 5.3   Hewlett-Packard's assets. *Source:* Hewlett-Packard SEC filings.

judging this: Although a construction firm could probably get a decent price if it needed to sell off some extra steel girders it had lying around in inventory, a retailer that needed to sell last fall's teen fashions would likely have to take pennies on the dollar.

More importantly, inventories soak up capital—cash that's been converted into inventory sitting in a warehouse can't be used for anything else. The speed at which a company turns over its inventory can have a huge impact on profitability because the less time cash is tied up in inventory, the more time it's available for use elsewhere. You can calculate a metric called *inventory turnover* by dividing a company's cost of goods sold by its inventory level.

For example, Dell's cost of goods sold for 2002 was $25.6 billion (see Figure 5.4) and inventory was $278 million (see Figure 5.2), yielding an incredible inventory turnover rate of 92. In other words, Dell went through its entire inventory 92 times over the course of the year. Contrast this with H-P, which had a cost of goods sold of $34.5 billion (see Figure 5.5) and inventory of $5.8 billion for 2002, yielding much lower inventory turns of just 6. As you

Dell Computer Corporation: Partial Income Statement

In millions Fiscal year ending	2003	2002	2001
Net revenue	$35,404	$31,168	$31,800
Cost of revenue	29,055	25,661	25,445

Figure 5.4   Dell's revenue and cost of revenue. *Source:* Dell SEC filings.

can see, H-P lets inventory sit around much longer than Dell, which is not a great idea when you consider how fast high-tech equipment loses its value.

Asset Accounts: Noncurrent Assets

Noncurrent assets are assets that are not expected to be converted into cash or used up within the reporting period. The big parts of this section are property, plant, and equipment (PP&E); investments; and intangible assets.

Property, Plant, and Equipment: These are long-term assets that form the infrastructure of the company: land, buildings, factories, furniture, equipment, and so forth. Dell, for example, had about $913 million in PP&E at the end of 2002, whereas H-P had $6.9 billion.

Hewlett-Packard: Partial Consolidated Statement of Income

For the following years ended October 31 In millions, except per share amounts	2002	2001	2000
Net revenue			
Products	$45,955	$38,005	$41,653
Costs and expenses			
Cost of products	$34,573	$28,863	$30,343

Figure 5.5   Hewlett-Packard's revenue breakdown. *Source:* Hewlett-Packard SEC filings.

Dell Computer Corporation: Partial Balance Sheet

Assets (millions)	2003	2002
Property, plant, and equipment, net	$ 913	$ 826
Investments	5,267	4,373
Other noncurrent assets	366	459
Total assets	$15,470	$13,535

Figure 5.6   Dell's assets. *Source:* Dell SEC filings.

If we compare these numbers to the firms' total assets (see Figures 5.6 and 5.7, we can get a feel for how capital-intensive the firms are—Dell's PP&E makes up about 6 percent of its total assets, whereas almost 10 percent of H-P's assets are in PP&E. Therefore, H-P is more capital-intensive than Dell.

Investments: This is money invested in either longer term bonds or in the stock of other companies, ranging from a token amount to a substantial stake. It's not nearly as liquid as cash and might be worth more or less on the

Hewlett-Packard Company and Subsidiaries: Partial Balance Sheet

Assets (millions)	2002	2001
Property, plant, and equipment, net of accumulated depreciation of $5,612 and $5,411 as of October 31, 2002 and 2001, respectively	$ 6,924	$ 4,397
Long-term financing receivables and other assets	7,760	6,126
Goodwill	15,089	667
Purchased intangible assets	4,862	89
Total assets	$70,710	$32,584

Figure 5.7   Hewlett-Packard's assets. *Source:* Hewlett-Packard SEC filings.

market than the amount shown on the balance sheet. You'll need to dig around in the notes to the financial statements to see what exactly is in this account and with how much skepticism you should view its value. You can see in Figures 5.6 and 5.7 that H-P has no long-term investments, but Dell has a pretty sizeable amount—about $5.3 billion—sitting on its balance sheet. Because that's almost a third of Dell's total assets, it's definitely something you'd want to dig into. (Turns out that Dell's investments were mainly bonds, so you wouldn't need to worry too much about them—if they were equities or venture capital, you'd want to find out more about that $5.3 billion value.)

Intangible Assets: The most common form of intangible assets is goodwill, which arises when one company acquires another. Goodwill is the difference between the price the acquiring company pays and tangible value—or equity—of the target company. Essentially, goodwill represents the value of all of the other stuff that one company gets when it acquires another. For example, the majority of Coca-Cola's value is not in the firm's buildings and equipment; it's in the powerful brand that Coke has built up over the past several decades. If some firm were to buy Coke, it would have to pay far more than the *book* value of Coke's equity, and that extra amount is called goodwill.

You should view this account with extreme skepticism because most companies tend to overpay for their targets, which means the value of goodwill that shows up on the balance sheet is very often far more than the asset is actually worth. (In 2003, for example, AOL Time Warner reduced the value of the goodwill on its balance sheet by an amazing 40 percent with the stroke of a pen, essentially admitting that it had far overpaid for AOL when the two companies merged. If you'd been counting on this goodwill account as an asset that the company had at its disposal, you'd have been sorely disappointed.)

As you can see in Figure 5.7, H-P had more than $15 billion—or almost 20 percent of its total assets of $71 billion—in its goodwill account for 2002. Was Compaq really worth $15 billion more than the value of its cash, inventory, fixed assets, customer lists, and patents? Maybe it was—but if it's not, H-P will have to reduce the value of this account at some point in the future, which means the value of the firm's total assets will also drop.

Liability Accounts: Current Liabilities

Now that we know what the company owns, we can look at the other side of the coin—what it owes.

Current liabilities are the flip side of current assets: money the company expects to pay out within a year. You should focus on accounts payable and short-term borrowings or payables.

Accounts Payable: These are bills the company owes to somebody else and are due to be paid within a year, like Mike's IOU to the grocer for the extra hot dog buns. Large companies that have a lot of leverage over their suppliers can push out some of their payables, which means they hold on to the cash longer—and that's good for cash flow.

Short-Term Borrowings: This refers to money the company has borrowed for a term of less than a year, usually to meet short-term needs. It's often a line of bank credit that the firm has temporarily drawn down, though it might also be a portion of long-term debt that's due within the next year. This line item becomes especially important for companies in financial distress because the entire amount often has to be paid back quickly. H-P's notes payable and short-term borrowings (see Figure 5.8) were about $1.8 billion, which is fairly small relative to the size of the firm's assets, so no worries there.

Liability Accounts: Noncurrent Liabilities

Noncurrent liabilities are the flip side of noncurrent assets. They represent money the company owes one year or more in the future. Though you'll sometimes see a variety of line items under this heading, the most important

Hewlett-Packard Company and Subsidiaries: Partial Balance Sheet		
Liabilities and Stockholder's Equity (millions)	2002	2001
Current liabilities		
Notes payable and short-term borrowings	$1,793	$1,722

Figure 5.8   Hewlett-Packard's current liabilities. *Source:* Hewlett-Packard SEC filings.

one by far is long-term debt. This represents money the company has borrowed—usually by issuing bonds, though sometimes from a bank—that doesn't need to be paid back for a few years.

Stockholders' Equity

Remember, shareholders' equity is equal to total assets minus total liabilities, and it represents the part of the company owned by shareholders. This can be the most confusing section of any firm's financial statements, because it's filled with many anachronistic line items that have little practical relevance.

The only account worth looking at is retained earnings, which basically records the amount of capital a company has generated over its lifetime—minus dividends and stock buybacks, which represent funds that have already been returned to shareholders. Retained earnings is a cumulative account; therefore, each year that the company makes a profit and doesn't pay it all out as dividends, retained earnings increase. Likewise, if a company has lost money over time, retained earnings can turn negative and is often renamed "accumulated deficit" on the balance sheet. Think of this account as a company's long-term track record at generating profits.

The Income Statement

Now that we know how much a company owns and how much it owes, we can move on to the good stuff—how much money it's making (or losing.) In a 10-K, you'll usually see the income statement labeled as the "consolidated statement of income" or the "consolidated statement of earnings" (see Figure 5.9).

Revenue

Sometimes labeled "sales," this is simply how much money the company has brought in during a quarter or a year. Larger companies sometimes break down revenues on the income statement according to business sector, geographic region, or products versus services.

Be sure to check the "revenue recognition policies" buried in the financial statements so you know what you're looking at—companies can record revenue at different times depending on the business that they're in. A software firm, for example, might record a big chunk of revenue when a product is

ACME Corporation: Income Statement

(In millions)	2002	2001	2000
Net sales	$5,444	$5,351	$5,566
Cost of goods sold	2,832	2,916	2,929
Gross profit	$2,612	$2,435	$2,637
Selling, general and administrative	$1,240	$1,345	$1,313
Research and development expenses	357	361	367
Other expenses (income)		-29	-62
Operating income	$1,015	$ 758	$1,019
Interest expense	$ 27	$ 41	$ 37
Interest and other income (loss)	13	12	9
Pretax income	$1,002	$ 729	$ 991
Provision for income taxes	$ 322	$ 234	$ 342
Net income	$ 680	$ 495	$ 650
Earnings per common share			
Basic	$ 2.78	$ 2.01	$ 2.63
Diluted	2.75	1.98	2.57
Weighted average shares outstanding			
Basic	244.2	246.7	246.7
Diluted	247.4	249.3	252.5

Figure 5.9   ACME Corporation's income statement. *Source:* Morningstar, Inc.

shipped to a customer, whereas a service firm might record revenue smoothly over the life of the service contract.

Cost of Sales

Also known as cost of goods sold, this number represents the expenses most directly involved in creating revenue, such as labor costs, raw materials (for manufacturers), or the wholesale price of goods (for retailers). Large companies that combine manufacturing with services (H-P, for example) sometimes break down this number into cost of goods sold and cost of services.

Gross Profit

This doesn't appear on all income statements, but it's simply revenue minus cost of sales. Once you have gross profit, you can calculate a gross margin, which is gross profit as a percentage of revenue. Essentially, this tells you how much a company is able to mark up its goods. As you can see in Figure 5.10, Dell has a gross margin of only 17.9 percent ($6.3 billion in gross profit divided by $35.4 billion in sales) because it sells commodity products. It's tough for Dell to charge much of a premium for the computers it sells.

H-P, meanwhile, sells higher end computer gear for which its customers are more willing to pay up. If you look at Figure 5.11, you can see this in its gross margin: Take product revenue of $45.9 billion, subtract product costs of $34.6 billion, and we have a gross profit of $11.4 billion. Divide that back into revenue, and we're left with a gross margin of 24.8 percent. As you can see, the more differentiated a company's products are, the more it can mark up its goods over what it costs to manufacture them. H-P also bundles proprietary software with a lot of the computers it sells, and software has very high gross margins.

Selling, General, and Administrative Expenses (SG&A)

This number, also known as operating expenses, includes items such as marketing, administrative salaries, and, sometimes, research and development.

Dell Computer Corporation: Partial Income Statement

In millions, except per share amounts

Fiscal year ending	2003	2002	2001
Net sales	$35,404	$31,168	$31,888
Cost of goods sold	29,055	25,661	25,445
Gross profit	$ 6,349	$ 5,507	$ 6,443

Figure 5.10 Dell's partial income statement. *Source:* Dell SEC filings.

Hewlett-Packard Company and Subsidiaries: Partial Income Statement

For the following years ended October 31 In millions, except per share amounts	2002	2001	2000
Net revenue			
Products	$45,955	$38,005	$41,653
Services	10,178	6,819	6,848
Financing income	455	402	369
Total net revenue	$56,588	$45,226	$48,870
Costs and expenses			
Cost of products	$34,573	$28,863	$30,343
Cost of services	6,817	4,396	4,470

Figure 5.11 Hewlett-Packard's partial income statement. *Source:* Hewlett-Packard SEC filings.

(Research and development is usually broken out as a separate line item, as is marketing for firms that spend large amounts on advertising.) You'll often see a relationship between SG&A and gross margin—firms that are able to charge more for their goods (e.g., H-P) have to spend more on salespeople and marketing. You can get a feel for how efficient a firm is by looking at SG&A as a percentage of revenues—a lower percentage of operating expenses relative to sales generally means a tighter, more cost-effective firm.

H-P, for example (see Figure 5.12), spent about 16 percent—or $9 billion—of its $56.5 billion in revenue on SG&A, whereas Dell spent only 8.9 percent of revenue on these types of costs.

Some of the difference results from the fact that Dell sells direct to customers and H-P has to pay salespeople to sell big-ticket computers to large corporations, but it still looks as though Dell runs a leaner shop than H-P.

Unfortunately, it's tough to give any hard-and-fast rules as to just how much a company should be spending on SG&A. Your best bet is to compare a company with its closest competitors to see which is able to do more with less and to look at SG&A as a percentage of sales over time. (If it's rising fast, watch out—the firm is spending more on overhead without reaping the benefit of higher sales.)

Dell Computer Corporation: Partial Income Statement			
(In millions)	2003	2002	2001
Selling, general, and administrative	$3,050	$2,784	$3,193

Hewlett-Packard Company and Subsidiaries: Partial Income Statement			
(In millions)	2002	2001	2000
Selling, general, and administrative	$9,033	$6,950	$6,984

Figure 5.12 Dell and Hewlett-Packard's partial income statements. *Source:* Dell/Hewlett-Packard SEC filings.

Depreciation and Amortization

When a company buys an asset intended to last a long time, such as a new building or a piece of machinery, it charges off a portion of the cost of that asset on its income statement over a series of years. (Think back to Mike's grilling tongs.) This number is occasionally broken out separately on the income statement, but it's usually rolled into operating expenses. It's always included in the cash flow statement, though, so you can look there to see how much a company's net income was affected by noncash charges such as depreciation.

Nonrecurring Charges/Gains

This is the catch-all area where companies put all the one-time charges or gains that aren't part of their regular, ongoing operations, such as the cost of closing a factory or the gain from selling a division. Ideally, you'd want to see this area of the income statement blank most of the time.

You should view one-time expenses with a great deal of skepticism. Companies have gotten into the habit of rolling many costs that really are part of doing business into charges, and firms that are *serial chargers*—meaning that they seem to take some kind of hit every year—are much more difficult to analyze because all kinds of expenses can be buried in one-time charges. The reasons behind these charges are always detailed in the notes section of a firm's financial statements, which you should certainly read to understand what caused the charges.

As you can see in Figure 5.13, H-P took a $1.8 billion charge in 2002 for restructuring, a $793 million charge for "in process research and development," and another $700 million in other assorted charges related to its merger with Compaq. Although a merger of this size doesn't occur every day, which means we can cut H-P some slack, we can also see that H-P had a good-sized restructuring charge of $384 million in 2001. If I owned H-P, I'd want to look very carefully at all of those charges to make sure they really were nonrecurring because serial charging is a sign of bad faith on management's part.

Operating Income

This number is equal to revenues minus cost of sales and all operating expenses. Theoretically, it represents the profit the company made from its actual operations, as opposed to interest income, one-time gains, and so forth. In practice, companies often include nonrecurring expenses (such as write-offs) in figuring operating income, and you have to add back one-time charges (or subtract one-time gains) yourself.

Operating income is as close to a solid bottom-line number as you're going to get for most firms. Because it excludes most one-time items, as well as income from nonoperational sources such as investments, you can use it to calculate an *operating margin,* which is fairly comparable across firms and across industries.

Hewlett-Packard Company and Subsidiaries: Partial Income Statement

For the following years ended October 31 In millions, except per share amounts	2002	2001	2000
Restructuring charges	$1,780	$384	$102
In-process research and development charges	793	35	—
Acquisition-related charges	701	25	—

Figure 5.13 Hewlett-Packard's partial income statement. *Source:* Hewlett-Packard SEC filings.

Interest Income/Expense

Sometimes interest income and interest expense are listed separately, and sometimes they are combined into net interest income (or expense, as the case may be). In either case, this number represents interest the company has paid on bonds it has issued or received on bonds or cash that it owns. You can get some insight into the financial health of a firm by looking at its earnings before interest and taxes relative to its interest expense, which is called an *interest coverage ratio*. This tells you the extent to which a firm's profits can cover needed interest payments. I talk more about such financial-health measures in the next chapter.

Taxes

Uncle Sam has to get paid, and tax information is usually the last expense listed before net income. Unfortunately, corporate taxation is an extremely complex topic because companies submit a completely separate set of financial statements to the IRS for tax purposes than the ones you and I see filed with the SEC. (There are a whole host of reasons for this—the biggest cause is different depreciation schedules—but it's not something you need to worry about.)

In general, the tax rate for U.S. corporations is around 35 percent. If the tax rate for a company you're analyzing is much lower than this, find out why, and find out whether that tax advantage is likely to be permanent or temporary. Some firms get tax breaks because they're located outside the United States, even if the bulk of their sales are made here in the States.

In addition, look at the tax rate of the firm you're analyzing over time. If it bounces around from year to year, the firm may be generating earnings by playing with tax loopholes rather than selling more goods or services. Tax advantages are nice to have, but politicians have a bad habit of taking them away at inopportune times, so it's not money you want to necessarily count on.

Net Income

This number represents (at least theoretically) the company's profit after all expenses have been paid, and it's the number most companies highlight in their quarterly earnings releases. As we saw in the Mike's hot dog example, net income may or may not be a good representation of the amount of cash the company has generated. For that, we'll need to look at the statement of cash flows. Although net income is the number you'll most often see companies tout in their press releases, don't forget that it can be wildly distorted by one-time charges and/or investment income.

Number of Shares (Basic and Diluted)

This figure represents the number of shares used in calculating earnings per share; it represents the average number of shares outstanding during the reporting period (a quarter or a year). Basic shares include only actual shares of stock, and you should pretty much ignore it—the fact that it's still recorded in financial statements is more of a historical legacy than anything else.

Diluted shares, however, include securities that could potentially be converted into shares of stock, such as stock options and convertible bonds. Given the amount of egregious granting of stock options that has occurred over the past several years, it's the diluted number that you'll want to look at, because you want to know the degree to which your stake in the firm could potentially be shrunk (or diluted) if all those option-holders convert their options into shares.

You can see in Figure 5.14 that H-P's basic and diluted shares are the same but that Dell has about 2 percent more diluted shares. Because diluted shares can be as much as 5 percent or more higher than basic shares, that's not a huge amount of dilution.

Earnings per Share (Basic and Diluted)

This number, which represents net income divided by number of shares, usually gets the most attention when a company reports its quarterly or annual results. It's not the end-all, be-all of corporate financial performance, though—in fact, without looking at cash flow and many other factors, it's mostly meaningless. So when you read in the paper that a firm "beat" or "missed" earnings per share estimates, don't get excited. Find out *why* instead.

The Statement of Cash Flows

This statement is the true touchstone for corporate value creation because it shows how much cash a company is generating from year to year—and cash is what counts (see Figure 5.15). In fact, I would almost recommend that you look at the statement of cash flows first when evaluating a company to see how much cash it's throwing off, then look at the balance sheet to test the

Dell Computer Corporation: Partial Income Statement

(In millions)	2003	2002	2001
Weighted average shares outstanding			
Basic	$2,584	$2,602	$2,582
Diluted	2,644	2,726	2,746

Hewlett-Packard Company and Subsidiaries: Partial Income Statement

(In millions)	2002	2001	2000
Weighted average shares used to compute net (loss) earnings per share			
Basic	$2,499	$1,936	$1,979
Diluted	2,499	1,974	2,077

Figure 5.14 Dell and Hewlett-Packard's partial income statements. *Source:* Dell/Hewlett-Packard SEC filings.

firmness of its financial foundation, and only then look at the income statement to check out margins and such.

The cash flow statement strips away all the abstract, noncash items such as depreciation that you see on the income statement and tells you how much actual cash the company has generated. Many of the items on this statement are also found on either the income statement or the balance sheet, but here they're rearranged to highlight the cash generated and how it relates to reported earnings. The cash flow statement is divided into three parts: cash flows from operating activities, from investing activities, and from financing activities.

The "cash flows from operating activities" section comes first and it tells you how much cash the company generated from its business. This is the area to focus most of your attention on because it's the cash-generating power of the business that we're most interested in. Dell's statement of cash flows is on page 70 so you can follow along (see Figure 5.16).

Net Income

This figure is simply taken from the income statement. All the items below it are added to or subtracted from net income to get the end result, "net cash provided by operating activities." In Dell's case, we start with the same $2.1 billion that was reported on the income statement.

ACME Corporation: Cash Flow Statement

(In millions)	2002	2001	2000
Cash flows from operating activities			
Net income	$ 680	$ 495	$ 650
Adjustments to reconcile net income to net cash provided by operating activities			
Depreciation and amortization	318	363	342
Deferred income tax provision	193	0	30
Pension contribution	-362	-52	-50
Changes in assets and liabilities			
Accounts receivable	-15	115	-57
Inventories	53	65	-87
Other current assets	41	-32	-23
Other assets	-25	36	-6
Accounts payable and other current liabilities	97	50	51
Other liabilities	83	5	-18
Net cash provided by operating activities	$1,063	$1,044	$ 831
Cash flows from investing activities			
(Capital expenditures)	$ -254	$ -327	$-372
(Acquisitions)	-419	-73	-157
Asset sales	28	38	35
Other investing cash flows	4	12	36
Net cash used in investing activities	$ -642	$ -350	$-458

Figure 5.15   ACME Corporation's cash flow statement. *Source:* Morningstar, Inc.

Cash flows from financing activities			
Purchase and retirement of short-term debt	$ -45	$ -7	$ -79
Purchases and retirement of long-term debt	207	43	157
Purchase or sale of stock	-140	-287	-130
Dividends paid to stockholders	-323	-316	-306
Other financing cash flows	-26	-6	-20
Net cash used in financing activities	$ -327	$ -572	$-377
Effect of exchange rate change on cash	$ -14	$ 1	$ 31
Increase (decrease) in cash and cash equivalents	$ 79	$ 123	$ 27
Cash and cash equivalents at beginning of period	$ 205	$ 82	$ 55
Cash and cash equivalents at end of period	284	205	82

Figure 5.15 *(Continued)*.

Depreciation and Amortization

This is not a cash charge—remember, Mike didn't have to pay anyone just because his grilling tongs started to wear out—so we need to add it back to net income. In Dell's case, we add back $211 million.

Tax Benefit from Employee Stock Plans

When an employee exercises stock options, the employer gets to deduct the gain received by the employee against its corporate income. (Employee compensation is generally tax deductible.) Because the result is a lower tax bill, we need to add back the tax benefit to the already-taxed net income. Be wary of this line item—if it's large relative to total operating cash flow and the company's stock has been zooming upwards, you shouldn't count on this cash being around in the future. When the shares sink, fewer employees will exercise their options, and the company will receive a smaller cash tax benefit. As you can see, Dell's tax benefit from stock option exercises dropped in half between 2001 and 2002 and sunk again in 2003. Over the same time period, Dell's stock wasn't such a hot performer—and that's not a coincidence.

Dell Computer Corporation: Partial Statement of Cash Flows

In millions Fiscal year ending	January 31, 2003	February 1, 2002	February 2, 2001
Cash flows from operating activities			
Net income	$2,122	$1,246	$2,177
Adjustments to reconcile net income to net cash provided by operating activities			
Depreciation and amortization	211	239	240
Tax benefits of employee stock plans	260	487	929
Special charges	—	742	105
(Gains)/losses on investments	(67)	17	(307)
Other, primarily effects of exchange rate changes on monetary assets and liabilities denominated in foreign currencies	(410)	178	135
Changes in			
Operating working capital	$1,210	$ 826	$ 642
Noncurrent assets and liabilities	212	62	274
Net cash provided by operating activities	$3,538	$3,797	$4,195

Figure 5.16 Dell's partial cash flow statement. *Source:* Dell SEC filings.

Changes in Working Capital

Remember when Mike let some folks buy hot dogs on credit and owed money to the grocer for those extra buns? Both of those actions affected working capital, and they'd be accounted for here. If a company is owed more money by customers this year than it was last year, accounts receivable increase and cash flow decreases; if it owes more money to suppliers, accounts payable increase and so does cash flow. Finally, if a firm pumps more money into inventory that doesn't sell, cash flow decreases. Remember, inventory ties up capital.

In Dell's case, we need to go back to the balance sheet to see where the $1.2 billion entry for the line item came from (see Figure 5.17).

Dell Computer Corporation: Partial Balance Sheet

For the following years ended October 31 In millions, except per share amounts	2003	2002
Current assets		
Cash and cash equivalents	$4,232	$3,641
Short-term investments	406	273
Accounts receivable—net	2,586	2,269
Inventories	306	278
Other	1,394	1,416

Figure 5.17 Dell's current assets. *Source:* Dell SEC filings.

As you can see, accounts receivable increased from $2.269 billion to $2.586 billion, which ate up $317 million ($2.586 minus $2.269) because Dell's customers owed it more money at the end of fiscal 2003 than they did at the end of fiscal 2002. In addition, inventory increased a bit from $278 million to $306 million, which also used up cash because Dell increased the amount of capital it had tied up in inventory.

Meanwhile, accounts payable increased from $5.075 billion to $5.989 billion, which means that Dell owed $914 million more to its suppliers at the end of 2003 than it did at the end of 2002—and that meant more cash in Dell's pocket (see Figure 5.18).

Dell Computer Corporation: Partial Balance Sheet

Liabilities and stockholder's equity	2003	2002
Current liabilities		
Accounts payable	$5,989	$5,075
Accrued and other	2,944	2,444

Figure 5.18 Dell's current liabilities. *Source:* Dell SEC filings.

So, we have $914 million in cash generated by an increase in accounts payable, minus the $317 million increase in accounts receivable, minus the $28 million change in inventory, which gives us $569 million in cash flow. Add in the $500 million increase in "accrued and other"—mainly warranties and employee bonuses that Dell may have to pay out in the future—as well as some other odds and ends detailed on the bowels of the financial filings, and you wind up with the $1.220 billion in "changes in operating working capital" that you see on Dell's cash flow statement.

You don't need to go through all of this every time you look at a statement of cash flows because everything gets neatly netted out for you in the "net cash provided by operating activities" line. But because the "changes in working capital" entry is often the biggest cause of differences between net income and operating cash flow, this is an area that you'll want to pay attention to—hence our detailed analysis.

One-Time Charges

Remember these? Dell didn't have any, but H-P did (see Figure 5.19). Because most of these charges were noncash charges—that is, H-P didn't write a check made out to someone named Restructuring—they need to be added back when figuring cash flow (similar to depreciation, which is also noncash).

Net Cash Provided by Operating Activities

This is your holy grail for figuring out whether a company is generating cash. Also known as *operating cash flow*, it's the result of adding or subtracting the

Hewlett-Packard Company and Subsidiaries: Partial Statement of Cash Flows			
For the following years ended October 31 In millions	2002	2001	2000
Restructuring charges	$1,780	$384	$102
Acquisition-related charges, including in-process research and development	1,494	60	—

Figure 5.19 Hewlett-Packard's partial cash flow statement. *Source:* Hewlett-Packard SEC filings.

previous items from net income. It doesn't replace net income, but if you don't look at it in addition to net income, you're not getting the full picture because the two can often tell very different stories.

Now we arrive at the second portion of the statement of cash flows, the "cash flow from investing activities" section. These are activities that involve acquiring or disposing of PP&E, corporate acquisitions, and any sales or purchases of investments.

Capital Expenditures

This figure represents money spent on items that last a long time, such as PP&E—basically, anything needed to keep the business running and growing at its current rate. Operating cash flow minus capital expenditures equals free cash flow, or the amount of cash the company generates after investing in its business. We can see in Figure 5.20 that Dell spent $305 million on capex.

Investment Proceeds

Companies often take some of their excess cash and invest it in bonds or stocks in an effort to get a better return than they could in a basic savings account. This number tells us how much money the company has made (or lost) on such investments. As you can see in Figure 5.20, Dell invested $8.7 billion of its cash in securities of one sort or another (purchases) and received

Dell Computer Corporation: Partial Statement of Cash Flows			
In millions Fiscal year ending	January 31, 2003	February 1, 2002	February 2, 2001
Cash flows from investing activities			
Investments:			
Purchases	$(8,736)	$(5,382)	$(2,606)
Maturities and sales	7,660	3,425	2,331
Capital expenditures	(305)	(303)	(402)
Net cash used in investing activities	$(1,381)	$(2,260)	$ (757)

Figure 5.20 Dell's partial cash flow statement. *Source:* Dell SEC filings.

$7.7 billion from previous investments that either reached maturity or were sold (maturities and sales).

The final portion of the statement of cash flows is the "cash flow from financing activities" section. Financing activities include any transactions with the company's owners or creditors. Items that typically show up in this section are briefly described next.

Dividends Paid

Unlike many line items, this one is just what it sounds like. You can see that H-P paid a total of $801 million in dividends in 2002 (see Figure 5.21).

Issuance/Purchase of Common Stock

This is an important number to look at because it indicates how a company is financing its activities. Rapidly growing companies often issue large amounts of new stock, which can dilute the value of existing shares but which also give the company cash for expansion. Slower growing companies that generate a lot of free cash flow tend to buy back significant amounts of their own stock, though companies that issue many stock options to their employees also buy back stock to minimize dilution.

You can see this kind of buyback activity in Figure 5.22 of Dell's financial statements printed to the right. Under "purchase of common stock," note that Dell spent $2.3 billion repurchasing its own stock, and on the income statement, you can see that the number of diluted shares outstanding fell about 3 percent, from 2.726 billion to 2.644 billion. Although share repurchases are generally a shareholder-friendly use of excess cash—after all, the fewer shares outstanding, the larger the piece of the company that each shareholder owns—

Hewlett-Packard Company and Subsidiaries: Partial Statement of Cash Flows			
For the following years ended October 31 In millions	2002	2001	2000
Dividends	$(801)	$(621)	$(638)

Figure 5.21 Hewlett-Packard's partial cash flow statement. *Source:* Hewlett-Packard SEC filings.

Dell Computer Corporation: Partial Statement of Cash Flows

In millions Fiscal year ending	January 31, 2003	February 1, 2002	February 2, 2001
Cash flows from financing activities			
Purchase of common stock	$(2,290)	$(3,000)	$(2,700)
Issuance of common stock under employee plans and other	265	298	395
Net cash used in financing activities	$(2,025)	$(2,702)	$(2,305)

Figure 5.22 Dell's partial cash flow statement. *Source:* Dell SEC filings.

you have to view share buybacks with caution when they come from firms such as Dell that grant large numbers of stock options. Firms that grant their employees a ton of options and then spend corporate cash on repurchases are essentially selling shares to their employees at low prices and buying it back on the open market at much higher prices, which is not the best use of capital.

Issuance/Repayments of Debt

This number tells you whether the company has borrowed money or repaid money it previously borrowed. In Figure 5.23, you can see that H-P received $2.5 billion from bondholders in exchange for some long-term debt and paid off $2.4 billion in short-term debt. You can see these two entries on the lines

Hewlett-Packard Company and Subsidiaries: Partial Statement of Cash Flows

For the following years ended October 31 In millions	2002	2001	2000
Cash flows from financing activities			
(Decrease) increase in notes payable and short-term borrowings	$(2,402)	$303	$(1,297)
Issuance of long-term debt	2,529	904	1,936
Payment of long-term debt	(472)	(290)	(474)

Figure 5.23 Hewlett-Packard's partial cash flow statement. *Source:* Hewlett-Packard SEC filings.

labeled "issuance of long-term debt" and "(decrease) in notes payable and short-term borrowings."

Conclusion

Painful though it may have been, you've just gained something very valuable: You now know enough about financial statements to meaningfully analyze a company. Although you can (and should) spend much more time learning the nooks and crannies of financial reporting, understanding how a company generates cash is now within your grasp, and that's what really matters. The details aren't nearly as important as the basic concepts that we've just walked through. Now that you've made it through most of this chapter, you're already ahead of the pack.

To wrap things up, let's follow a dollar through Dell to see what happens to it. A customer—let's call him Steven, just for kicks—buys a computer for $1,000 from Dell. Dell turns around and uses $821 to pay manufacturing employees and parts suppliers (cost of goods sold). How do I know this? Look at Dell's income statement (Figure 5.24): The firm spent $29,055/$35,404, or 82.1 percent, of every dollar in sales paying for the cost of manufacturing the computer, and 82.1 percent of $1,000 is $821. So. Dell has $179 of the $1,000 it received for the computer left over after paying for the cost of making the computer.

Now, look at the rest of the income statement (Figure 5.25) to see what happens to the remaining $179. About $86 is spent on television ads and corporate overhead (selling, general, and administrative), $13 goes to research and development, and another $25.50 goes to Uncle Sam. After adding back a little

Dell Computer Corporation: Partial Income Statement	
	2003
Net revenue	$35,404
Cost of revenue	29,055
Gross margin	6,349

Figure 5.24 Dell's revenue breakdown. *Source:* Dell SEC filings.

Dell Computer Corporation: Partial Income Statement

	2003
Operating expenses	
Selling, general, and administrative	$3,050
Research, development, and engineering	455
Special charges	—
Total operating expenses	$3,505
Operating income	2,844
Investment and other income (loss)—net	183
Income before income taxes and cumulative effect of change in accounting principle	3,027
Provision for income taxes	905
Income before cumulative effect of change in accounting principle	2,122
Cumulative effect of change in accounting principle—net	—
Net income	$2,122

Figure 5.25 Dell's partial income statement. *Source:* Dell SEC filings.

bit of investment income generated by Dell's huge cash balance, we're left with about $60 in net profit from the $1,000 computer sale. That $60 can be reinvested in the business, used to buy back stock, or simply kept in a bank account until a good opportunity comes along. You can calculate every single one of these numbers yourself right from Dell's income statement—just divide the line item by total sales, and multiply the resulting percentage by $1,000.

What do we now know about Dell's business? For one thing, we know that the profit margins are pretty low—with only about $60 in net profits of every $1,000 in sales, we can see that most of Dell's revenue goes right back out the door to the folks who build the computers, supply the parts, and run the company.

We also know that Dell doesn't spend much on R&D or marketing, which makes sense because the company is striving to be the low-cost producer in a commodity market. If Dell were a pharmaceutical company and spent only 1.5 percent of revenue on research, we'd get mighty worried. But R&D isn't all that important to Dell, so we're not too concerned about it.

There's much more you can learn about a company than this, and that's exactly what we do in the next chapter—we take what we've learned about financial statements and use it to generate analytical insights into how a business is functioning.

But don't overlook the power of this simple test: If you can't understand how a dollar flows from a company's customers back through to shareholders, something's amiss. Either the company's business model is too confusing or you need to do more digging before committing any of your money.

Investor's Checklist: Financial Statements Explained

▶ The balance sheet tells you how much a company owns, how much it owes, and the difference between the two, which represents the value of the money that shareholders have invested in the firm. Shareholders' equity in a firm is the value of the firm's assets minus its liabilities.

▶ Because the balance sheet must balance at all times, any change in assets or liabilities will cause a corresponding change in equity. If a firm generates huge profits that drive an increase in assets, equity will also increase.

▶ Keep an eye on the trend in accounts receivable compared with sales. If the firm is booking a large amount of revenue that hasn't yet been paid for, this can be a sign of trouble.

▶ When you're evaluating a company's liabilities, remember that debt is a fixed cost. A big chunk of long-term debt can be risky for a company because the interest has to be paid no matter how business is doing.

▶ Be wary of companies that report "nonrecurring" charges, particularly if they make a habit of it. All kinds of expenses can be buried in "one-time" charges.

▶ The statement of cash flows is the true touchstone for corporate value creation because it shows how much cash a company is generating from year to year—and cash is what counts. Look at the cash flow statement first.

▶ When you're analyzing a company, make sure you can understand how a dollar flows through the business. If you can't do this, you probably don't understand the company well enough to buy the stock.

Analyzing a Company—
The Basics

Now that we have the basic tools of financial statement analysis in hand, we can start tearing into companies. Because this can be a daunting task, I suggest that you break down the process into five areas:

1. *Growth:* How fast has the company grown, what are the sources of its growth, and how sustainable is that growth likely to be?
2. *Profitability:* What kind of a return does the company generate on the capital it invests?
3. *Financial health:* How solid is the firm's financial footing?
4. *Risks/bear case:* What are the risks to your investment case? There are excellent reasons *not* to invest in even the best-looking firms. Make sure you look at the full story and investigate the negatives as well as the positives.
5. *Management:* Who's running the show? Are they running the company for the benefit of shareholders or themselves? This is such a critical topic that I've devoted an entire chapter (Chapter 7) to it.

One word of caution: In this chapter and the next, we'll be concerned only with evaluating the quality of the *company.* However, this is only half the story because even the best companies are poor investments if purchased at too high a price. We'll cover how to evaluate *stocks* in Chapters 9 and 10, where I'll show you how to estimate the right price to pay for a company's shares.

Growth

The allure of strong growth has probably led more investors into temptation than anything else. High growth rates are heady stuff—a company that manages to increase its earnings at 15 percent for five years will double its profits, and who wouldn't want to do that? Unfortunately, a slew of academic research shows that strong earnings growth is not very persistent over a series of years; in other words, a track record of high earnings growth does not necessarily lead to high earnings growth in the future.

Why is this? Because the total economic pie is growing only so fast—after all, the long-run aggregate growth of corporate earnings has historically been slightly slower than the growth of the economy—strong and rapidly growing profits attract intense competition. Companies that are growing fast and piling up profits soon find other companies trying to get a piece of the action for themselves.

You can't just look at a series of past growth rates and assume that they'll predict the future—if investing were that easy, money managers would be paid much less, and this book would be much shorter. It's critical to investigate the *sources* of a company's growth rate and assess the *quality* of the growth. High-quality growth that comes from selling more goods and entering new markets is more sustainable than low-quality growth that's generated by cost-cutting or accounting tricks.

The Four Sources

In the long run, sales growth drives earnings growth. Although profit growth can outpace sales growth for a while if a company is able to do an excellent job cutting costs or fiddling with the financial statements, this kind of situation simply isn't sustainable over the long haul—there's a limit to how much costs can be cut, and there are only so many financial tricks that companies can use to boost the bottom line. In general, sales growth stems from one of four areas:

1. Selling more goods or services
2. Raising prices
3. Selling new goods or services
4. Buying another company

The easiest way to grow is to do whatever you're doing better than your competitors, sell more products than they do, and steal market share from them. Mobile-phone giant Nokia, for example, increased its share of the global mobile phone market from around 15 percent in the mid-1990s to around 35 percent today by simply doing a better job selling phones.

Raising prices can also be a great way for companies to boost their top lines, although it takes a strong brand or a captive market to be able to do it successfully for very long. Anheuser-Busch, for example, has historically been able to raise prices by 1 percent to 3 percent per year because it has a strong portfolio of popular brands such as Budweiser, Bud Lite, and Michelob.

Cable companies have also used pricing power to increase their top lines, though it's due more to monopoly power than strong brands. Throughout the 1990s, most markets had only one cable provider for any given consumer, so cable firms were able to push through annual price increases of 6 percent to 7 percent.

If there's not much more market share to be taken or your customers are very price-sensitive, you can do what Wal-Mart did and expand your market by selling products that you hadn't sold before. In the mid-1980s, founder and then-CEO Sam Walton saw that the firm's growth was likely to hit a wall at some point in the ensuing decade, so he began investigating new markets. After a trip to Europe, where European retailers had begun to build hypermarkets that sold everything from clothes to toys to ketchup under one roof, Walton figured that groceries could be Wal-Mart's next big market. Fifteen years later, Wal-Mart is the largest seller of groceries in the United States, and supercenters that include food sales account for an ever-larger percentage of its sales.

Remember, the goal of this type of analysis is simply to know why a company is growing. In Anheuser-Busch's case, you'd want to know how much growth is coming from price increases (more expensive beer), how much is coming from volume increases (more beer drinkers), and how much is coming from market share growth (more Budweiser drinkers). Once you're able to segment a firm's growth rate into its components, you'll have a much better handle on where that growth is likely to come from in the future—and when it may tap out.

The fourth source of sales growth—acquisitions—deserves special attention. Acquisitive firms are often darlings of Wall Street because they're major consumers of investment banking services. They're often looking to either raise capital for a new acquisition or find a new target, which means they constantly have folks in suits lining up at their door trying to pitch them on deals. It shouldn't come as any surprise, then, that the analysts that follow acquisition-hungry firms usually have nice things to say.

Unfortunately, the historical track record for acquisitions is mixed. Most acquisitions fail to produce positive gains for shareholders of the acquiring firm, and one study showed that even acquisitions of small, related businesses—which you'd think would have a good chance of working out well—succeeded only about half the time.[1]

There are a host of reasons for this. For one, acquisitive firms have to keep buying bigger and bigger firms to keep growing at the same rate—and the bigger a target firm is, the harder it is to check out thoroughly, which increases the risk of buying a pig in a poke. Even Warren Buffett found this out when Berkshire Hathaway bought GenRe, a huge reinsurance firm, in 1998. Buffett knows more about insurance than almost anyone alive, but the GenRe purchase turned out to be less than stellar. Buffett himself said some time after the deal that GenRe was in worse shape than he'd thought when he bought it. Not even the savviest of CEOs can know all the skeletons that may be lurking in a huge target firm.

Another reason to be skeptical of acquisitive firms is simply that buying other companies takes time and money. Targets have to be investigated, investment bankers have to be paid, and acquired firms have to be integrated into the new owner, all of which steals resources away from running the core business. If executives are spending all of their energy looking for ways to

---

[1] Mark L. Sirower, *The Synergy Trap* (New York: Free Press, 1997).

make the firm bigger, rather than better, the wheels are sure to come off the cart eventually.

From the investor's perspective, however, the biggest reason to be leery of a growth-by-acquisition strategy is even simpler: It makes the company more difficult to understand. Acquisitive firms usually post many merger-related charges and often wind up restating their financial results, which means the results of the acquiring company can be obscured in all the merger-related confusion. As a result, two things can happen:

1. An unscrupulous management team can use the fog created by constant acquisitions to artificially juice results, and this financial tinkering can take a long time to come to light because it's buried in the necessary financial rejiggering that comes with any sizeable acquisition.
2. The true growth rate of the underlying business may be impossible to figure out, especially if management is evasive about giving out information on the firm's organic growth rate.

Bottom line: If you don't know how fast the company would have grown *without* acquisitions, don't buy the shares—because you never know when the acquisitions will stop. Remember, the goal of a successful investor is to buy great businesses, not successful merger and acquisition machines.

Questioning Quality

As you might have guessed, I generally view acquisitions as a very low-quality way of generating growth. Unfortunately, there are plenty of other ways of making growth look better than it really is, especially when we turn our attention to *earnings* growth rather than *sales* growth. (Sales growth is much more difficult to fake.) Although the list of tricks that companies can use to boost earnings growth even as sales growth falters is a long one, there are a few basic areas to watch out for. Changing tax rates, changing share counts, pension gains, one-time gains (often from selling off businesses), and rampant cost cutting are among the most common. (I'll show you the full spectrum of earnings-management tricks in Chapter 8.)

In general, any time that earnings growth outstrips sales growth over a long period—for example, 5 to 10 years—you need to dig into the numbers to

IBM Growth Rates	1995	1996	1997	1998	1999	2000	2001	2002
Revenue %	12.3	5.6	3.4	4.0	7.2	1.0	-2.9	-5.5
Operating income %	51.7	13.2	5.8	0.7	30.2	-2.5	-20.1	-26.9
Earnings per share %	43.7	41.4	17.6	9.3	25.2	7.8	-2.0	-28.0

Figure 6.1   Annual growth rates for IBM.

see how the company keeps squeezing out more profits from stagnant sales. A big difference between the growth rate of net income and operating income or cash flow from operations can also hint at something unsustainable.

IBM is a classic example of what I call "manufactured growth," because it used almost all of the previously mentioned techniques to pump up its bottom line during the 1990s. As shown in Figure 6.1, Big Blue's earnings per share growth looks pretty good since the Lou Gerstner-led turnaround began in the early 1990s—close to double digits most years, which is not bad for a company of this size.

But when we look at operating income, it looks as though the company was growing much slower, while sales growth was stuck around 5 percent on average. As a double-check, take a quick look at cash flow from operations—unfortunately, this also looks pretty stagnant from 1995 through the end of the decade (see Figure 6.2).

So what was driving those great earnings-per-share results that Gerstner's IBM kept turning like clockwork? A whole host of items: For one, the firm's tax rate plunged from 46 percent in 1995 to around 30 percent by the end of the decade. For another, the firm cut overhead spending substantially during the 1990s—a laudable accomplishment, given the bureaucratic nature of the firm.

Finally, IBM bought back about a quarter of its shares during the latter half of the 1990s—fewer shares outstanding meant more earnings per share—and benefited from an overfunded pension plan that boosted earnings. As you can see, a simple comparison of IBM's earnings per share relative to its

IBM	95	96	97	98	99	00	01	02
Cash flow ($bil)	10.7	10.3	8.9	9.3	10.1	9.3	14.3	13.8

Figure 6.2   Annual cash flow from operations for IBM.

operating income and cash flow raised many red flags—enough that any investor looking at the company in the late 1990s could have been skeptical about the quality of the firm's earnings growth. (Note: Low-quality growth doesn't imply that a company is cooking the books, merely that the growth rate isn't likely to be sustained over the long haul.)

You should also keep an eye out for one-time gains and losses that can distort a historical growth rate. A big gain from the sale of a division, for example, can make growth look better than it really was. Large losses can also affect growth rates—if a company's earnings were depressed in the first year of a three- or five-year period, the firm's growth rate will be overstated because growth will be calculated from a depressed base. So don't take the trailing three-year and five-year growth rates that you see as gospel—always check to see what's behind the numbers.

In general, any time you can't pinpoint the sources of a company's growth rate—or the reasons for a sharp divergence between the top and bottom lines, as was the case with Big Blue—you should be wary of the quality of that growth rate. Paying less taxes and buying back shares are good things for shareholders, no question, but they're short-term fixes rather than long-term sources of earnings growth.

A word on cost cutting: All things equal, I'd rather own a more efficient firm—one with lower overhead costs—than a less efficient firm. However, cost cuts are not a sustainable long-term source of earnings growth, and if you're looking at a firm that's been slashing costs, you should be aware that at some point there won't be any more costs to cut. Earnings growth will eventually slow unless sales growth speeds up.

At some point, a cost-cutting firm is going to find that it has become as efficient as possible, and sales and earnings growth will converge unless the firm manages to boost revenue growth. So when you see a firm with earnings gains being driven by cost cutting, make sure you think about the sustainability of those cost cuts because they won't be around forever.

Profitability

Now we come to the second—and, in many ways, most crucial—part of the analysis process: How much profit is the company generating relative to the amount of money invested in the business? This is the real key to separating great companies from average ones, because the job of any company is to take money from outside investors and invest it to generate a return. The higher that return, the more attractive the business.

I've already briefly discussed profit margins and the importance of understanding whether cost cuts or price hikes are driving an increase in profit margins. Comparing cash flow from operations to reported earnings per share is another good way to get a rough idea of a firm's profitability because cash flow from operations represents real profits.

But neither net margin nor cash flow from operations accounts for the amount of capital that's tied up in the business, and that's something we can't ignore. We need to know how much economic profit a firm is able to generate per *dollar of capital employed* because it will have more excess profits to reinvest, which will give it an advantage over less-efficient competitors.

Think about it this way—a company's management is similar to the manager of a mutual fund. A mutual fund manager takes investors' money and earns a return on it by investing in stocks and bonds. Wouldn't you rather put your money with an equity manager who has consistently generated returns of 12 percent per year than one who has returned an average of only 9 percent per year?

Companies aren't much different. They take shareholders' money and invest it in their own businesses to create wealth. By measuring the return that a company's management has achieved through this investment process, we know how good they are at efficiently transforming capital into profits. Just like a mutual fund, a company whose management is investing well enough to generate returns on capital of 12 percent is usually a more attractive investment than a company that returns only 9 percent on its capital.

Our two tools for assessing corporate profitability are return on capital and free cash flow. I start with return on assets (ROA) and return on equity (ROE), which we first saw in Chapter 3 when we evaluated economic moats. Then I'll show you how to compare free cash flow to ROE and I'll finish up with a quick discussion of a sophisticated measure of profitability called return on invested capital (ROIC).

Return on Assets (ROA)

You already know the first component of ROA. It's simply net margin, or net income divided by sales, and it tells us how much of each dollar of sales a company keeps as earnings after paying all the costs of doing business. The second component is asset turnover, or sales divided by assets, which tells us roughly how efficient a firm is at generating revenue from each dollar of assets. Multiply these two together, and you have return on assets, which is simply the amount of profits that a company is able to generate per dollar of assets.

$$\frac{\text{Net income}}{\text{Sales}} = \text{Net margin}$$

$$\frac{\text{Sales}}{\text{Assets}} = \text{Asset turnover}$$

$$\text{Net margin} \times \text{Asset turnover} = \text{Return on assets}$$

Think of ROA as a measure of efficiency. Companies with high ROAs are better at translating assets into profits. We can see this easily when we compare a top-notch retailer such as Best Buy with a firm like Circuit City, which was struggling in the late 1990s and early 2000s. Since 1998, Circuit City's returns on assets have been around 4 percent to 5 percent, whereas Best Buy's improved from 5 percent to almost 10 percent (see Figures 6.3 and 6.4.)

Higher profit margins—almost 3 percent for Best Buy and below 2 percent for Circuit City—are part of the picture, but higher asset turnover is a bigger differentiator between the two. In 2002, for example, each dollar that Circuit City had invested in property and inventory (the two biggest assets for most retailers) generated about $2.50 in sales, while the same dollar invested by Best Buy generated $3.20 in sales. Clearly, Best Buy was running a more efficient shop than Circuit City and was much better at transforming its assets into profits.

Circuit City Profitability	1998	1999	2000	2001	2002
Net margin (%)	1.4	1.6	1.9	1.4	2.0
Asset turnover (average)	2.6	3.0	3.2	3.0	2.5
Return on assets (%)	3.6	4.8	6.1	4.2	5.0

Figure 6.3 Annual profitability figures for Circuit City.

Best Buy Profitability	1998	1999	2000	2001	2002
Net margin (%)	1.1	2.2	2.8	2.6	2.9
Asset turnover (average)	4.4	4.4	4.5	3.9	3.2
Return on assets (%)	4.8	9.7	12.6	10.1	9.3

Figure 6.4 Annual profitability figures for Best Buy.

ROA helps us understand that there are two routes to excellent operational profitability: You can charge high prices for your products (high margins), or you can turn over your assets quickly. Often, you'll see companies with lower profit margins, such as grocery stores and discount retailers, emphasize high asset turnover as a way to achieve solid ROAs. For any business that can't charge a big premium for its goods, tight inventory management is critical because it keeps down the amount of capital tied up in assets, which helps pump up return on assets. On the flip side, companies that can mark up their goods in a big way—a luxury retailer such as Tiffany, for example—can afford to have more capital tied up in their assets because they make up for low asset turnover with high profit margins.

Just using ROA would be fine if all companies were big piles of assets, but many firms are at least partially financed with debt, which gives their returns a leverage component that we need to take into account. Our next measure of returns on capital, return on equity, lets us do this.

Return on Equity (ROE)

Return on equity is a great overall measure of a company's profitability because it measures the efficiency with which a company uses shareholders' equity—in other words, it measures how good the company is at earning a decent return on the shareholder's money. Think of it as measuring profits per dollar of shareholders' capital.

To calculate ROE, multiply ROA by a firm's financial leverage ratio:

$$\text{Financial leverage} = \frac{\text{Assets}}{\text{Shareholders' equity}}$$

$$\text{Return on equity} = \text{Return on assets} \times \text{Financial leverage}$$

Because Return on assets = Net margin × Asset turnover, ROE in all its glory equals:

$$\text{Net margin} \times \text{Asset turnover} \times \text{Financial leverage}$$

You'll notice that we've introduced a new metric—financial leverage, which is essentially a measure of how much debt a company carries, relative to shareholders' equity. Unlike net margin and asset turnover—for which higher ratios are almost unequivocally better—financial leverage is something you need to watch carefully. As with any kind of debt, a judicious amount can boost returns, but too much can lead to disaster.

Look at the kind of business the firm is in. If it's fairly steady, a company can probably take on large amounts of debt without too much risk because there's only a small chance of the business falling off a cliff and the company being caught short when bondholders demand their interest payments. On the flip side, be very wary of a high financial leverage ratio if a company's business is cyclical or volatile. Because interest payments are fixed, the company has to pay them whether business is good or bad.

Therefore, we have three levers that can boost ROE—net margins, asset turnover, and financial leverage. For example, a firm could have only so-so margins and modest levels of financial leverage, but it could do a great job with asset turnover (e.g., a well-run discount retailer such as Wal-Mart). Companies with high asset turnover are extremely efficient at extracting more dollars of revenue for each dollar they have invested in hard assets. A firm could also excel at convincing customers to pay up for its products—asset turns might be just middling, and the firm might not have much leverage, but it would have great profit margins (e.g., a luxury goods company such as Coach). Finally, a firm can boost its ROE to respectable territory by taking on good size amounts of leverage (e.g., mature firms such as utilities).

Although it's tough to generalize, let me offer some rough benchmarks for evaluating firms' ROEs. In general, any nonfinancial firm that can generate consistent ROEs above 10 percent *without excessive leverage* is at least worth investigating. As of mid-2003, only about one-tenth of the nonfinancial firms in Morningstar's database were able to post an ROE above 10 percent for each of the past five years, so you can see how tough it is to post this kind of performance. And if you can find a company with the potential for consistent ROEs over 20 percent, there's a good chance you're really on to something.

Two caveats when you're using ROE to evaluate firms: First, banks always have enormous financial leverage ratios, so don't be scared off by a leverage ratio that looks high relative to a nonbank. (We go over how to evaluate banks' financial health in Chapter 17.) In addition, because banks' leverage is always so high, you want to raise the bar for financial firms—look for consistent ROEs above 12 percent or so.

The second caveat concerns firms with ROEs that look too good to be true because they're usually just that. ROEs above 40 percent or so are often meaningless because they've probably been distorted by the firm's financial structure. Firms that have been recently spun off from parent firms, companies that have bought back many of their shares, and companies that have taken massive charges often have very skewed ROEs because their equity base is depressed. If you see an ROE over 40 percent, check to see if the company has any of these characteristics.

Free Cash Flow

In the previous chapter, I introduced you to cash flow from operations (CFO), which measures how much cash a company generates. As useful as CFO is, it doesn't take into account the money that a firm has to spend on maintaining and expanding its business. To do this, we need to subtract capital expenditures, which is money used to buy fixed assets. The result is free cash flow:

$$\text{Free cash flow} = \text{Cash flow from operations} - \text{Capital spending}$$

Thinking back to our hot dog stand example, suppose Mike was so successful that he decided to use the cash he'd generated to build a second hot dog stand. The cost of building that stand would be posted to "capital spending," and subtracted from free cash flow.

Why? We need to be able to separate out businesses that are net users of capital—ones that spend more than they take in—from businesses that are net producers of capital because it's only that excess cash that really belongs to us as shareholders. You may sometimes see free cash flow referred to as "owner earnings," because that's exactly what it is: the amount of money the owner of a company could withdraw from the treasury without harming the company's ongoing business.

A firm that generates a great deal of free cash flow can do all sorts of things with the money—save it for future investment opportunities, use it for acquisitions, buy back shares, and so forth. Free cash flow gives financial flexibility because the firm isn't relying on the capital markets to fund its expansion. Firms that have negative free cash flow have to take out loans or sell additional shares to keep things going, and that can become a risky proposition if the market becomes unsettled at a critical time for the company.

As with ROE, it's tough to generalize about how much free cash flow is enough. However, I think it's reasonable to say that any firm that's able to convert more than 5 percent of sales to free cash flow—just divide free cash flow by sales to get this percentage—is doing a solid job at generating excess cash.

Putting Return on Equity and Free Cash Flow Together

One good way to think about the returns a company is generating is to use the *profitability matrix,* which looks at a company's ROE relative to the amount of free cash flow it's generating. Figure 6.5 shows free cash flow along one side and ROE on the other side, and this matrix can tell you a great deal about the kind of company you're analyzing.

Companies such as Microsoft, Pfizer, and First Data all have very high ROEs. People write books about how to manage a business as well as these companies do, and it's easy to see why—they're all money machines. Investors pour new money into them, and large amounts of extra money get spit out. Their managements are very, very good at earning a high return on shareholders' money.

If you follow any of these companies at all, you'll notice they have another thing in common besides high ROEs—their stocks all had valuations that were high during the bull market of the 1990s. Again, it's easy to see why: A company that can earn a high return on its shareholders' money is worth more to those same shareholders.

Looking at the other axis, we see that these companies are also very good at generating free cash flow. Pfizer, for example, generated more than $8 billion in free cash flow in 2002. That's $8 billion Pfizer made *after* spending whatever it needed to invest in its business. Pfizer could have chosen to pay

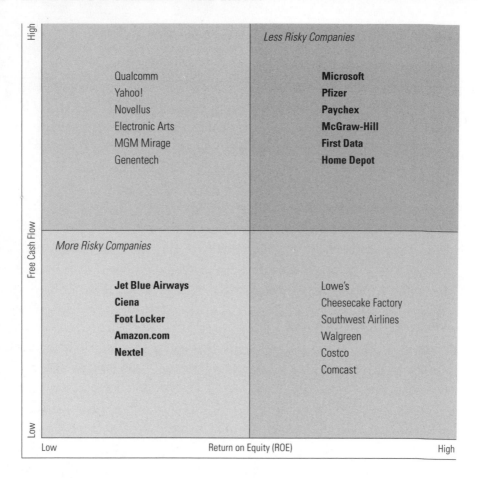

Figure 6.5   The Profitability Matrix: High ROEs and strong free cash flows are worth paying up for.
Source: Morningstar, Inc.

that $8 billion—which worked out to about $1.31 per share—out to share-holders. In fact, that's exactly what older, more mature companies often do with their free cash flow. Their businesses aren't growing very fast, and they figure that shareholders can earn a better return on the free cash flow than they can. So, they return it to shareholders in the form of dividends. (This is why slow-growth firms often have such high yields.)

Pfizer, on the other hand, thinks that it can figure out a way to invest that $8 billion more profitably than its shareholders. Because the company is in a relatively fast-growing area of the economy—health care—and has a solid track record of turning out profitable new drugs, it may very well be able to do so. However, if Pfizer started to pile up cash on its balance sheet the way Microsoft has over the past several years, we'd probably conclude that the company doesn't have many profitable avenues for reinvesting its excess profits. In this case, we'd want the firm to pay a dividend or buy back shares. Although Microsoft's dividend isn't very large at this writing, at least the company has one, which means that it has recognized that internal reinvestment opportunities are diminishing.

On the bottom half of the matrix, we have companies such as Amazon .com, JetBlue, Comcast, and Lowe's, which generate low or negative free cash flow. Companies like these aren't generating much free cash because they're using all the cash their businesses generate—and then some—to invest in expansion. They're investing heavily because they hope that those expansion efforts will pay off in the form of fat profits in the future. Amazon, for example, is spending heavily on building a brand and expanding its Web site, while JetBlue is spending heavily on new airplanes so that it can expand its service to new cities.

JetBlue and Amazon are like young entrepreneurs. They've taken out loans and maxed out their credit cards, and they're plowing every cent they have into building and expanding their businesses. Although they're not earning much in the way of profits right now, folks are investing in their businesses because they expect these companies to be very profitable sometime in the future, which is when investors will be rewarded. Pfizer, on the other hand, is more like a successful, middle-age businessman. He's already proven he can earn a good return on shareholders' money, so folks line up outside his door for the privilege of investing in his ventures.

You'd be taking a lot less risk investing with the older businessman than you would with the young entrepreneur—though that entrepreneur might just pay you back many, many times over. Just remember that for every Jeff Bezos or Steve Jobs, there are literally hundreds of entrepreneurs who never paid their investors a dime.

There's nothing wrong with investing in the entrepreneurs of the world, as long as you know what you're getting into. A profitability matrix can help you separate your long shots from your core holdings.

Think of the profitability matrix like this: That upper right-hand corner, where Pfizer sits, is the sweet spot—excess cash and the ability to earn a high return on it. Companies in this square tend to be the cream of the crop and have a low level of business risk. (They might be very risky *stocks,* though, if they're trading at high valuations.)

Moving down to the bottom right, where Lowe's is, you see companies that are reinvesting all of their cash in expansion but are still able to generate a high return on shareholders' money. If these firms still have profitable reinvestment opportunities, they *should* be spending all the cash they generate on expansion. For example, Starbucks and Home Depot posted high ROEs and negative free cash flow all through the 1990s because they were plowing every cent they earned into building more stores.

In the bottom left are young companies growing like weeds, but which haven't yet proven that they can earn a decent ROE—they're spending tons of money, but they're not yet making it pay off very well. This is where the most speculative companies hang out. These companies are generally long shots because it's still unclear whether all of that heavy investment will ever generate an attractive return.

Return on Invested Capital (ROIC)

Return on invested capital is a sophisticated way of analyzing return on capital that adjusts for some peculiarities of ROA and ROE. Although you needn't worry about calculating it for yourself—it's pretty complicated—it's worth knowing how to interpret it because it's overall a better measure of profitability than ROA and ROE. (If you *are* interested in how to calculate it, see the ROIC box.)

Essentially, ROIC improves on ROA and ROE because it puts debt and equity financing on an equal footing: It removes the debt-related distortion that can make highly leveraged companies look very profitable when using ROE. It also uses a different definition of profits than ROE and ROA, both of which use net income. ROIC uses operating profits *after* taxes, but *before* interest expenses. Again, the goal is to remove any effects caused by a company's financing decisions—does it use debt or equity?—so that we can focus as closely as possible on the profitability of the core business.

What does all this mean to you if you hear someone talking about ROIC? Simply that you should interpret ROIC just as you would ROA and ROE— a higher return on invested capital is preferable to a lower one.

Return on Invested Capital (ROIC)

Warning: The material in this box drifts dangerously close to finance-geek territory. If hard-core finance puts you to sleep, ignore this box and don't worry about the inner workings of ROIC and WACC.

The true operating performance of a firm is best measured by return on invested capital (ROIC), which measures the return on all capital invested in the firm regardless of the source of the capital. The formula for ROIC is deceptively simple:

$$ROIC = \frac{\text{Net operating profit after taxes (NOPAT)}}{\text{Invested capital}}$$

The numerator of this equation is easy: profits after taxes, but before interest costs. The denominator is a bit trickier, and although there are many different ways to calculate it, you'll do just fine if you use this version:

$$\frac{\text{Invested}}{\text{capital}} = \frac{\text{Total}}{\text{assets}} - \begin{array}{c}\text{Non-interest-bearing}\\\text{current liabilities (usually}\\\text{accounts payable and}\\\text{other current assets)}\end{array} - \begin{array}{c}\text{Excess cash (cash}\\\text{not needed for}\\\text{day-to-day}\\\text{business needs)}\end{array}$$

You may also want to subtract goodwill if it's a large percentage of assets.

Let's run through an example: At the end of fiscal 2002, Wal-Mart's total assets were worth $94.7 billion. Subtract accounts payable, accrued liabilities, and accrued income taxes, and $67.7 billion remains, which is Wal-Mart's invested capital. Looking at the firm's income statement, we see that operating profit was $13.6 billion. If we multiply this by the firm's 36 percent tax rate, we get a rough idea of what taxes would have been without any interest income or interest expense (remember, interest is tax deductible for corporations), and we find that NOPAT equals $13.6 − ($13.6 × 0.36) = $8.7 billion.

Next, divide NOPAT by invested capital, or $8.7 billion by $67.7 billion, and ROIC is 12.9 percent—pretty respectable for a firm as large and mature as Wal-Mart.

Financial Health

Once we've figured out how fast (and why) a company has grown and how profitable it is, we need to look at its financial health. Even the most beautiful home needs a solid foundation, after all.

The bottom line about financial health is that when a company increases its debt, it increases its fixed costs as a percentage of total costs. In years when business is good, a company with high fixed costs can be extremely profitable because once those costs are covered, any additional sales the company makes fall straight to the bottom line. When business is bad, however, the fixed costs of debt push earnings even lower.

Look at what debt does to the earnings volatility of the creatively named Acme (see Figure 6.6). With more debt, Acme's earnings fluctuate a lot: They're up more in good times and down more in bad times.

A common measure of leverage is simply the financial leverage ratio that we used in calculating ROE, equal to assets divided by equity. Think of financial leverage like a mortgage—a homebuyer who puts $20,000 down on a $100,000 house has a financial leverage ratio of 5. For every dollar in equity, the buyer has $5 in assets.

The same holds true for companies. In 2002, home improvement retailer Lowe's had a financial leverage ratio of 2.1, meaning that for every dollar in equity, the firm had $2.10 in total assets. (It borrowed the other $1.10.) A financial leverage ratio of 2.1 is fairly conservative, even for a fast-growing retailer. It's when we see ratios of 4, 5, or more that companies start to get really risky.

In addition to financial leverage, make sure to examine a few other key metrics when assessing a company's financial health.

Debt to Equity

This is just what it sounds like—long-term debt divided by shareholder's equity. It's a little like the financial leverage ratio, except that it's more narrowly focused on how much long-term debt the firm has per dollar of equity.

Times Interest Earned

This one requires a little more work to calculate, but it's worth it. Look up pretax earnings, and add back interest expense—this gives earnings before

Acme: Conservatively financed with a little debt.	2002
Sales	5,000
Gross profit	1,000
Less: Interest Expense	**200**
Earnings before taxes	800
Less: Taxes (35% rate)	280
Net income	520

2003 Hypothetical Scenarios: Good Year (Sales up 20%)	Bad Year (Sales down 20%)
6,000	4,000
1,200	800
200	**200**
1,000	600
350	210
650	390
Profits up 25%	**Profits down 25%**

Acme: Aggressively financed with a lot of debt.	2002
Sales	5,000
Gross profit	1,000
Less: Interest Expense	**600**
Earnings before taxes	400
Less: Taxes (35% rate)	140
Net income	260

2003 Hypothetical Scenarios: Good Year (Sales up 20%)	Bad Year (Sales down 20%)
6,000	4,000
1,200	800
600	**600**
600	200
210	70
390	130
Profits up 50%	**Profits down 50%**

Figure 6.6   The impact of financial leverage. *Source:* Morningstar, Inc.

interest and taxes (EBIT). Divide EBIT by interest expense, and you'll know how many times (hence the name) the company could have paid the interest expense on its debt. The more times that the company can pay its interest expense, the less likely that it will run into difficulty if earnings should fall unexpectedly.

For home improvement retailer Lowe's, for example, we add $182 million in interest expenses to $2.36 billion in pretax earnings to get $2.54 billion in EBIT, and we divide $2.54 million by the $182 million in interest expense to get times interest earned of 14. In other words, Lowe's earned enough money in 2003 to cover its interest obligation 14 times over, which is a pretty safe margin (see Figure 6.7).

Lowe's Companies: Partial Income Statement	
Year ending January 31	2003
Net sales	$26,491
Cost of sales	18,465
Gross margin	8,026
Expenses:	
Selling, general, and administrative	4,730
Store opening costs	129
Depreciation	626
Interest	**182**
Total expenses	5,667
Pre-Tax Earnings	**2,359**
Income tax provision	888
Net earnings	$1,471

Figure 6.7   Lowe's Income Statement. *Source:* Lowe's SEC filings.

It's tough to say precisely how low this metric can go before you should be concerned—but higher is *definitely* better. You want to see higher times interest earned for a company with a more volatile business than for a firm in a more stable industry. Be sure to look at the trend in times interest earned over time, as well. Calculate the ratio for the past five years, and you'll be able to see whether the company is becoming riskier—times interest earned is falling—or whether its financial health is improving.

Current and Quick Ratios

The current ratio (current assets divided by current liabilities) simply tells you how much liquidity a firm has—in other words, how much cash it could raise if it absolutely had to pay off its liabilities all at once. A low ratio means the company may not be able to source enough cash to meet near-term liabilities, which would force it to seek outside financing or to divert operating income to pay off those liabilities. As a *very* general rule, a current ratio of 1.5 or more means the firm should be able to meet operating needs without much trouble.

Unfortunately, some current assets—such as inventories—may be worth less than their value on the balance sheet. (Imagine trying to sell old PCs or last year's fashions to generate cash—you'd be unlikely to receive anything close to what you paid for them.) So there's an even more conservative test of a company's liquidity, the *quick ratio,* which is simply current assets less inventories divided by current liabilities. This ratio is especially useful for manufacturing firms and for retailers because both of these types of firms tend to have a lot of their cash tied up in inventories. In general, a quick ratio higher than 1.0 puts a company in fine shape, but always look at other firms in the same industry to be sure.

The Bear Case

After you've assessed growth, profitability, and financial health, your next task is to look at the bear case for the stock you're analyzing. Start by listing all of the potential negatives, from the most obvious to the least likely. What could go wrong with your investment thesis? Why might someone prefer to be a seller of the stock than a buyer? Constructing a convincing bear case is especially important for those who like to buy high-quality companies that have hit temporary speed bumps, because what looks like a speed bump may very well be a roadblock on closer inspection.

Equally important, your bear case will be a great reference point even if you do decide to buy the stock. You'll know in advance what signs of trouble to watch for, which will help you make better decisions when bad news comes down the pike in the future. Having already investigated the negatives, you'll have the confidence to hang on to the stock during a temporary rough patch as well as the savvy to know when the rough patch might really be a serious turn for the worse.

I'll admit to a painful example from my own history that shows the importance of developing a bear case before buying a stock. In the mid-1990s, I purchased some shares of a small firm called Ballantyne of Omaha, which was one of the world's largest manufacturer of motion picture projectors in the world at the time. (The big ones in movie theaters—not the ones your teacher used in elementary school.) The firm was growing at a decent clip, had few competitors, and management seemed to have their heads on straight. The stock was selling for what I thought was a pretty reasonable price, as well.

Unfortunately, the movie theater industry—Ballantyne's main customer—was in the midst of a huge debt-fueled building boom at the time. Remember all of those 10- and 20-screen suburban theaters that got thrown up during the 1990s? That's what was pumping up Ballantyne's sales, and the expansion wasn't sustainable. Many of the big theater chains had liquidity crunches, and a few even went belly up. Needless to say, this did not do wonders for movie-projector demand, and Ballantyne's financial results (and stock price) went into a fast slide.

The lesson? I should have constructed a convincing bear case for Ballantyne before I bought it. If I'd looked deeper into the financial health of Ballantyne's customers, I might have asked myself what would happen if the multiplex boom slowed down. I didn't and, as a result, I made a poor investment that could have been avoided.

Conclusion

To this point, we've investigated the financial performance of companies. We've assessed their competitive strengths by investigating their economic moats, and we've analyzed their financial statements.

In Chapter 7, I'll discuss how to assess the quality of management. In Chapter 8, I'll give you some tips on how to spot aggressive accounting, after which we'll turn to perhaps the toughest task faced by any serious investor: Deciding on a fair price for the stock. How can we avoid paying too much for excellent companies, while not being so cheap that we let wonderful opportunities pass us by? In Chapters 9 and 10, I'll show you how to value stocks.

Investor's Checklist: Analyzing a Company—The Basics

▶ When you're evaluating a company's growth rate, don't get swept away by heady historical growth. Make sure you understand where the growth is coming from and how it can be sustained over time.

▶ Be wary of companies that have relied on acquisitions to boost growth. Most acquisitions fail to produce positive returns for shareholders of the acquiring firm, and they make it tough to evaluate a company's true growth rate.

▶ If earnings growth outstrips sales growth over a long period, this might be a sign of *manufactured growth.* Make sure to dig into the numbers to see how the company keeps squeezing out more profits from stagnant sales.

▶ Return on assets measures the amount of profits that a company is able to generate per dollar of assets. Companies with high ROAs are better at translating assets into profits.

▶ ROE is a good measure of profitability because it measures how the company is at earning a return on shareholders' money. But because companies can boost their ROEs by taking on more debt, don't take it as gospel. For a nonfinancial company, look for an ROE of at least 10 percent, without excessive leverage.

▶ Free cash flow gives financial flexibility because the firm isn't relying on the capital markets to fund its expansion. Firms with negative free cash flow have to take out loans or sell additional shares to keep things going, and that can become a risky proposition if the market becomes unsettled at a critical time for the company.

▶ Be wary of companies with too much financial leverage. Because debt is a fixed cost, it magnifies earnings volatility and leads to more risk.

▶ Before you buy a stock, think through all the potential negatives. This can help you make better decisions if bad news does come down the pike.

7

Analyzing a Company—
Management

Excellent management can make the difference between a mediocre
business and an outstanding one, and poor management can run even a great
business into the ground. Your goal is to find management teams that think
like shareholders—executives that treat the business as if they owned a piece
of it, rather than as hired hands. Unfortunately, managers like this are more
rare than you might think.

People buy stocks all the time without checking out the folks in the executive suite, and the excuse I hear most often is that it's tough to assess management without meeting them face-to-face. Hogwash. There are many,
many ways to get a feel for the folks running a company that have nothing to
do with looking the CEO in the eye. No one can run a public company without leaving a trail of pretty strong objective evidence behind. My advice is to
divide the management-assessment process into three parts: compensation,
character, and operations.

Compensation

Compensation is the easiest of the three areas to assess because the bulk of the information is contained in a single document, usually called the *proxy statement*. This is the form that companies mail shareholders around the time of the annual meeting, and it details how much executives are paid and what perks they get. (You can find this form online at www.sec.gov or www.freeedgar.com. Look for form DEF14A.)

Here's what to look for in a company's compensation plan. First and most important, how much does management pay itself? (This is detailed in the aptly named "summary compensation table.") Generally, I prefer big bonuses to big base salaries and restricted stock grants to generous option packages. Bonuses mean that a good portion of the pay is at least theoretically at risk, and restricted stock means the executive loses money if the share price declines. That's just the tip of the iceberg, though.

First, look at the raw level of cash compensation to see if it's reasonable. There's not necessarily a strict limit here, though I personally think an $8 million cash bonus is silly no matter how well the company has done. (For reference, the average CEO of a large U.S. firm currently earns about 500 times as much as the average employee. Twenty years ago, this multiple was just 40.)

In any case, use your own judgment—if the amount that executives earn makes you cringe, it's probably too much. Also look at competing firms to see what their CEOs are paid, so you can see how the boss that you're investigating stacks up. In general, the larger the firm and the better its financial performance, the more an executive should be paid. But some executives think they have a license to print money just because they manage a huge company, no matter how poor a job they're doing, which is why you need to determine whether their pay is tied to the firm's operational performance. (Case in point: After retiring as chairman and co–CEO of Verizon, Charles Lee became a "consultant" to the firm at the exorbitant rate of $250,000 per *month*. To me, that's a cringe-worthy retirement package.)

Pay for Performance

What's even more important is whether executives' pay is truly tied to the company's performance. At many companies, so-called "performance targets" are set by a subcommittee of the board of directors, which can often rewrite the rules of the game if the CEO appears to be losing. In 2001, for example, Coca-Cola's board reduced CEO Douglas Daft's goal of 15 percent earnings growth over five years to 11 percent. Moving the goalposts like this can be justified in one sense—after all, if the performance target isn't achievable, it's hardly going to motivate the CEO—but you can also fault the board for not setting more realistic goals in the first place. In any case, I think it's a negative sign when the targets are changed but the potential reward stays the same, because it indicates that the board is unwilling to stand up to the CEO and punish him or her by slashing the bonus when performance slumps.

At least Coke's shareholders knew what the target was, though. According to the 2001 proxy, Walt Disney's compensation gurus decided that bonuses:

> may be based on one or more of the following business criteria, or on any combination thereof, on a consolidated basis: net income (or adjusted net income), return on equity (or adjusted return on equity), return on assets (or adjusted return on assets), earnings per share (diluted) (or adjusted earnings per share [diluted]).

In other words, Disney's CEO was going to get paid no matter what. To add insult to injury, the gang at Disney wrote that "[we believe] that the specific target constitutes confidential business information the disclosure of which could adversely affect the Company." More likely, it would have adversely affected Disney management because the board wouldn't have been able to move the goalposts in the middle of the game. This kind of nondisclosure on the compensation front is a bad sign when you're looking for good managers.

Another sign of poor compensation procedures is paying managers for actions that make the company bigger, but not better. In 2001, for example, Disney wrote the following in its proxy statement:

> As permitted by the plan, special bonuses were paid outside the plan to three executives . . . Peter Murphy, Thomas Staggs and Louis Meisinger—for extraordinary services to the Company unrelated to the plan's performance targets, including, in the case of Messrs. Murphy and Staggs, *services related to the Company's acquisition of Fox Family Worldwide, Inc.*

Rewarding management for consummating an acquisition is an absolutely terrible idea—paying big bonuses just for getting a deal done simply encourages executives to go out and do more dubious deals. A better idea, though not one I've ever seen implemented, would be to wait a couple of years and pay a bonus only if an acquisition has provided an adequate—and predetermined—return on the investment.

The bottom line is this: Executives' pay should rise and fall based on the performance of the company. So, after reviewing a company's historical financials, read the past few years' proxies to see whether this has truly been the case or whether some lackeys on the board of directors have cooked up justifications for big bonuses even in bad times. Firms with good corporate governance standards won't hesitate to pay managers less in bad times and more in good times, and that's the kind of pattern you want to see as a shareholder.

Other Red Flags

Aside from the big-picture question of whether executives' pay truly is linked to company performance, keep an eye out for the following issues when you're assessing executive compensation.

Were Executives Given "Loans" that Were Subsequently Forgiven? This was a common—and disgusting—practice before the Sarbanes-Oxley Act banned it in 2002. Companies would give loans to senior managers at below-market rates of interest and then often quietly forgive the loans a few years later. In my book, a loan that's not repaid is a bonus, and companies that tried to fudge executive pay in this fashion weren't treating shareholders with respect. If the executive needed a loan, he should have asked his bank, not his employer. Don't tolerate this kind of behavior from companies you're investigating—even though it's not legal any longer, companies that did this sort of thing in past should be viewed with skepticism. After all, would they have stopped unless they were forced to? (Loans of this sort are usually disclosed in the "other compensation" column of the executive compensation table in the footnotes.)

Do Executives Get Perks Paid for by the Company that They Should Really Be Paying for Themselves? It's a sure sign of corporate excess when execs get country club memberships and other frippery paid for by shareholders. After all, when you're paying someone several hundred thousand dollars per year, making shareholders foot the bill for their greens fees seems rather silly. More importantly, such behavior at the top sets a poor example for everyone else in the firm. Managers who enjoy ridiculous perks are acting like latter-day royalty rather than prudent custodians of shareholders' money. Conversely, thrifty CEOs are a plus: Managers who do things such as paying for their own parking and eschewing pricey perks set a good tone for the rest of the organization.

Does Management Hog Most of the Stock Options Granted in a Given Year, or Do Rank-and-File Employees Share in the Wealth? Generally, firms with more equitable distribution schemes perform better over the long run. Most firms break out the percentage of options granted to executives relative to the total granted in the proxy statement.

Does Management Use Stock Options Excessively? Even if they're distributed beyond the executive suite, giving out too many options dilutes existing shareholders' equity. If a company gives out more than 1 or 2 percent of the outstanding shares each year, they're giving away too much of the firm's equity every year. Conversely, it's a great sign if the firm issues restricted stock instead of options. Restricted stock has to be counted as an expense on the income statement (options don't, as of this writing), and restricted stock also forces the recipient to participate on the downside if the stock falls.

If a Founder or Large Owner Is Still Involved in the Company, Does He or She Also Get a Big Stock Option Grant Each Year? This makes me queasy. After all, it's hard to argue that, for example, CEO Larry Ellison of Oracle needs additional options to motivate him when he already owns 25 percent of the firm.

Do Executives Have Some Skin in the Game? That is, do they have substantial holdings of company stock, or do they tend to sell shares right after they exercise options? As a shareholder, I want management to have meaningful equity in the company. After all, selling shares in the name of "diversification" means not being exposed if the company goes downhill. Generally, I'm happier owning companies where executives own stock right alongside me because large unexercised option positions are cold comfort. You can find this information in the footnotes of the proxy. Companies indicate executives' percentage ownership *including* options prominently in a table labeled "security owner-ship of certain beneficial owners," but they declare only how many actual *shares* are owned in the footnotes. In Peoplesoft's 2003 proxy, for example, CEO Craig Conway was listed as owning 3.8 million shares, or 1.2 percent of the company. But if you looked at the footnote, you'd have seen that he owned only 626,000 shares, 625,000 of which weren't even vested yet.

Character

Compensation by itself is often a good litmus test for character—anecdotally, there's a pretty strong relationship between management teams that are in it for the money and management teams that treat shareholders poorly. How-ever, there are some other important questions you should ask to get a handle on whether a firm's management deserves your trust.

Does Management Use Its Position to Enrich Friends and Relatives?

In a company's annual 10-K filing, look for a section called "related-party transactions." If a friend or relative of a company officer has substantial busi-ness dealings with the firm, you'll read about it here. Often, this stuff is pretty innocuous—an ex-officer or director is paid some nominal amount each year for consulting services. As long as the firm isn't paying out hundreds of thou-sands of dollars, this kind of thing doesn't get my hackles up.

But when the firm pays substantial amounts of money to, for example, an interior-design firm run by the CEO's wife or to a law firm in which the CFO's son-in-law is a partner, I sit up and take notice. The key here is to make sure that (1) the firm isn't sending a great amount of business in the di-rection of related parties and (2) there's not an egregious pattern of abuse. One or two small related-party transactions aren't a big deal, but they do cause me to raise an eyebrow because they may be signs of a deeper problem. And if it looks as though virtually all family members of the company officers have their hands in the till, you have a big character issue.

Is the Board of Directors Stacked with Management's Family Members or Former Managers?

Look at the biographies of the board, which are also in the proxy statement. If many of them are closely related to top management—or are former managers themselves, it's a good bet the board isn't going to be as hard-nosed when questioning management's actions as it could be. And because the board is shareholders' last line of defense against a CEO running amok, that's hardly a good thing.

Is Management Candid about Its Mistakes?

Not even the smartest executives get everything right, and it's important that a management team be able to honestly discuss poor decisions and why they were made. CEOs who bury mistakes might be burying other things as well. Look for this type of candor in annual reports and in quarterly conference calls. I especially like to look at the letter to shareholders in the annual report. Is it a candid assessment of the past year's successes and failures or a fluff piece?

How Promotional Is Management?

Although a certain amount of rallying the troops is the job of a CEO, watch out for company officers who cross the line and begin blindly pumping up the stock or themselves. This is a red flag because management's job is to worry about running the company—if executives get that right, the stock price will take care of itself over time. Executives who complain about how undervalued their firm's shares are or who opine about its true worth are probably more concerned with the value of their options than with making solid, long-term business decisions. Self-promotional managers, meanwhile, are not likely to make decisions that are in the best interests of long-term shareholders. If you read a number of glowing media articles in which a CEO paints himself or herself as a latter-day savior, watch out. The cult of the CEO-as-hero is dangerous.

Can the CEO Retain High-Quality Talent?

This one is subtler, but it can tell you a great deal about the firm you're analyzing. Some firms judge the quality of managers by the turnover rate of their subordinates because turnover is seen as the ultimate acid test of the working environment and employees' views of a company's potential. Extend this view to the executive team: How often do officers turn over? What is the tenure of key officers? Is executive hiring done from the outside? (All of this can be uncovered by reviewing several years' worth of proxy statements.) Long tenure is a great signal of intrinsic motivation and confidence in the business, whereas a CEO who keeps forcing out immediate subordinates is likely spending too much time on internal power struggles and not enough on running the business.

Does Management Make Tough Decisions that Hurt Results but Give a More Honest Picture of the Company?

If a management team makes decisions that actually hurt reported results, you're in luck. Management teams that use restricted stock grants instead of options—because the former has to be expensed, while the latter doesn't—or who expense rather than capitalize items such as research and development or software costs are the kinds of folks who are more interested in running the business than playing numbers games. And those are precisely the kind of people you want running the companies you own.

Running the Business

In addition to managers who are paid reasonably and are honest, you also want folks who can run the business well.

Performance

The first stop is simply the financial performance of the company during the tenure of the current management team. Look for high and increasing ROEs and ROAs—but don't forget to check whether increasing ROE was driven by higher leverage, as opposed to improved profitability or asset efficiency.

Are there any big jumps in revenue? If so, the firm probably did an acquisition, and you should check to see whether management paid a reasonable price and whether the acquired firm wound up adding to shareholder value. Most acquisitions do not pay off, so digging into past merger and acquisition (M&A) activity is definitely worth your while.

Finally, look at the share count over a long period of time. If the number of shares outstanding has increased substantially because of aggressive options programs or frequent equity issuance, the firm is essentially giving away part of your stake without asking you. That's not a great recipe for long-term share performance.

Follow-Through

When management identifies a problem and promises a solution, does it actually implement the plan, or does it hope you forget about it? The same goes for any "new strategic initiatives" that are announced: Does the firm go ahead with a new plan once it's announced, or does every year see the firm announcing a grand new strategy that's never realized? One way to vet this is to look at past annual reports and see what new initiatives were discussed three to seven years ago. It's fine if they weren't all successful, but where are they now? Has management kept shareholders up to date on them, or do the initiatives just disappear from the radar screen? In the latter case, management is probably spending more time hiring consultants with grandiose plans than actually figuring out what's broken.

Candor

Does the firm provide enough information to properly analyze the business, or does it clam up about certain issues? Generally, management teams will talk ad nauseam about parts of the business that are hitting on all cylinders, but questions about a problem area are sometimes met with evasion or a straight, "We don't disclose that."

For example, Merck changed the way it reported its drug sales figures in 2001, but it wouldn't provide comparable data for past periods—which made it difficult to get a clear picture of what was going on. Lucent was another offender in this department because it grouped together high-growth and low-growth product lines when it broke out segment data. It's entirely proper for firms not to report certain things, but selective reticence about problem areas is never a good sign.

Self-Confidence

I generally applaud firms that do something markedly different from their peers or from conventional opinion. It's tough to take a pass on a hot consulting fad when all of your golfing buddies are singing its praises or to buy a beaten-down competitor when your industry is in the tank—but these are both moves that can pay off in spades. Maintaining research and development spending during an industry downturn is another good example of self-confidence that shows management is more concerned with beating competitors over the long haul than beating its quarterly earnings guidance.

Flexibility

Has management made decisions that will give the firm flexibility in the future? These include simple decisions such as not taking on too much debt and controlling fixed expenses (even in good years), as well as more strategic decisions such as issuing equity when the stock is high. Attaching call options to debt, retiring high-rate debt when the opportunity presents itself, and buying back stock only when the price is low are also good examples of capital allocation decisions that evidence a solid operational hand on the tiller.

Investor's Checklist: Analyzing a Company—Management

▶ Evaluating management is a critical component of analyzing a stock. Look for management teams that act like shareholders, rather than hired hands.

▶ Get compensation information from the proxy statement—SEC form DEF-14A. Check out how much management is paid and whether pay varies with the company's performance. If a pay package makes you cringe, it's too high.

▶ Avoid companies that give loans to executives, have many related-party transactions, or give out too many stock options. Look for executives that have substantial stock ownership positions.

▶ Make sure the company discloses enough information for you to properly analyze the business. "We don't disclose that" is often code for, "The news is bad, so we'd rather not say."

8

Avoiding Financial Fakery

As YOU'VE LIKELY figured out by now, picking great stocks is not a black-and-white process. Unfortunately, neither is accounting. There are literally dozens of techniques that are perfectly legal and aboveboard, but which have the effect of fooling an observer into thinking that a firm has posted true operational improvements when all it has really done is moved some numbers around. You need to know how to identify what's known as *aggressive accounting* so you can avoid the companies that practice it.

Even worse than aggressive accounting, of course, is outright fraud—the hucksters of the world are naturally attracted to the stock market because it's the perfect arena for profiting from the greed and carelessness of others. Knowing the signs of potential fraud can save you a lot of financial pain.

It's not that hard, either. Although you might need a CPA to understand *exactly* how an aggressive or fraudulent firm is exaggerating its results, you don't need to be an expert to recognize the warning signs of accounting chicanery. As long as you avoid the companies that bristle with red flags, you won't be caught owning them when the SEC starts investigating.

Six Red Flags

When you're giving a company the once-over, there are six major red flags to watch out for. Though some of these issues can pop up for innocent reasons, be sure you thoroughly investigate them before giving the firm a clean bill of health—or your money.

Declining Cash Flow

Even if accounting gobbledygook makes your head spin, there is one very simple thing you can do: Watch cash flow. Over time, increases in a company's cash flow from operations should roughly track increases in net income. If you see cash from operations decline even as net income keeps marching upward—or if cash from operations increases much more slowly than net income—watch out. This usually means that the company is generating sales without necessarily collecting the cash, and that's a very good recipe for a blowup down the road.

My favorite example of this is former high-flyer Lucent. Between 1997 and 1999, Lucent's net income soared from $449 million, to just over $1 billion, to almost $3.5 billion—an incredible growth rate for such a large company. At the same time, however, cash flow from operations was plunging precipitously, from $2.1 billion in 1997 to $1.9 billion in 1998, to *negative* $276 million in 1999. Why? It's a long and sordid story, but it boiled down to three big reasons:

1. Lucent was extending credit to anyone who could spell photon, which meant it was booking many sales without receiving the cash. (Think back to our hot dog stand example in Chapter 4—as long as a firm ships a product and has reasonable certainty that it will eventually collect the cash, it can post the sale.) Accounts receivable (A/R) ballooned from 20 percent of sales to 27 percent of sales between 1997 and 1999, a clear sign that the firm was having trouble collecting the money it was owed.
2. Lucent kept building more gear than it could ship, which sent inventories upward. (Remember, manufacturing something and then storing it in a warehouse uses cash.) This effect showed up in the "increase in inventories" line item in the firm's statement of cash flows.
3. Lucent's pension plan was pumping up net income with noncash gains.

If you do nothing else, watch cash flow like a hawk.

Serial Chargers

Be wary of firms that take frequent one-time charges and write-downs. This practice makes the historical financials muddier because every charge has a long explanation and usually has various components that affect different accounts—all of which need to be adjusted if you want to look at comparable year-to-year financial results.

More importantly, frequent charges are an open invitation to accounting hanky-panky because firms can bury bad decisions in a single restructuring charge. Usually, the rationale for a charge is pretty vague, which means there's a fair amount of leeway for management.

When a firm takes a big restructuring charge, it's essentially improving future results by pulling future expenses into the present. In other words, poor decisions that might need to be paid for in future quarters—an unsuccessful product that may need to be terminated or a bloated division that will need to pay severance payments to redundant employees—all get rolled into a single one-time charge in the current quarter, which improves future results.

If you run across a firm that has frequent restructuring charges, don't ignore them, despite the firm's blandishments about what earnings would be after excluding the charge. After all, if a firm dug itself into a deep enough hole that it needs quarter after quarter of charges to make things right, those charges are a normal cost of improving the business.

Serial Acquirers

As I mentioned earlier in the book, firms that make numerous acquisitions can be problematic—their financials have been restated and rejiggered so many times that it's tough to know which end is up. Aside from muddying the waters, acquisitions increase the risk that the firm will report a nasty surprise some time in the future, because acquisitive firms that want to beat their competitors to the punch often don't spend as much time checking out their targets as they should.

The Chief Financial Officer or Auditors Leave the Company

Quis custodiet ipsos custodes? is Latin for "who watches the watchmen?" And when it comes to financial reporting, those watchmen are the chief financial officer (CFO) and the corporate auditors. If a CFO leaves the company for reasons that seem at all strange—or inexplicable—you should be on your guard. It's normal for CFOs to move around just like other executives, but if you see a CFO leave a company that's already under suspicion for accounting issues, you should think very hard about whether there might be more going on than meets the eye. The same applies to corporate auditors. If a company changes auditors frequently or fires its auditors after some potentially damaging accounting issue has come to light, watch out. This one may not be a big deal by itself, but it's definitely something to watch with firms that have already displayed other warning signs.

The Bills Aren't Being Paid

There are few things Wall Street loves more than growth, and companies go to great lengths to keep their top line increasing as rapidly as possible. One of the sneakier ways for a company to pump up its growth rate is to loosen customers' credit terms, which induces them to buy more products or services. (Companies can also ship out more products than their customers ask for—known as "stuffing the channel"—but this is less common.)

The trick here is that even though the company has recorded a sale—which increases revenues—the customer has not yet paid for the product. If enough customers don't pay—and those looser credit terms are probably attracting financially shakier customers—the pumped-up growth rate will eventually come back to bite the company in the form of a nasty write-down or charge against earnings.

You should track how fast A/R are increasing relative to sales—the two should roughly track each other. But if sales increase by, for example, 15 percent, while A/R increases 25 percent, the company is booking sales faster than it's receiving cash from its customers. (Remember, A/R measures goods that are sold, but not yet paid for.) As a general rule, it's simply not possible for A/R to increase faster than sales for a long time—the company is paying out more money (as finished goods) than it's taking in (through cash payments).

On the credit front, watch the "allowance for doubtful accounts," which is essentially the company's estimate of how much money it won't be able to collect from deadbeat customers. If this amount doesn't move up in sync with A/R, the company may be artificially boosting its results by being overly optimistic about how many of its new customers will pay their bills.

Changes in Credit Terms and Accounts Receivable

Finally, check the company's 10-Q filing for any mentions of changes in credit terms for customers, as well as for any explanation by management as to why A/R has jumped. (Look in the management's discussion and analysis section for the latter and in the accounting footnotes for the former.)

Seven Other Pitfalls to Watch Out For

Watching for these six warning signs will help you avoid maybe two-thirds of potential accounting-related blowups. Unfortunately, though, there are many other ways that firms can embellish their financial results. When you're reading a 10-K or annual report, watch for the following pitfalls.

Gains from Investments

It's reasonably common for large firms—especially in the technology sector—to make small investments in other companies. Occasionally, these investments work out well, the owner sells some of the shares, and records the capital gain as income. This is no different from the way you or I would report a capital gain as income when we're doing our taxes every year, and it's perfectly legal and aboveboard.

An honest company breaks out these sales, however, and reports them below the "operating income" line on its income statement. The problem arises when companies try to boost their operating results—in other words, the performance of their core business—by shoehorning investment income into other parts of their financial statements.

The most blatant means of using investment income to boost results is to include it as part of revenue, though this isn't very common. Companies can also record the income "above the line" so that it is included as part of operating income and thus boosts their operating margins. This is manifestly a no-no because accounting rules require any piece of one-time income to be separated from income that comes from normal operations. Finally, companies can hide investment gains in their expense accounts by using them to reduce operating expenses, which makes the firm look more efficient than it really is.

If the firm you're analyzing is using investment gains or asset sales to boost operating income or reduce expenses, you know you're dealing with a company that might be less than forthcoming in other areas as well.

Pension Pitfalls

Pensions can be a big ball-and-chain for companies with many retirees because if the assets in the pension plan don't increase quickly enough, the firm has to divert profits to prop up the pension. To fund pension payments to future retirees, companies shovel money into pension plans that then are invested in stocks, bonds, real estate, and so forth. If a company winds up with fewer pension assets than pension liabilities, it has an *underfunded* plan, and if the company has more than enough pension assets to meet its projected obligations to retirees, it has an *overfunded* plan. (More on overfunded plans in the next section of this chapter.)

To see whether the company has an over- or underfunded pension plan, go to the footnotes of a 10-K filing and look for the note labeled "pension and other postretirement benefits," "employee retirement benefits," or some variation. Then look at the line labeled "projected benefit obligation." This is the first key number. It's the estimated amount the company will owe to employees after they retire, and it's based on assumptions about how long retirees will live, the rate that salary levels at the company will grow over time, and the interest rate that the company uses to discount its future obligations to their present value. Compare this with the line labeled "fair value of plan assets at end of year," which is the second key number.

If the benefit obligation exceeds the plan assets, the company has an underfunded pension plan and is likely to have to shovel in more money in the future, reducing profits. This can be a huge number for a large company with many retirees—General Motors, for example, had pension obligations of $80 billion at year-end 2002 versus pension assets of $61 billion. One way or another, GM will need to make up the $19 billion difference. (As recently as 2000, GM had a $1.7 billion *surplus* in its pension plan. When Wall Street goes south, so do pension plans—but the obligation keeps growing as employees earn benefits.)

What did this mean for GM? In 2002, the firm chucked in a whopping $4.9 billion to the plan. (You can see this in the pension footnote under "employer contributions.") That's almost $5 billion in cold, hard cash that an unwary shareholder might have been expecting to increase the firm's value, but which actually went straight to GM retirees.

So, always check out the pension footnote. There's a lot of accounting gobbledygook there, but you can also find out whether the firm you're looking at is going to wind up owing its retirees more money than it actually has. And if that's the case, they'll get the money before you will as a shareholder.

Pension Padding

Pensions can be a boon as well as a burden. When stocks and bonds do really well, as they did in the 1990s, pension plans go gangbusters. And if those annual returns exceed the annual pension costs, the excess can be counted as profit. Flowing gains from an overfunded pension plan through the income statement is a perfectly legal practice that pumped up earnings at General Electric for years and boosted earnings at many defense companies by 30 percent to 40 percent during the 1990s.

However, this pension-related income is a strange kind of profit. It's not available to pay out to shareholders—it belongs to the pension plan. And the only way to unlock that excess is to terminate the plan, which is highly unusual. But the excess does benefit shareholders: It should mean the company will have to contribute less to the pension plan in the future to keep it solvent. As a shareholder, you'd much rather have an overfunded pension plan than an underfunded one. But this income is completely dependent on the stock market, so it's not money you want to rely on in the future. You should subtract it from net income when trying to figure out just how profitable a company really is.

To find out how much profits decreased because of pension costs or increased because of pension gains, go to the line in the pension footnote labeled either "net pension/postretirement expense," "net pension credit/loss," "net periodic pension cost," or some variation. Companies usually break out the contribution of pension costs to profits for the trailing three years; therefore, you can see not only the absolute level of pension profit or loss, but also the trend. You won't see these numbers in the income statement—they get lumped in with other categories there.

Vanishing Cash Flow

There's one important caveat to the general rule that cash flow is a number to be trusted: You can't count on cash flow generated by employees exercising options. I mentioned this wrinkle in Chapter 5—the amount is labeled "tax benefits from employee stock plans," or "tax benefit of stock options exercised" on the statement of cash flows. Here's why you don't want to count on this cash flow.

When employees exercise their stock options, the amount of cash taxes that their employer has to pay declines. Let's say your employer gives you 100 options with an exercise price of $10. A few years later, the stock is trading for $30, and you decide to cash in. You pay taxes on the $2,000 difference (the $30 market price less the $10 exercise price), and your employer gets to take a tax deduction of $2,000 against its corporate income because taxable employee compensation is tax deductible for employers. In other words, your employer reduced its tax bill by $700—assuming a 35 percent tax rate—just because you exercised your 100 options.

As long as the firm's stock keeps going up and it keeps giving out options, this process continues. More options are exercised, tax deductions are taken, and the firm saves cash by lowering its tax bill. But what happens if the stock takes a tumble? Many people's options will be worthless—their exercise prices will be higher than the market price—and, consequently, fewer options will be exercised. Fewer options are now exercised, the company's tax deduction gets smaller, and it has to pay more taxes than before, which means lower cash flow.

Therefore, when the stock price declines, the firm generates less cash than it did when the stock was flying. Sun Microsystems, for example, reported about $2.1 billion in cash flow from operations in fiscal 2001, $816 million of which resulted from this lovely tax benefit. In other words, Sun would have generated 40 percent less cash in 2001 if its employees hadn't exercised tons of options. But the next year, when Sun's shares plunged to below $5, this portion of cash flow dried up very fast as fewer options were exercised. In 2002, Sun's option-related tax benefits dropped by almost 90 percent, to only $98 million.

If you're analyzing a company with great cash flow that also has a high-flying stock, check to see how much of that cash flow growth is coming from options-related tax benefits. Unless you think you can predict the stock market, that's not cash you want to count on in years to come.

Overstuffed Warehouses

When inventories rise faster than sales, there's likely to be trouble on the horizon. Sometimes the buildup is just temporary as a company prepares for a new product launch, but that's usually more the exception than the rule.

When a company produces more than it's selling, either demand has dried up or the company has been overly ambitious in forecasting demand. In any case, the unsold goods will have to get sold eventually—probably at a discount—or written off, which would result in a big charge to earnings.

This is what happened in late 2000 to virtually every company selling communications-related gear—inventories started to balloon as demand from telecom carriers started to slow. At the time, many analysts (including, I'm humbled to say, me) thought that the gear-makers had simply overestimated demand temporarily and that the situation would correct itself once telecom carriers used up the gear they'd already ordered. But it turned out that demand was not just pausing—it was falling off a cliff. Therefore, inventories continued to pile up until sales started to slow as well, and companies such as Cisco had to write off billions in unsold goods.

Change Is Bad

Another way firms can make themselves look better is by changing any one of a number of assumptions in their financial statements. As a very general rule, you should look skeptically on any optional change—some accounting changes are mandated by rule makers—that improves reported results. Odds are good that the motivation for making the change wasn't altruistic.

One item that can be altered is a firm's depreciation expense. If a firm is assuming that an asset—such as a building or factory—will wear out in 10 years, it subtracts (or depreciates) one-tenth of the building's value from its earnings each year. As you can imagine, the longer the depreciation period, the smaller the annual hit to earnings. Therefore, if a firm suddenly decides that an asset has a longer useful life and stretches out the depreciation period, it's essentially pushing costs out into the future and inflating current earnings.

Firms can also change their *allowance for doubtful accounts.* If the allowance for doubtful accounts doesn't increase at the same rate as accounts receivable, a firm is essentially saying that its new customers are much more creditworthy than the previous ones—which is pretty unlikely. If the allowance actually *declines* as accounts receivable rise, the company is stretching the truth even further. In either case, if more customers wind up not paying than the firm estimated, the firm will have to take a charge to earnings at some point in the future, which means current results are overstated.

Firms can also change things as basic as how expenses are recorded and when revenue is recognized (one of those gray accounting areas). You'll generally find this kind of information in the "summary of significant accounting policies" section of the 10-K—and if a firm chooses to make changes that materially reduce expenses or increase revenue, watch out. Unless these moves were required by the accounting rule makers, the firm is probably trying to cover up deteriorating results.

To Expense or Not to Expense

Companies can also fiddle with their costs by capitalizing them. As I discussed in Chapter 4, the basis of accrual accounting is that benefits have to be matched with expenses on the income statement. Operating costs—such as office supplies, office rents, and so forth—are expensed because they produce a short-term benefit. (You pay the rent only one month or year at a time, and the benefit you receive expires at the end of that period unless you make another payment.) On the other hand, costs such as a new piece of machinery are *capitalized*—that is, their value is recorded as an asset that slowly declines in value over time—because they produce long-term benefits. (A machine that you buy today will still be cranking out products three years from now, just at a lower rate because of wear and tear.)

The tricky part is that certain types of costs, such as marketing and some kinds of software development, can be treated either way. As you can imagine, a company that wants to inflate profits can easily do so by capitalizing $100 in marketing costs and spreading the expense out over several years, rather than expensing the entire $100 in the current period. This is exactly what AOL did in the mid-1990s—the firm argued that the subscribers it was acquiring were likely to produce long-term benefits, so it should be allowed to capitalize its marketing costs. The SEC disagreed, and AOL had to reverse course.

Finding this kind of information will take some digging around in the footnotes of a company's 10-K form, but it's time well spent. Any time you see expenses being capitalized, ask some hard questions about just how long that "asset" will generate an economic benefit. Looking at the *useful life* assumption will generally do the trick—a building might be useful for 40 years, but a piece of office furniture or a chunk of software won't.

Investor's Checklist: Avoiding Financial Fakery

▶ The simplest way to detect aggressive accounting is to compare the trend of net income with the trend in cash flow from operations. If net income is growing quickly while cash flow is flat or declining, there's a good chance of trouble lurking.

▶ Companies that make numerous acquisitions or take many one-time charges are more likely to have aggressive accounting. Be wary if a firm's chief financial officer leaves or if the firm changes auditors.

▶ Watch the trend of accounts receivable relative to sales. If accounts receivable is growing much faster than sales, the company may be having trouble collecting cash from its customers.

▶ Pension income and gains from investments can boost reported net income, but don't confuse them with solid results from the company's core operations.

9

Valuation—The Basics

So far, we've spent all of our time analyzing companies. If the investment process were as simple as identifying great companies with shareholder-friendly management teams and wide economic moats, we'd be finished—and investing would be much easier. But even the most wonderful business is a poor investment if purchased for too high a price. To invest successfully means you need to buy great companies at attractive prices.

This is an idea that lost credence during the bull market of the 1990s and was thrown completely out the window during the tech bubble. Valuations mattered less and less because investors were always willing to pay more and more—in fact, one popular investment commentary service stated baldly that business quality was 100 times more important than valuation.

For a while, this strategy—relying on a greater fool to take an asset off your hands at a higher price—was lucrative and made many people rich, at least on paper. The trouble was that no one knew when the music would stop. When it did, investors who bought overpriced assets hoping to sell them at even more inflated prices were sorely disappointed.

This is the difference between investors and speculators. Investors purchase an asset for less than their estimate of its value and receive a return more or less in line with the financial performance of that asset. Specula-tors, by contrast, purchase an asset not because they believe it's actually worth more, but because they think another investor will pay more for it at some point. The return that investors receive on assets depends largely on the accuracy of their analysis, whereas a speculator's return depends on the gullibility of others.

Over time, the stock market's returns come from two key components: investment return and speculative return. As Vanguard founder John Bogle has pointed out, the investment return is the appreciation of a stock because of its dividend yield and subsequent earnings growth, whereas the speculative return comes from the impact of changes in the price-to-earnings (P/E) ratio. Over the entire twentieth century, Bogle found that the 10.4 percent average annual return of U.S. equities broke down into 5 percentage points from div-idends, 4.8 percentage points from earnings growth, and just 0.6 percentage points from P/E changes. In other words, over a long time span, the impact of investment returns trump the impact of speculative returns.[1]

However, the picture is much different when we look at it over shorter time frames. From 1980 through 2000, for example, the market's approxi-mately 17 percent annual return was composed of 4 percentage points divi-dends, 6 percentage points earnings growth—and a whopping 7 percentage points per year from the increase in the P/E ratio.

During the horrific bear market of the 1970s, the market's *investment* return was a solid 13.4 percent per year, but as the aftermath of the early-1970s Nifty Fifty craze dragged the market's P/E ratio down from 16 times to 7 times, the market's *speculative* return was a crushing −7.5 percentage points per year. The market returned an average of only 5.9 percent per year during the 1970s, not because earnings and dividends refused to cooperate, but because the average investor paid less for the average stock in 1980 than in 1970.

Paying Up Rarely Pays Off

What does all this have to do with picking solid stocks? By paying close atten-tion to the price you pay for a stock, you minimize your speculative risk, which

---

[1] John C. Bogle, "After the Fall: What Lies Ahead for Capitalism and the Financial Markets?" (address given at the University of Missouri, Columbia, October 22, 2002).

helps maximize your total return. No one knows what a stock's speculative return will be over the next year—or even 10 years—but we can make some pretty good educated guesses about the investment return. If you find great companies, value them carefully, and purchase them only at a discount to a reasonable valuation estimate, you'll be fairly well insulated against the vicissitudes of market emotion.

For example, let's take a stock that trades for $30 per share, earns $1.50 per share, and pays a $1.00 annual dividend. Assume that earnings and dividends grow at 6 percent per year, and the initial P/E ratio of 20 doesn't change.

After five years, earnings will be $2.01, so our shares would theoretically trade for $2.01 × 20 = $40.20. We've also received $5.64 in dividends, which means we have $45.84 after five years. That works out to an annualized return of 8.8 percent, which is our investment return. Because the P/E remained at 20, we didn't receive any speculative return.

However, if earnings and dividends grow at the same rate, *but* the P/E ratio decreases from its starting point of 20 to 15, our returns change dramatically. Although we still have $2.01 in earnings after five years, our shares are worth only $2.01 × 15 = $30.15. Add in $5.64 in dividends, and annualized return shrinks to just 3.6 percent—our 8.8 percent investment return was damaged by a −5.2 percent speculative return. Conversely, a rise in the P/E ratio from 20 to 25 would yield a fat 13.3 percent annual return because the speculative return builds on our investment return.

Thus, a change in the market's mood can reduce our solid 8.8 percent return to a paltry 3.6 percent or boost it to a wonderful 13.3 percent. You can buy an excellent company that kicks out earnings and dividends like clockwork, but the negative effects of a sharp decline in the stock's valuation can wipe out even the most robust investment return—and a P/E decline from 20 to 15 is hardly a worst-case scenario. In fact, declines in valuation are usually coupled with deteriorating corporate fundamentals—slowing earnings growth or some similar setback. When this happens, the investor gets socked with a decline in the speculative return as the valuation shrinks and a decline in the investment return as earnings growth slows down.

Careful attention to valuation lessens the risk that something truly unknown—what other investors will pay for our asset in the future—will hurt the return of our portfolio. As investors, we can diligently work to identify wonderful businesses, but we can't predict how other market participants will value stocks, so we shouldn't try.

Being picky about valuation isn't fun. It means letting many pitches go by and watching many stocks run—stocks that never met your strict valuation criteria. But when it's done properly, disciplined valuation also greatly increases your batting average—the number of stocks you pick that do well versus the number that do poorly—and it also limits the odds of a real blow-up damaging your portfolio.

Using Price Multiples Wisely

Our first stop in learning how to value stocks is traditional measures such as the price-to-sales (P/S) or P/E ratios. Although these measures do have some advantages—for example, they're very easy to compute and use—they also have some significant pitfalls that can lead the unwary investor to fuzzy conclusions.

Price-to-Sales

The most basic ratio of all is the P/S ratio, which is the current price of the stock divided by sales per share. The nice thing about the P/S ratio is that sales are typically cleaner than reported earnings because companies that use accounting tricks usually seek to boost earnings. (Firms can use accounting tricks to boost sales, but it's much less frequent and it's easier to catch.) In addition, sales are not as volatile as earnings—one-time charges can depress earnings temporarily, and the bottom line of economically cyclical companies can vary significantly from year to year.

This relative smoothness of sales makes the P/S ratio useful for quickly valuing companies with highly variable earnings, by comparing the current P/S ratio with historical P/S ratios. Motorola, for example, takes special charges so often that they're no longer very special, and, as a result, it had negative net income in three of the five years between 1998 and 2002. With such spotty earnings, a P/E ratio isn't going to help us very much. But over that same time period, sales haven't jumped around nearly as much, which makes the P/S ratio useful. In mid-2003, Motorola's P/S ratio was about 1.0, close to a five-year low, which made the stock look relatively inexpensive compared with where it traded in the past (see Figure 9.1).

However, the P/S ratio has one big flaw: Sales may be worth a little or a lot, depending on a company's profitability. If a company is posting billions

Motorola	1998	1999	2000	2001	2002
Price/Earnings	NA	119.7	34.9	NA	NA
Price/Sales	1.3	3.2	1.2	1.1	0.7

NA = Earnings are negative, therefore, P/E ratios cannot be calculated.

Figure 9.1   When earnings are negative, price/sales can be a useful metric.

in sales, but it's losing money on every transaction, we'd have a hard time pinning an appropriate P/S ratio on the shares because we have no idea what level (if any) profits the company will generate. We can see the drawbacks of using sales as a proxy for value in the marketplace every day.

Retailers, which typically have very low net margins—that is, they convert a relatively small percentage of every dollar of sales into profits—tend to have very low P/S ratios. The average grocery store, for example, had a P/S ratio of 0.4 in mid-2003, whereas the average medical device firm had a P/S of around 4.3. The reason for this huge difference isn't that grocery stores happened to be dirt cheap—it was that the average grocery store had a net margin of 2.5 percent, whereas the average medical device firm had a net margin of 11 percent. A grocer with a P/S of just 1.0 would look ridiculously overvalued, but a medical device manufacturer with the same P/S ratio would be an absolute steal.

Therefore, although the P/S ratio might be useful if you're looking at a firm with highly variable earnings—because you can compare today's P/S with a historical P/S ratio—it's not something you want to rely on very much. In particular, don't compare companies in different industries on a price-to-sales basis, unless the two industries have very similar levels of profitability.

Price-to-Book

Another common valuation measure is price-to-book (P/B), which compares a stock's market value with the book value (also known as shareholder's equity or net worth) on the company's most recent balance sheet. The idea here is that future earnings or cash flows are ephemeral, and all we can really count on is the net value of a firm's tangible assets in the here-and-now. Legendary value investor Benjamin Graham, one of Warren Buffett's mentors, was a big advocate of book value and P/B in valuing stocks.

Although P/B still has some utility today, the world has changed since Ben Graham's day. When the market was dominated by capital-intensive firms that owned factories, land, rail track, and inventory—all of which had some objective tangible worth—it made sense to value firms based on their accounting book value. After all, not only would those hard assets have value in a liquidation, but also they were the source of many firms' cash flow. But now, many companies are creating wealth through intangible assets such as processes, brand names, and databases, most of which are not directly included in book value.

For service firms, in particular, P/B has little meaning. If you used P/B to value eBay, for example, you wouldn't be according a shred of worth to the firm's dominant market position, which is the single biggest factor that has made the firm so successful. Price-to-book can also lead you astray for a manufacturing firm such as 3M, which derives much of its value from its brand name and innovative products, not from the size of its factories or the quantity of its inventory.

Another item to be wary of when using P/B to value stocks is goodwill, which can inflate book value to the point that even the most expensive firm looks like a value. When one company buys another, the difference between the target firm's tangible book value and the purchase price is called *goodwill,* and it's supposed to represent the value of all the intangible assets—smart employees, strong customer relationships, efficient internal processes—that made the target firm worth buying.

Unfortunately, goodwill often represents little else but the desperation of the acquiring firm to buy the target before someone else did, because acquiring firms often overpay for target companies. Be highly skeptical of firms for which goodwill makes up a sizable portion of their book value. The P/B may be low, but the bulk of the *B* could disappear in a hurry if the firm declares the goodwill as "impaired" (in other words, the firm admits that it grossly overpaid for a past acquisition) and writes down its value.

Price-to-book is also tied to return on equity (equal to net income divided by book value) in the same way that price-to-sales is tied to net margin (equal to net income divided by sales). Given two companies that are otherwise equal, the one with a higher ROE will have a higher P/B ratio. For example, over the past five years, Nokia's P/B ratio has averaged about 14, whereas rival mobile-phone giant Motorola's has averaged 3.1. One major reason for this difference is that Nokia's average ROE of 29 percent over the same period left Motorola's average ROE of 3 percent in the dust. The reason is clear—a firm that can compound book equity at a much higher rate is worth far more because book value will increase more quickly.

Therefore, when you're looking at P/B, make sure you relate it to ROE. A firm with a low P/B relative to its peers or to the market and a high ROE might be a potential bargain, but you'll want to do some digging before making that assessment based solely on the P/B.

A caveat: Although P/B isn't terribly useful for service firms, it's very good for valuing financial services firms because most financial firms have considerable liquid assets on their balance sheets. The nice thing about financial firms is that many of the assets included in their book value are marked-to-market—in other words, they're revalued every quarter to reflect shifts in the marketplace, which means that book value is reasonably current. (A factory or piece of land, by contrast, is recorded on the balance sheet at whatever value the firm paid for it, which is often very different from the asset's current value.)

As long as you make sure that the firm doesn't have a large number of bad loans on its books—see Chapter 17 for more on banks and bad loans—P/B can be a solid way to screen for undervalued financial firms. Just remember that financial firms trading below book value (a P/B lower than 1.0) are often experiencing some kind of trouble, so you'll want to investigate just how solid that book value is before investing.

Price-to-Earnings: The Benefits

Now we come to the most popular valuation ratio, which can take you pretty far as long as you're aware of its limitations. The nice thing about P/E is that accounting earnings are a much better proxy for cash flow than sales, and they're more up-to-date than book value. Moreover, earnings per share results and estimates are easily available from just about any financial data source imaginable, so it's an easy ratio to calculate.

The easiest way to use a P/E ratio is to compare it to a benchmark, such as another company in the same industry, the entire market, or the same company at a different point in time. Each of these approaches has some value, as long as you know the limitations. A company that's trading at a lower P/E than its industry peers could be a good value, but remember that even firms in the same industry can have very different capital structures, risk levels, and growth rates, all of which affect the P/E ratio. All else equal, it makes sense to pay a higher P/E for a firm that's growing faster, has less debt, and has lower capital reinvestment needs.

You can also compare a stock's P/E to the average P/E of the entire market. However, the same limitations of industry comparisons apply to this process as well. The stock you're investigating might be growing faster (or slower) than the average stock, or it might be riskier (or less risky). In general, comparing a company's P/E with industry peers or with the market has some value, but these aren't approaches that you should rely on to make a final buy or sell decision.

However, comparing a stock's current P/E with its historical P/E ratios can be useful, especially for stable firms that haven't undergone major shifts in their business. If you see a solid company that's growing at roughly the same rate with roughly the same business prospects as in the past, but it's trading at a lower P/E than its long-term average, you should start getting interested. It's entirely possible that the company's risk level or business outlook has changed, in which case a lower P/E is warranted, but it's also possible that the market is simply pricing the shares at an irrationally low level.

This method generally works better with more stable, established firms than with young companies with more uncertain business prospects. Firms that are growing rapidly are changing a great deal from year to year, which means their current P/Es are less comparable to their historical P/Es.

Price-to-Earnings: The Drawbacks

Relative P/Es have one huge drawback: A P/E of 12, for example, is neither good nor bad in a vacuum. Using P/E ratios only on a relative basis means that your analysis can be skewed by the benchmark you're using.

So, let's try to look at the P/E ratio on an absolute level. What factors would cause a firm to deserve a higher P/E ratio? Because risk, growth, and capital needs are all fundamental determinants of a stock's P/E ratio, higher growth firms should have *higher* P/E ratios, higher risk firms should have *lower* P/E ratios, and firms with higher capital needs should have *lower* P/E ratios.

We can see why this is true intuitively, without breaking out any equations, by thinking about the basics of valuation—the three big factors that affect value are the amount, timing, and riskiness of a firm's future cash flows.

Firms that have to shovel in large amounts of capital to generate their earnings run the risk of needing to tap additional funding, either through debt (which increases the risk level of the company) or through additional equity offerings (which may dilute the value of current shareholders' stake). Either way, it's rational to pay less for firms with high reinvestment needs because each dollar of earnings requires more of shareholders' capital to produce it.

Meanwhile, a firm that's expected to grow quickly will likely have a larger stream of future cash flows than one that's growing slowly, so all else equal, it's rational to pay more for the shares (thus, the higher P/E ratio). On the flip side, a firm that's riskier—maybe it has high debt, maybe it's highly cyclical, or maybe it's still developing its first product—has a good chance of having lower future cash flows than we originally expected, so it's rational to pay less for the stock.

When you're using the P/E ratio, remember that firms with an abundance of free cash flow are likely to have low reinvestment needs, which means that a reasonable P/E ratio will be somewhat higher than for a run-of-the-mill company. The same goes for firms with higher growth rates, as long as that growth isn't being generated using too much risk.

A few other things can distort a P/E ratio. Keep these questions in the back of your mind when looking at P/E ratios, and you'll be less likely to misuse them.

Has the Firm Sold a Business or an Asset Recently? When you're looking at a P/E ratio, you must be sure that the E makes sense. If a firm has recently sold off a business or perhaps a stake in another firm, it's going to have an artificially inflated E, and thus a lower P/E. Because you don't want to value the firm based on one-time gains such as this, you need to strip out the proceeds from the sale before calculating the P/E. In late 2000, it looked as though Oracle had a ridiculously low P/E based on the past four quarters' earnings—until you dug into the numbers and saw that the company had booked a $7 billion gain by selling part of its stake in Oracle Japan. Based on operating earnings, the stock wasn't all that cheap.

Has the Firm Taken a Big Charge Recently? If a firm is restructuring or closing down plants, earnings could be artificially depressed, which would push the P/E up. For valuation purposes, it's useful to add back the charge to get a sense of the firm's normalized P/E.

Is the Firm Cyclical? Firms that go through boom and bust cycles—semiconductor companies and auto manufacturers are good examples—require a bit more care. Although you'd typically think of a firm with a very low trailing P/E as cheap, this is precisely the wrong time to buy a cyclical firm because it means earnings have been very high in the recent past, which in turn means they're likely to fall off soon. For cyclical stocks, your best bet is to look at the most recent cyclical peak, make a judgment whether the next peak is likely to be lower or higher than the last one, and calculate a P/E based on the current price relative to what you think earnings per share will be at the next peak.

Does the Firm Capitalize or Expense Its Cash Flow-Generating Assets? A firm that makes money by building factories and making products gets to spread the expense of those factories over many years by depreciating them bit by bit. On the other hand, a firm that makes money by inventing new products—drug firms are the classic example—has to expense all of its spending on research and development every year. Arguably, it's that spending on R&D that's really creating value for shareholders. Therefore, the firm that expenses assets will have lower earnings—and thus a higher P/E—in any given year than a firm that capitalizes assets.

Is the E Real or Imagined? There are two kinds of P/Es—a *trailing P/E*, which uses the past four quarters' worth of earnings to calculate the ratio, and a *forward P/E*, which uses analysts' estimates of next year's earnings to calculate the ratio. Because most companies are increasing earnings from year to year, the forward P/E is almost always lower than the trailing P/E, sometimes markedly so for firms that are increasing earnings at a very rapid clip. Unfortunately, estimates of future earnings by Wall Street analysts—the *consensus* numbers that you often read about—are consistently too optimistic. As a result, buying a stock because its forward P/E is low means counting on that future E to materialize in its entirety, and that's usually not the case.

Price-to-Earnings Growth (PEG)

The PEG is an offshoot of the P/E ratio that's calculated by dividing a company's P/E by its growth rate. The PEG is extremely popular with some investors because it seeks to relate the P/E to a piece of fundamental information—a company's growth rate. On the surface, this makes sense because a firm that's growing faster will be worth more in the future, all else equal.

The problem is that risk and growth often go hand in glove—fast-growing firms tend to be riskier than average. This conflation of risk and growth is why the PEG is so frequently misused. When you use a PEG ratio, you're assuming that all growth is equal, generated with the same amount of capital and the same amount of risk.

But firms that are able to generate growth with less capital should be more valuable, as should firms that take less risk. If you look at a stock that's expected to grow at 15 percent trading at 15 times earnings and another one that's expected to grow at 15 percent trading at 25 times earnings, don't just plunk your money down on the one with the lower PEG ratio. Look at the capital that needs to be invested to generate the expected growth, as well as the likelihood that those expectations will actually materialize, and you may very well wind up making a very different decision.

Say Yes to Yield

In addition to multiple-based measures, you can also use yield-based measures to value stocks. For example, if we invert the P/E and divide a firm's earnings per share by its market price, we get an earnings yield. If a stock sells for $20 per share and has $1 in earnings, it has a P/E of 20 ($20/$1) but an earnings yield of 5 percent ($1/$20). The nice thing about yields, as opposed to P/Es, is that we can compare them with alternative investments, such as bonds, to see what kind of a return we can expect from each investment. (The difference is that earnings generally grow over time, whereas bond payments are fixed.)

In late-2003, for example, I could get a risk-free return from Uncle Sam of about 4.5 percent by buying a 10-year treasury bond. Therefore, I'd want to demand a higher rate of return from my stocks because they're riskier than treasuries. A stock with a P/E of 20 would have an earnings yield of 5 percent, which is a bit better than treasuries, but not much considering the additional risk I'm taking. A stock with a P/E of 12, however, would have an earnings yield of 8.3 percent ($1/$12), which is much better than those poky treasuries. Thus, I might be induced to take the additional risk.

The best yield-based valuation measure is a relatively little-known metric called *cash return*. In many ways, it's actually a more useful tool than the P/E.

To calculate a cash return, divide free cash flow by enterprise value. (Enterprise value is simply a stock's market capitalization plus its long-term debt minus its cash.) The goal of the cash return is to measure how efficiently the business is using its capital—both equity and debt—to generate free cash flow.

Essentially, cash return tells you how much free cash flow a company generates as a percentage of how much it would cost an investor to buy the whole shebang, including the debt burden. An investor buying the whole company would not only need to buy all the shares at market value, but also would be taking on the burden of any debt (net of cash) the company has.

Let's use household-products giant Clorox as an example of how to use cash return to find reasonably valued investments. In late 2003, Clorox had a market cap of about $9.8 billion and carried $495 million in long-term debt and $172 million in cash on its balance sheet. Its enterprise value was $9,800 + $495 − $172, or $10.1 billion. That's half of our ratio.

The other half is free cash flow. Figure 9.2 shows Clorox's free cash flow over the past decade; the firm generated about $600 million in free cash flow in 2003. So, our cash return on Clorox will be $600 million/$10,100 million, or 5.9 percent.

With 10-year treasuries yielding just 4.5 percent in late 2003 and corporate bonds yielding a higher (but still relatively paltry) 4.9 percent, that 5.9 percent cash return from Clorox looks pretty good. Throw in the fact that Clorox's free cash flow is likely to grow over time, whereas those bond payments are fixed, and Clorox starts to look like a pretty solid value.

Cash return is a great first step to finding cash cows trading at reasonable prices, but don't use cash return for financials or foreign stocks. As I discuss in Chapter 17, cash flow isn't terribly meaningful for banks and other firms that earn money via their balance sheets. And because definitions of cash flow can

Free Cash Flow ($mil)	94	95	96	97	98	99	00	01	02	03
Cash operations ($mil)	266.8	290.9	406.7	362.1	312.7	588.0	658.0	747.0	876.0	803.0
Cap expenses ($mil)	-56.6	-62.9	-84.8	-95.2	-99.0	-176.0	-158.0	-192.0	-177.0	-205.0
Free cash flow ($mil)	**210.2**	**228.0**	**321.9**	**266.9**	**213.7**	**412.0**	**500.0**	**555.0**	**699.0**	**598.0**

Figure 9.2 Annual cash flows for Clorox.

vary widely in other countries, a foreign stock that looks cheap based on its cash return may simply be defining cash flow more liberally.

Investor's Checklist: Valuation—The Basics

▶ Be picky about valuation. You'll do well over the long haul by buying companies that are undervalued relative to their earnings potential.

▶ Don't rely on any single valuation metric because no individual ratio tells the whole story. Apply a number of different valuation tools when you're assessing a stock.

▶ If the firm is cyclical or has a spotty earnings history, use the price-to-sales ratio. Companies with P/S ratios lower than their historical average can sometimes be bargains.

▶ The price-to-book ratio is most useful for financial firms and firms with numerous tangible assets, and it's least useful for service-oriented firms. In addition, firms with higher ROEs will typically be worth a higher P/B ratio.

▶ You can compare a company's P/E with the market, with a similar firm, or with the company's historical P/E. In each case, you'll want the company's P/E to be lower than the benchmark, but make sure you're aware of any differences in risk or growth rates between the company you're valuing and the benchmark. The most reliable benchmark is likely to be the company's own historical valuations, assuming the company hasn't changed very much over time.

▶ Use the PEG with caution because fast-growing firms also tend to be riskier. Don't overpay for expected growth that may never materialize.

▶ The lowest P/E isn't always the best. Firms with high growth, low risk, and low capital reinvestment needs should have higher P/E ratios. You'll likely be better off in the long run paying more for a low-risk firm that's generating large amounts of cash than paying less for a cyclical company that's very capital intensive.

▶ Check the earnings yield and cash return, and compare them with the rates available on bonds. An earnings yield or cash return above current bond rates can indicate an undervalued stock.

10

Valuation:—Intrinsic Value

THE BIG DRAWBACK of the ratios we discussed in the previous chapter is that they're all based on *price*—they compare what investors are currently paying for one stock to what they're paying for another stock. Ratios do not, however, tell you anything about *value*, which is what a stock is actually worth.

Without knowing what a stock is worth, how can you know how much you should pay for it? At Morningstar, we're firm believers that stocks should be purchased because they're trading at some discount to their intrinsic value, not simply because they're priced at a higher or lower point than similar companies. Comparing ratios across companies and across time can help us understand whether our valuation estimate is close to or far from the mark, but estimating the intrinsic value of a company gives us a better target.

Having an intrinsic value estimate keeps you focused on the value of the business, rather than the price of the stock—and that's what you want because, as an investor, you're buying a small piece of a business. Intrinsic valuation also forces you to think about the cash flows that a business is generating today and the cash it could generate in the future, as well as the returns on capital that the firm creates. It makes you ask yourself: If I could buy the whole company, what would I pay?

Second, having an intrinsic value gives you a stronger basis for making investment decisions. Without looking at the true determinants of value, such as cash flow and return on capital, we have no way of assessing whether a P/E of, for example, 15 or 20 is too low, too high, or right on target. After all, the company with the P/E of 20 might have much lower capital needs and a less risky business than the company with the P/E of 15, in which case it might actually be the better investment.

In this chapter, I'm going to walk you through a simplified version of how we estimate intrinsic values at Morningstar. Even if you choose not to go through the entire exercise yourself for every stock you think about buying—and you very well may not—knowing the basic principles will help you make better investment decisions.

A warning: This can be some difficult stuff, so don't be discouraged if you're a bit confused. It does get easier with practice, though—I promise!

Cash Flow, Present Value, and Discount Rates

Our first step is answering a basic question—what's a stock worth? Luckily, we can stand on the shoulders of giants such as economists Irving Fisher and John Burr Williams, who answered this question for us more than 60 years ago: The value of a stock is equal to the present value of its future cash flows. No more and no less.

Let's take this idea apart carefully, because understanding it is crucial to properly valuing stocks. Companies create economic value by investing capital and generating a return. Some of that return pays operating expenses, some gets reinvested in the business, and the rest is free cash flow.

Remember, we care about free cash flow because that's the amount of money that could be taken out of the business each year without harming its operations. A firm can use free cash flow to benefit shareholders in a number of ways. It can pay a dividend, which essentially converts a portion of each investor's interest in the firm to cash. It can buy back stock, which reduces the number of shares outstanding and thus increases the percentage ownership of each shareholder. Or, the firm can retain the free cash flow and reinvest it in the business.

These free cash flows are what give the firm its investment value. A *present value* calculation simply adjusts those future cash flows to reflect the fact that money we plan to receive in the future is worth less than money we receive today.

Why are future cash flows worth less than current ones? First, money that we receive today can be invested to generate some kind of return, whereas we can't invest future cash flows until we receive them. This is the *time value of money*. Second, there's a chance we may never receive those future cash flows, and we need to be compensated for that risk, called the "risk premium."

The time value of money is essentially the opportunity cost of receiving money in the future versus receiving it today, and it's often represented by the interest rates being paid on government bonds. It's pretty certain that the U.S. government will be around to pay us our interest in a few years.

Of course, not many cash flows are as certain as those from the feds, so we need to tack on an additional premium to compensate us for the risk that we may never receive the money that we've been promised. Add the government bond rate to the risk premium, and you have what's known as a *discount rate*.

The oddly named discount rate makes more sense when you think about it in these terms: What rate of return would you need to make you indifferent between receiving some quantity of money right now versus at some time in the future? The old saying that a bird in the hand is worth two in the bush expresses the same concept in a different way: We know we have the bird in the hand, so we need two birds in the bush to make us indifferent between the two options. In a similar vein, money to be received in the future is worth less to us because we don't know if we'll get it, and if we get it today, we could invest it to earn a return.

For example, if you were about to take a one-week vacation, but your boss asked you at the last minute to postpone it for a year, you might ask your boss for an extra day off to compensate for the delay. In other words, six days off next year is equivalent to five days off right now, because you'd rather take the trip now and because something else could crop up over the next year that would force you to delay the trip again.

So, your mental discount rate for vacation time is 20 percent. That's the rate at which five days becomes six days in a year (6 days − 5 days/5 days). And if you thought your boss might get fired—which would make it less certain that her promise of an extra day would be honored—you might ask for two extra days off next year. In that case, your mental discount rate would be

40 percent, which is the rate at which five days becomes seven days in a year (7 days − 5 days/5 days).

Now you can start to see why stocks with stable, predictable earnings often have such high valuations—investors discount their future cash flows at a lower rate, because they believe that there's a lower risk attached to the likelihood that those future cash flows will actually show up. Conversely, a business with an extremely uncertain future should logically have a lower valuation because there's a substantial risk that the potential future cash flows will never materialize.

You can see why a rational investor should be willing to pay more for a company that's profitable now relative to one that promises profitability only at some point in the future. Not only does the latter carry higher risk (and thus a higher discount rate), but the promised cash flows won't arrive until some years in the future, diminishing their value still further.

This can be a tough concept, so let's look at an example with some real numbers. Figure 10.1 illustrates the difference that changing discount rates and

	StableCorp		CycliCorp		RiskCorp	
Year	Free Cash Flow ($)	Discounted at 9%	Free Cash Flow ($)	Discounted at 12%	Free Cash Flow ($)	Discounted at 15%
2003	2,000	2,000	2,000	2,000	0	0
2004	2,200	2,018	2,200	1,964	0	0
2005	2,420	2,037	1,980	1,578	0	0
2006	2,662	2,056	2,376	1,691	2,000	1,315
2007	2,928	2,074	2,851	1,812	2,540	1,452
2008	3,221	2,093	3,421	1,941	3,226	1,604
2009	3,543	2,113	3,207	1,625	4,097	1,771
2010	3,953	2,162	3,900	1,764	5,203	1,956
2011	4,327	2,172	4,681	1,891	6,608	2,160
2012	4,746	2,185	5,383	1,941	8,325	2,366
Sum	32,000	**20,910**	31,999	**18,207**	31,999	**12,624**

Figure 10.1 Timing and uncertainty have a big effect on present value. The longer you have to wait to receive a set of cash flows and the less certain you are that you'll eventually receive them, the less they're worth to you today. *Source:* Morningstar, Inc.

the timing of cash flows can have on present value. In all three examples—StableCorp, CycliCorp, and RiskCorp—the sum of the *undiscounted* cash flows is about $32,000.

However, the value of the *discounted* cash flows is quite different from company to company. In present value terms, CycliCorp is worth about $2,700 less than StableCorp. That's because StableCorp is more predictable, which means that investors' discount rate isn't as high. CycliCorp's cash flow increases by 20 percent some years and shrinks in some years, so investors perceive it as a riskier investment and use a higher discount rate when they're valuing its shares. As a result, the *present value* of the *discounted* cash flows is lower.

The difference in the present value of the cash flows is even more acute when you look at RiskCorp, which is worth almost $8,300 less than StableCorp. Not only are the bulk of RiskCorp's cash flows far off in the future, but also, we're less certain that they'll come to pass, so we assign an even higher discount rate.

Believe it or not, you now know the basic principles behind a discounted cash flow model. Value is determined by the *amount, timing,* and *riskiness* of a firm's future cash flows, and these are the three items you should always be thinking about when deciding how much to pay for a stock. That's all it really boils down to.

Calculating Present Value

Now that you know the theory behind an intrinsic value calculation, here's how you can do it in practice. To find the present value of a $100 future cash flow, divide that future cash flow by 1.0 plus the discount rate. Using a 10 percent discount rate, for example, a cash flow of $100 one year in the future is worth $100/1.10, or $90.91. A $100 cash flow two years in the future is worth $100/(1.10)^2$, or $82.64. In other words, $82.64 invested at 10 percent becomes $90.91 in a year and $100 in two years. Discount rates are really just interest rates that go backwards through time instead of forwards.

Generalizing the previous formula, if we represent the discount rate as R, the present value of a future cash flow in year N equals $CF_n/(1 + R)^n$. Suppose, for example, that we have a $500 cash flow two years in the future with a 7 percent discount rate. The present value of that cash flow is:

$$\frac{\$500}{\left(1.07\right)^2} = \frac{\$500}{1.1449} = \$436.72$$

That same cash flow three years in the future is worth \$408.16 today:

$$\frac{\$500}{\left(1.07\right)^3} = \frac{\$500}{1.225} = \$408.16$$

Looking three years into the future and changing our discount rate back to 10 percent, our present value is \$375.66 today:

$$\frac{\$500}{\left(1.10\right)^3}$$

(If you want to do this in a spreadsheet program such as Excel, remember to use the carat [^] symbol to insert an exponent. Thus, 1.10^4 would be written as 1.10^4 in an Excel formula.)

Fun with Discount Rates

Now that we have the formula down, we need to figure out what factors determine discount rates. How do we know whether to use 7 percent or 10 percent? From our previous example of the delayed vacation, we know that opportunity cost—or time value—is one factor and that the other big determinant of our discount rate is risk.

Unfortunately, there is no precise way to calculate the exact discount rate that you should use in a discounted cash flow (DCF) model, and academics have filled entire journal issues with nothing but discussions about the right way to estimate discount rates—but trust me, it's not a discussion in which you want to be involved.

Here's what you need to know for practical purposes: As interest rates increase, so will discount rates. As a firm's risk level increases, so will its discount rate. Let's put these two together. For interest rates, you can use a long-term average of Treasury rates as a reasonable proxy. (Remember, we use the interest rate on treasuries to represent opportunity costs because we're pretty certain that the government will pay us our promised interest.) In mid-2003, the average yield of the 10-year bond over the past decade was about 5.5 percent, so we'll use that. Because this isn't an exact science, you may want to use 5 percent or 6 percent.

Now for risk, which is an even less exact factor to measure. According to standard finance theorists, risk is the same thing as volatility, and the risk level of a company can be estimated simply by looking at how much its shares have bounced around relative to how much the market has bounced around. Thus, if a firm's shares suddenly drop from $30 to $20, this theory holds that the stock has just become much riskier.

We're not big fans of this definition of risk at Morningstar because we think stocks that are cheap are generally less risky than stocks with high price tags. (This assumes that nothing dramatic has changed with the underlying business, which isn't always the case when a stock drops.) We think it's better to assess risk by looking at the company, rather than by looking at the stock, and that a firm's riskiness is determined by the likelihood that it will or won't generate the cash flows that we're forecasting.

Why? Because what the share price has done in the *past* may have little bearing on what cash flows the company generates in the future. We think it makes more sense to define risk as the chance of permanent capital impairment—in other words, the likelihood that our investment will be worth much less when we go to sell it than it is today. Here are some factors we think should be taken into account when estimating discount rates.

Size

Smaller firms are generally riskier than larger firms because they're more vulnerable to adverse events. They also usually have less diversified product lines and customer bases.

Financial Leverage

Firms with more debt are generally riskier than firms with less debt because they have a higher proportion of fixed expenses (debt payments) relative to other expenses. Earnings will be better in good times, but worse in bad times, with an increased risk of financial distress. (Financial distress means that the firm is having trouble paying its debts.) Look at a firm's debt-to-equity ratio, interest coverage, and a few other factors to determine the degree of a company's risk from financial leverage.

Cyclicality

Is the firm in a cyclical industry (such as appliances or semiconductors) or a stable industry (such as breakfast cereal or beer)? Because the cash flows of cyclical firms are much tougher to forecast than stable firms, their level of risk increases.

Management/Corporate Governance

This factor boils down to a simple question: How much do you trust the folks running the shop? Although it's rarely black or white, firms with promotional managers, managers who draw egregious salaries, or who exhibit any of the other red flags covered in Chapter 7 are definitely riskier than companies with managers who don't display these traits.

Economic Moat

Does the firm have a wide moat, a narrow moat, or no economic moat? The stronger a firm's competitive advantage—that is, the wider its moat—the more likely it will be able to keep competitors at bay and generate a reliable stream of cash flows.

Complexity

The essence of risk is uncertainty, and it's tough to value what you can't see. Firms with extremely complex businesses or financial structures are riskier than simple, easy-to-understand firms because there's a greater chance that something unpleasant is hiding in a footnote that you missed. Even if you think management is as honest as the day is long and that the firm does a great job running its operations, it's wise to incorporate a *complexity discount* into your mental assessment of risk—unless you really want to memorize all 700 pages of the last 10-K filing.

How should you incorporate all of these risk factors into a discount rate? As I said earlier, there's no *right* answer. At Morningstar, we use 10.5 percent as the discount rate for an average company based on the factors in the preceding list, and we create a distribution of discount rates based on whether firms are riskier or less risky than the average. As of mid-2003, firms such as Johnson & Johnson, Colgate, and Wal-Mart fall at the bottom of the range, at around 9 percent, whereas riskier firms—such as Micron Technology, JetBlue Airways, and E*Trade—top out at 13 percent to 15 percent.

The key is to pick a discount rate you're comfortable with. Don't worry about being exact—just think about whether the company you're evaluating is riskier or less risky than the average firm, along with how much riskier or less risky it is, and you'll be fine. In addition, remember that assigning discount rates is an inexact science—there is no "right" discount rate for a company.

Calculating Perpetuity Values

We're almost there—we have cash flow estimates, and we have a discount rate. We need only one more element, called a *perpetuity value,* and we're ready to put the whole thing together. We need a perpetuity because it's not feasible to project a company's future cash flows out to infinity, year-by-year, and because companies have theoretically infinite lives.

The most common way to calculate a perpetuity is to take the last cash flow (*CF*) that you estimate, increase it by the rate at which you expect cash flows to grow over the very long term (*g*), and divide the result by the discount rate (*R*) minus the expected long-term growth rate. In formula terms, this equals:

$$\frac{CF_n(1+g)}{(R-g)}$$

The result of this calculation then must be discounted back to the present, using the method I discussed previously. Let's run through an example to show you what I mean.

For example, suppose we're using a 10-year DCF model for a company with an 11 percent discount rate. We estimate that the company's cash flow in year 10 will be $1 billion and its cash flows will grow at a steady 3 percent annual rate after that. (Three percent is generally a good number to use as your long-run growth rate because it's roughly the average rate of U.S. gross domestic product [GDP] growth. If you're valuing a firm in a declining industry, you might use 2 percent.)

First, multiply $1 billion by 1.03 to get an estimated $1.03 billion cash flow in year 11.

$$\$1 \text{ billion} \times 1.03 = \$1.03 \text{ billion}$$

Divide $1.03 billion by 0.08 (our 11 percent discount rate minus 3 percent long-run growth rate) to get $12.88 billion in estimated cash flows from year 11 onward.

$$\frac{\$1.03 \text{ billion}}{0.11 - 0.03} = \$12.88 \text{ billion}$$

To get the present value of these cash flows, we need to discount them using the formula we saw earlier: $CF_n/(1 + R)^n$, where n is the number of years in the future, CF_n is the cash flow in year n, and R is the discount rate. Plugging in the numbers:

$$N = 10$$
$$CF_n = \$12.88 \text{ billion}$$
$$R = 0.11$$
$$\frac{\$12.88}{(1.11)^{10}} = \frac{\$1288}{2.839} = \$4.536 \text{ billion}$$

Now, all we need to do is add this discounted perpetuity value to the discounted value of our estimated cash flows in years 1 through 10, and divide by the number of shares outstanding (see Figure 10.2).

I'll go through a couple of detailed examples in the next chapter, but here's a brief outline of the process. I'll use Clorox as an example again. You can follow along by matching the following steps to Figure 10.3:

1. Estimate free cash flows for the next four quarters. This amount will depend on all of the factors we discussed earlier in the book—how fast the

Simple 10-Year Valuation Model

Step 1	Forecast free cash flow (FCF) for the next 10 years.
Step 2	Discount these FCFs to reflect the present value: ▸ Discounted FCF = FCF for that year ÷ $(1 + R)^N$ *(where R = discount rate and N = year being discounted)*
Step 3	Calculate the perpetuity value and discount it to the present: ▸ Perpetuity Value = $FCF_{10} \times (1 + g) \div (R - g)$ ▸ Discounted Perpetuity Value = Perpetuity Value ÷ $(1 + R)^{10}$
Step 4	Calculate total equity value by adding the discounted perpetuity value to the sum of the 10 discounted cash flows (calculated in step 2): ▸ Total Equity Value = Discounted Perpetuity Value + 10 Discounted Cash Flows
Step 5	Calculate per share value by dividing total equity value by shares outstanding: ▸ Per Share Value = Total Equity Value ÷ Shares Outstanding

Figure 10.2   A step-by-step discounted cash flow model for calculating the equity value of a company. *Source:* Morningstar, Inc.

company is growing, the strength of its competitors, its capital needs, and so on. (We get into more detail on estimating cash flows in the next chapter when we analyze and value two firms top to bottom.) For Clorox, our first step is to see how fast free cash flow has grown over the past decade, which turns out to be about 9 percent when you do the math. We could just increase the $600 million in free cash flow that Clorox generated in 2003 by 9 percent, but that would assume that the future will be as rosy as the past. During the 1990s, the rise of mega-retailers like Wal-Mart—which now accounts for almost a quarter of Clorox's sales—has hurt the bargaining power of consumer-products firms. So, let's be conservative and assume free cash flow increases by only 5 percent over last year, which would work out to $630 million.

2. Estimate how fast you think free cash flow will grow over the next 5 to 10 years. Remember, only firms with very strong competitive advantages and low capital needs are able to sustain above-average growth rates for very long. If the firm is cyclical, don't forget to throw in some bad years. We won't do this for Clorox because selling bleach and Glad bags is a very stable business. We will, however, be conservative on our growth rate

Assumptions for Clorox

Current stock price:	$45.00
Shares outstanding (mil)	221.0
Next year's free cash flow (mil)	$630.00
Perpetuity growth rate (g)	3.0%
Discount rate (R)	9.0%

10-Year Valuation Model for Clorox

Step 1: Forecast free cash flow (FCF) for the next 10 years.
Assumes constant 5% growth rate, free cash flows in $ millions.

		Yr 1	Yr 2	Yr 3	Yr 4	Yr 5	Yr 6	Yr 7	Yr 8	Yr 9	Yr 10
Free cash flow	→	630.0	661.5	694.6	729.3	765.8	804.1	844.3	886.5	930.8	977.3

Step 2: Discount these free cash flows to reflect the present value.
Discount Factor = $(1 + R)^N$ (where R = discount rate and N = year being discounted)

		Yr 1	Yr 2	Yr 3	Yr 4	Yr 5	Yr 6	Yr 7	Yr 8	Yr 9	Yr 10
Free cash flow		630.0	661.5	694.6	729.3	765.8	804.1	844.3	886.5	930.8	977.3
÷ Discount factor		1.09^1	1.09^2	1.09^3	1.09^4	1.09^5	1.09^6	1.09^7	1.09^8	1.09^9	1.09^{10}
= Discounted FCF	→	577.9	556.8	536.3	516.7	497.7	479.4	461.8	444.9	428.6	412.8

Step 3: Calculate the perpetuity value and discount it to the present.
Perpetuity Value = Yr 10 FCF × (1 + g) ÷ (R − g) (where g = perpetuity growth rate and R = discount rate)

Perpetuity value	→	(977.3 × 1.03) ÷ (.09−.03) = $16,776.98
Discounted	→	$16,776.98 ÷ 1.09^{10} = $7,086.78

Step 4: Calculate total equity value.
Add the discounted perpetuity value (see above) to the sum of the 10 discounted cash flows (see step 2).

Total equity value	→	$7,087.05 + $4,913.01 = $12,000.06

Step 5: Calculate per share value.
Divide total equity value by shares outstanding.

Per share value	→	$12,000.06 ÷ 221.00 = $54.30

Figure 10.3   Valuing Clorox using discounted cash flow. *Source:* Morningstar, Inc.

because of the "Wal-Mart factor," and we'll assume free cash flow increases at 5 percent annually over the next decade.

3. Estimate a discount rate. Financially, Clorox is rock-solid, with little debt, tons of free cash flow, and a noncyclical business. So, we'll use 9 percent for our discount rate, which is meaningfully lower than the 10.5 percent average we discussed earlier. Clorox is a pretty predictable company, after all.

4. Estimate a long-run growth rate. Because I think people will still need bleach and trash bags in the future, and it's a good bet that Clorox will continue to get a piece of that market, I use the long-run GDP average of 3 percent.

5. That's it! We discount the first 10 years of cash flows, add that value to the present value of the perpetuity, and divide by shares outstanding.

This is a very simple DCF model—the one we use at Morningstar has about a dozen Excel tabs, adjusts for complicated items such as pensions and operating leases, and explicitly models competitive advantage periods, among many other things. But a model doesn't need to be super complex to get you most of the way there and help you clarify your thinking. For example, our valuation of Clorox—which pegs the value of the stock at about 15 percent higher than the stock price in late 2003—has the company generating free cash flow of about $800 million per year 10 years from now.

How realistic is this? As of late 2003, only 125 companies in Morningstar's database of more than 6,500 firms were able to accomplish such a feat, so it's certainly a high hurdle. However, given Clorox's portfolio of strong brands and solid track record of product innovation it's not unreasonable. Moreover, our 5 percent estimated annual growth rate in free cash flow is a good deal lower than the firm's past growth rate, which makes the model somewhat conservative. After all, Clorox has so many strong brands—including the eponymous bleach, Pine-Sol, and Formula 409—that it may be able to hold the line when it negotiates with big retailers like Wal-Mart.

The important thing is that we forced ourselves to think through these kinds of issues, which we wouldn't have if we'd just looked at Clorox's stock chart or if we'd just said, "Sixteen times earnings seems reasonable." By thinking about the business, we arrived at a better valuation in which we have more confidence.

Margin of Safety

We've analyzed a company, we've valued it—now we need to know when to buy it. If you really want to succeed as an investor, you should seek to buy companies at a discount to your estimate of their intrinsic value. Any valuation and any analysis is subject to error, and we can minimize the effect of these errors by buying stocks only at a significant discount to our estimated intrinsic value. This discount is called the *margin of safety,* a term first popularized by investing great Benjamin Graham.

Here's how it works. Let's say we think Clorox is worth $54, and the stock is trading at $45. If we buy the stock and we're exactly right about our analysis, the return we receive should be the difference between $45 and $54 (20 percent) plus the discount rate of about 9 percent. (The discount rate for a stock is sometimes called the *required return* for precisely this reason.) That would be 29 percent, which is a pretty darn good return, all things considered.

But what if we're wrong? What if Clorox grows even more slowly than we'd anticipated—maybe a competitor takes market share—or the firm's pricing power erodes faster than we'd thought? If that's the case, then Clorox's fair value might actually be $40, which means we would have overpaid for the stock by buying it at $45.

Having a margin of safety is like an insurance policy that helps prevent us from overpaying—it mitigates the damage caused by overoptimistic estimates. If, for example, we'd required a margin of safety of 20 percent before buying Clorox, we wouldn't have purchased the stock until it fell to $43. In that case, even if our initial analysis had been wrong and the fair value had really been $40, the damage to our portfolio wouldn't have been as severe.

Because all stocks aren't created equal, not all margins of safety should be the same. It's much easier to forecast the cash flows of, for example, Anheuser-Busch over the next five years than the cash flows of Boeing. One company has tons of pricing power, dominant market share, and relatively stable demand, whereas the other has relatively little pricing power, equal market share, and highly cyclical demand. Because I'm less confident about my forecasts for Boeing, I'll want a larger margin of safety before I buy the shares. There's simply a greater chance that something might go wrong and that my forecasts will be too optimistic.

Paying more for better businesses makes sense, within reason. The price you pay for a stock should be closely tied to the quality of the company, and great businesses are worth buying at smaller discounts to fair value. Why? Because high-quality businesses—those that have wide economic moats—are more likely to increase in value over time, and it's better to pay a fair price for a great business than a great price for a fair business.

How large should your margin of safety be? At Morningstar, it ranges all the way from just 20 percent for very stable firms with wide economic moats to 60 percent for high-risk stocks with no competitive advantages. On average, we require a 30 percent to 40 percent margin of safety for most firms.

Having a margin of safety is critical to being a disciplined investor because it acknowledges that as humans, we're flawed. Simply investing in the stock market requires some degree of optimism about the future, which is one of the biggest reasons that buyers of stocks are too optimistic far more often than they're too pessimistic. Once we know this, we can correct for it by requiring a margin of safety for all of our share purchases.

Conclusion

Every approach to equity investing has its own warts. Being disciplined about valuation may mean that you'll miss out on some great opportunities because some companies wind up performing better for longer periods of time than almost anyone would have anticipated. Companies such as Microsoft and Starbucks, for example, looked very pricey back in their heyday, and it's unlikely that many investors who were very strict about valuation would have bought them early in their corporate lives. Why? Because both firms managed to fend off their competitors for very long periods of time—much longer than a conservative estimate would have given them credit for.

Being disciplined about valuation would have meant missing these opportunities, but it also would have kept you out of many investments that were priced like the next Microsoft, but which wound up disappointing investors in a big way. Think about how many software firms have fallen by the wayside over the past decade, for example, or when bagel stocks were priced as if they were going to all become the next McDonald's back in the early 1990s. Although we acknowledge that some high-potential companies are worth a leap of faith and a high valuation, on balance, we think it's better to miss a solid investment because you're too cautious in your initial valuation than it is to buy stocks at prices that turn out to be too high.

After all, the *real* cost of losing money is much worse than the *opportunity* cost of missing out on gains. That's why the price you pay is just as important as the company you buy.

Investor's Checklist: Valuation—Intrinsic Value

- ► Estimating an intrinsic value keeps you focused on the value of the business, rather than on the price of the stock.
- ► Stocks are worth the present value of their future cash flows, and that value is determined by the amount, timing, and riskiness of the cash flows.
- ► A discount rate is equal to the time value of money plus a risk premium.
- ► The risk premium is tied to factors like the size, financial health, cyclicality, and competitive position of the firm you're evaluating.
- ► To calculate an intrinsic value, follow these five steps: Estimate cash flows for the next year, forecast a growth rate, estimate a discount rate, estimate a long-run growth rate, and add the discounted cash flows to the perpetuity value.

Putting It All Together

Now, IT'S TIME for the fun part. You now have an investment philosophy, you know what economic moats are, and you know how to read financial statements and evaluate companies. Let's put all this knowledge to work by analyzing two real-world companies: chipmaker Advanced Micro Devices (AMD) and Biomet, a medical device firm.

(Note: All of the financial data in this chapter is available free on Morningstar.com in the same format that you see it here.)

Advanced Micro Devices

At first, AMD might look like an attractive investment. It's one of only two companies that manufacture microprocessors—the brains in a PC or server—and computers are pretty ubiquitous devices. AMD also makes flash memory chips that are used in a variety of devices that should have solid long-term demand, such as mobile phones and network routers. In the microprocessor market, AMD has caught up to archrival Intel on the technological front over the past several years, and for a brief spell in the late 1990s, the firm was selling chips that were arguably faster and better than those being sold by Intel.

In addition, AMD has been working on a powerful next-generation chip that may be better than anything Intel has to offer.

This is the AMD story that you might know if you followed the news a bit and casually flipped through the company's Web site and its recent annual reports. However, it's not enough information to make a sound investment decision, so let's approach the firm systematically to see just how solid an investment AMD really is.

Economic Moat

First, look for evidence of an economic moat. As we discussed in Chapter 3, we can do this by examining how profitable AMD has been in the past by analyzing free cash flow, margins, return on equity, and return on assets (see Figure 11.1).

It looks like AMD has had a pretty spotty history of generating free cash flow. After a few good years in the early 1990s, free cash flow turned negative as the firm heavily increased capital spending, and AMD didn't throw off any free cash again until the technology boom in 2000. That's not a good sign that the firm has much of an economic moat. However, some rapidly growing firms spend years plowing all of their money back into capital spending, which means their free cash flow is negative because they're still building their economic moat. (Starbucks was a great example of this during the 1990s.) Even these kinds of firms should have solid profits, however, so let's turn to AMD's margins and returns on capital (see Figure 11.2).

Looking at operating and net margins, we see that although AMD scores better on this front than it does on free cash flow, it still lost money for 6 of the past 10 years. The trend doesn't indicate that these were simply cyclical

Free Cash Flow ($mil)	93	94	95	96	97	98	99	00	01	02
Cash operations ($mil)	456.2	573.2	611.9	73.2	398.8	144.4	259.9	1,205.6	167.7	-88.9
Cap expenses ($mil)	-323.7	-548.7	-620.8	-485.0	-685.1	-996.2	-619.8	-805.5	-678.9	-705.2
Free Cash Flow ($mil)	**132.5**	**24.5**	**-8.9**	**-411.8**	**-286.3**	**-851.8**	**-359.9**	**400.1**	**-511.2**	**-794.1**
FCF/Sales (%)	**8.0**	**1.1**	**-0.4**	**-21.1**	**-12.2**	**-33.5**	**-12.6**	**8.6**	**-13.1**	**-29.4**

Figure 11.1 AMD's free cash flow.

AMD Profitability	93	94	95	96	97	98	99	00	01	02
Operating margin (%)	18.5	24.0	14.3	-13.0	-3.8	-6.4	-11.2	19.1	-1.5	-45.4
Net margin (%)	13.3	13.8	12.4	-3.5	-0.9	-4.1	-3.1	21.2	-1.6	-48.3
Asset turnover (avg)	1.0	1.0	0.9	0.6	0.7	0.7	0.7	0.9	0.7	0.5
Return on Assets (%)	**13.3**	**13.8**	**11.2**	**-2.1**	**-0.6**	**-2.9**	**-2.2**	**19.1**	**-1.1**	**-24.2**
Financial leverage (avg)	1.4	1.4	1.4	1.5	1.6	1.9	2.2	2.0	1.7	1.9
Return on Equity (%)	**18.6**	**19.3**	**15.7**	**-3.2**	**-1.0**	**-5.5**	**-4.8**	**38.2**	**-1.9**	**-46.0**

Figure 11.2   AMD's profitability numbers.

losses—the firm lost money for four straight years between 1996 and 1999, even though the U.S. economy was going gangbusters.

ROE and ROA tell a similar story. After some salad days in the early 1990s—ROEs in the high teens are pretty good—AMD's performance went into a big slump until the tech boom in 2000. We can also see that asset turnover has declined, which means that AMD has become less efficient and financial leverage has gradually edged upward, indicating that AMD has probably taken on more debt.

AMD has had one great year recently—ROE, free cash flow, and margins were all excellent in 2000—and it's worth our time to find out why so we can determine whether it was an aberration or a sign of better times to come. After reading through some recent annual reports, we find that AMD made money in 2000 the old-fashioned way: It rolled out a chip that was faster and cheaper than anything Intel had at the moment. This made the company a ton of money until 2001, when the demand for PCs slowed down and Intel rolled out a competing chip.

So, AMD's one big recent success was due to a product with superior technology, which we know from Chapter 3 is the least sustainable source of an economic moat. It shouldn't come as a surprise to us that Intel quickly used its superior size and cash hoard to accelerate the rollout of a competing chip and regain the market share it briefly lost to AMD.

Overall, there's not much evidence of a sustainable economic moat in AMD's historical financials. It's not difficult to understand why: Intel dominates the microprocessor market, and AMD's market share has typically been around 15 percent for the past several years. Intel's size lets it spend four times as much on research and development as AMD does, which is a big advantage when you consider how fast semiconductor technology changes. Intel's size has also allowed it to attain much greater economies of scale, because it can spread the fixed costs of its manufacturing plants across a much larger volume of chips.

AMD's lack of an economic moat means we'd want a big margin of safety if we wanted to buy the stock, but even no-moat companies can sometimes be decent investments if the fundamentals aren't too shaky and the stock is cheap enough. Let's complete our analysis by looking at the five areas I discussed in Chapter 6—growth, profitability, financial health, risks, and management—and then by doing a rough valuation of the stock.

Growth

Figure 11.3 shows that revenue growth has been somewhat volatile for AMD over the past decade. Overall, it's not been terrible, but a 6 percent average annual growth rate over a decade when PC demand was pretty hot is nothing to crow about.

It's tough to say much that's meaningful about growth in profits because AMD had so many money-losing years during the 1990s. About the best we can do is note that AMD made a lot more money in its most recent profitable year (2000) than it did in the previous profitable year (1995), but it also lost much more money in 2002 than it ever had before—a spotty track record, at best (see Figure 11.4).

Profitability

We looked at free cash flow and returns on capital when we were assessing whether AMD had an economic moat, and the verdict was pretty negative. Let's dig a bit deeper to see what else we can understand about how AMD

AMD Revenue Growth	93	94	95	96	97	98	99	00	01	02
Year over year (%)	8.8	29.5	13.8	-19.6	20.7	7.9	12.4	62.5	-16.2	-30.7
3-Year average (%)	—	—	17.1	5.8	3.3	1.5	13.5	25.4	15.3	-1.9
10-Year average (%)	—	—	—	—	—	—	—	—	—	5.9

Figure 11.3 AMD's revenue growth.

	93	94	95	96	97	98	99	00	01	02
Net income ($mil)	218.4	294.9	300.5	-69.0	-21.1	-104.0	-88.9	983.0	-60.6	-1,303.0

Figure 11.4   AMD's net income.

makes (and loses) money. Look at Figure 11.5, which is a *common size* income statement. Common size statements are great tools for evaluating companies because they put every line item in context by looking at each of them as a percentage of sales.

These numbers show some disturbing trends. In the early 1990s, gross margins were around 50 percent, and they've steadily slid to between 20 percent and 30 percent in 2001 and 2002. Spending on overhead (SG&A) has been pretty steady at 16 percent to 19 percent of sales, while R&D spending has increased dramatically. The big increase in R&D spending helps support our previous intuition that chip companies need to spend large amounts on R&D to stay competitive. It also correlates with the big increase in capital spending we saw on the statement of cash flows—AMD was spending boatloads of money on expanding its manufacturing capabilities.

Overall, we have a company making less money per chip, not becoming much more efficient in terms of overhead spending, and having to increase research spending in a big way. Couple these trends with highly variable sales—see the revenue growth line in Figure 11.3—and you have a pretty dismal profitability picture.

AMD	93	94	95	96	97	98	99	00	01	02
Revenue (%)	100.0	100.0	100.0	100.0	100.0	100.0	100.0	100.0	100.0	100.0
COGS (%)	47.9	46.0	53.5	73.8	67.0	67.6	68.7	54.1	66.5	78.1
Gross Margin (%)	**52.1**	**54.0**	**46.5**	**26.2**	**33.0**	**32.4**	**31.3**	**45.9**	**33.5**	**21.9**
SG&A (%)	17.6	16.8	15.8	18.7	17.0	16.5	18.9	12.9	15.9	24.8
R&D (%)	15.9	13.1	16.4	20.5	19.9	22.3	22.2	13.8	16.7	30.3
Other (%)	0.0	0.0	0.0	0.0	0.0	0.0	1.3	0.0	2.3	12.3
Operating Margin (%)	**18.5**	**24.0**	**14.3**	**-13.0**	**-3.8**	**-6.4**	**-11.2**	**19.1**	**-1.5**	**-45.4**

Figure 11.5   AMD's common size income statement, representing each line item as a percent of revenue.

Financial Health

Unfortunately, things don't look much better when we examine AMD's financial health.

At the end of 2002, the firm had $1.9 billion in debt and $2.5 billion in shareholders' equity. The resulting debt-to-equity ratio of 0.7 isn't terribly high relative to the market, but it's not great for a firm that has as much trouble generating profits as AMD does. AMD's current ratio—which, remember, is simply current assets divided by current liabilities—was about 1.5. Again, not terrible, but not comforting either, given AMD's second-tier industry position and spotty history of profitability.

Finally, we learn by digging into AMD's 10-K filing that the firm has some big loans outstanding with banks in Germany, relating to a large manufacturing facility that the firm is building there. Adding these loans to other contractual obligations, we see that AMD will need to pay out more than $950 million to various parties between 2004 and 2006. That's a huge amount of money for a company that has generated only $250 million in net operating income since 1993 and has bled about $2.7 billion in free cash flow over the same period.

(You can calculate the cumulative operating income and free cash flow amounts yourself from the previous figures.) I'd say AMD doesn't score very well on the financial health front.

The Bear Case

Although I normally recommend developing a strong bear case for any company you analyze, we've uncovered many more negatives than positives about AMD so far, so let's move on.

Management

Let's look at some of AMD's proxy statements to see what we can find out about management. For one thing, they're paid pretty well: Outgoing CEO Jerry Sanders pulled in about $1 million in salary every year between 1997 and 2002, an additional $400,000 in "deferred retirement compensation" for each of those years, and bonuses ranging from zero to $5.1 million. He also received a good-sized amount of additional "in-kind" compensation from use of company vehicles and the company plane. In 2002, for example, he received about $184,000 worth of company-provided vehicle services. That's either an expensive car or a well-paid chauffeur.

Other top executives also did well in 2002, with the top five individuals receiving salaries of between $450,000 and $900,000, and three of the five receiving hefty bonuses despite AMD's $1.2 billion loss that year. Incoming CEO Hector Ruiz didn't get a cash bonus, but don't feel too sorry for him—he received 1.2 million options (about 10 percent of the total granted that year) instead. Depending on the assumptions used, Ruiz's options will be worth between $12 and $30 million over the next decade.

Speaking of options, it looks to me as though AMD has been giving away the store to its employees and diluting shareholder value as a result. From 2000 through 2003, AMD issued about 46 million stock options to its employees and officers, increasing the number of shares outstanding by 15 percent. (You can find the total number of options granted each year in that year's proxy statement.) Therefore, anyone who bought AMD shares in 2000 and held them through 2003 saw their stake in the company shrink meaningfully after three years, simply because the firm gave away so many options to its employees. This kind of egregious options granting tells me that management cares little for outside shareholders.

Overall, I'd say that AMD's management is overpaid, and they are not the type of folks to whom I'd entrust my money.

Valuation

Valuation is tough, because AMD has lost money for the past two years. On a price-to-sales basis, AMD was trading at about 1.5 times sales in September, 2003, which was much cheaper than the seven times sales valuation of the chip industry average and in line with AMD's own 1.6 times sales average valuation over the past five years—not too bad.

We can't use a P/E because AMD was forecasted to lose about $0.30 per share in 2004. In any event, it would be tough to have much confidence in earnings estimates for a company that's been as volatile as AMD—for example, 2004 earnings estimates for AMD ranged from a low of −$0.85 per share to a high of $0.20 per share in September, 2003. In other words, no one has the

faintest clue how much money AMD will be making (if any) in the near future, which tells us that we should demand a big margin of safety from our valuation we arrive at.

Because AMD is highly cyclical, we could also attempt to predict its earnings at the peak of the next cycle and value the company based on the resulting P/E ratio. Figure 11.6 shows that AMD's last peak earnings per share was
almost $3 in 2000. However, we'd be wise to take this figure with a grain of
salt because the earnings occurred during a technology boom that's unlikely
to repeat and during a rare time when AMD was able to catch Intel napping.
Still, even if we assume that AMD will earn only $1 per share during its next
cyclical peak, the stock doesn't look too expensive—it was trading at $12 in
September 2003, which is 12 times peak earnings.

The problem is that we have no idea when (or if) AMD's next cyclical
peak will arrive. After all, the company has a weak competitive position and
a troublesome balance sheet. Thus, I don't think valuing it on peak earnings
makes much sense.

Finally, we can attempt to forecast cash flows and use a DCF approach.
This is also tough because AMD has generated positive annual free cash flow
only three times in the past decade. Let's give it a whirl, though.

If we conservatively estimate that AMD returns to positive free cash flow
in 2005, generates $200 million that year, and increases free cash flow at 5 per-
cent annually for the next 10 years, it will generate about $2.2 billion in free
cash over the next decade. Discounted back to the present at 14 percent, that's
about $1.0 billion. (I used 14 percent because AMD had a poor track record of
profitability, had considerable balance sheet risk, and operated from a weak
competitive position in a cyclical industry.) Add in our perpetuity value of
$750 million, and AMD is worth about $1.8 billion, or about $5 per share (see
Figure 11.7).

AMD Net Income	93	94	95	96	97	98	99	00	01	02
Net income ($mil)	218.4	294.9	300.5	-69.0	-21.1	-104.0	-88.9	983.0	-60.6	-1,303.0
Basic EPS ($)	1.15	1.51	1.42	-0.25	-0.08	-0.36	-0.30	3.18	-0.18	-3.81
Total shares	190.2	195	211.2	271.4	280.9	287.3	294.1	309.3	332.4	342.3

Figure 11.6 AMD's net income and shares outstanding.

Assumptions for AMD

Current stock price	$7.00
Shares outstanding (mil)	342.0
Next year's free cash flow (mil)	—
Perpetuity growth rate (g)	3.0%
Discount rate (R)	14.0%

10-Year Valuation Model for AMD

Step 1: Forecast free cash flow (FCF) for the next 10 years.
Assumes constant 5% growth rate, free cash flows in $ millions.

	Yr 1	Yr 2	Yr 3	Yr 4	Yr 5	Yr 6	Yr 7	Yr 8	Yr 9	Yr 10
Free cash flow →	—	200.0	210.0	220.5	231.5	243.1	255.3	268.0	281.4	295.5

Step 2: Discount these free cash flows to reflect the present value.
Discount Factor $= (1 + R)^N$ (where R = discount rate and N = year being discounted)

	Yr 1	Yr 2	Yr 3	Yr 4	Yr 5	Yr 6	Yr 7	Yr 8	Yr 9	Yr 10
Free cash flow	—	200.0	210.0	220.5	231.5	243.1	255.3	268.0	281.4	295.5
÷ Discount factor	—	1.14^2	1.14^3	1.14^4	1.14^5	1.14^6	1.14^7	1.14^8	1.14^9	1.14^{10}
= Discounted FCF →	—	153.9	141.7	130.6	120.3	110.8	102.0	94.0	86.5	79.7

Step 3: Calculate the perpetuity value and discount it to the present.
Perpetuity Value = Yr 10 FCF $\times$ (1 + g) ÷ (R − g) (where g = perpetuity growth rate and R = discount rate)

Perpetuity value → (295.5 $\times$ 1.03) ÷ (.14−.03) = $2,766.86
Discounted → $2,766.86 ÷ 1.14^{10} = $746.34

Step 4: Calculate total equity value.
Add the discounted perpetuity value (above) to the sum of the 10 discounted cash flows (see step 2).

Total equity value → $1,019.40 + $746.34 = $1,765.74

Step 5: Calculate per share value.
Divide total equity value by shares outstanding.

Per share value → $1,765.74 ÷ 342 = $5.16

Figure 11.7   Valuing AMD using discounted cash flow. *Source:* Morningstar, Inc.

With the stock trading at $12 as of this writing, I'd take a pass. With such an uncertain future, this is a stock that I would buy only at a big discount to a conservative estimate of intrinsic value—and perhaps not even then, given how many strikes the firm has against it. The intrinsic value could be much lower if AMD fails to generate free cash flow in the near future or runs into liquidity troubles, or it could be much higher if AMD gains some kind of competitive edge against Intel. In particular, the next-generation "Hammer" family of chips AMD has rolled out could give the firm a boost. Given the firm's poor track record of holding its own against Intel, though, that's not a bet I'd want to make. The stock could move higher if the market gets enthusiastic about AMD's prospects—it tends to be pretty volatile—but it seems like a poor long-term investment.

Biomet

Medical-device firm Biomet, which will hopefully be more promising than AMD, makes artificial joints—mainly hips and knees—as well as a variety of other products used in orthopedic surgery, such as pins and screws for setting broken bones. The firm has been around for about 25 years, is still run by one of the founders, and competes with a relatively small group of firms. (The top five firms in Biomet's main market control about 85 percent of sales.)

The orthopedic device industry is pretty attractive. Developed-country populations are aging, and better health care means that people are staying active longer—which increases the demand for artificial joints. Moreover, artificial joints became a mass-market product only during the 1980s and 1990s. Because joints typically have a 10- to 12-year life span, the number of revision procedures, which replace or repair a worn-out artificial joint, is just now starting to climb. Add these revisions to the demand for first-time procedures, and the market is growing at 7 percent to 10 percent. And because annual price hikes of 3 percent to 4 percent are pretty usual in the orthopedic industry, sales growth of 10 percent to 14 percent looks pretty doable for the average orthopedic device company. Companies that gradually gain market share or compete in the high-end segment of the market might be able to grow a touch faster, as well.

Margins are fat because the industry has high barriers to entry and high switching costs. Surgeons prefer products with long clinical track records, which means it would be tough for an upstart to quickly gain market share. In addition, this is a heavily research-dependent business, so having decades of product development experience and expertise helps keep incumbents ahead of potential new entrants. Finally, each company's products are slightly different, which means that orthopedic surgeons develop product preferences and are reluctant to take time off from surgery to get retrained on a competitor's product unless it offers a large potential benefit. Because artificial joint innovations tend to be incremental, rather than revolutionary, this isn't terribly likely, so market share in the industry stays fairly stable.

You can learn all of this information by reading Biomet's 10-K and those of a few of its competitors, as well as surfing a few industry-oriented Web sites. Let's see if the financials bear out what seems to be an attractive company.

Economic Moat

First, we need to look for evidence that the firm has an economic moat—what sounds good in words may not always show up in the numbers. As with AMD earlier in the chapter, we can do this by examining the trends in Biomet's free cash flow, margins, return on equity, and return on assets (see Figure 11.8).

These are the kinds of consistently excellent financial results that serious stock investors dream about—consistent and constantly increasing free cash flow, a free cash-to-sales ratio well above 5 percent (and usually above 10 percent), and very consistent operating and net margins. There's little to quibble with here—any company that can convert more than 10 percent of sales into free cash flow for a decade is doing something right.

Trends in ROA and ROE also look stellar, with high margins, decent asset turns, and modest financial leverage (see Figure 11.9). Asset efficiency

Free Cash Flow	93	94	95	96	97	98	99	00	01	02
Cash operations ($mil)	43.0	65.7	52.6	68.5	123.0	121.8	148.5	131.6	190.5	184.2
Cap expenses ($mil)	-14.9	-6.6	-28.9	-14.1	-21.4	-44.1	-51.1	-43.1	-35.3	-62.3
Free Cash Flow ($mil)	**28.9**	**59.1**	**23.7**	**54.4**	**101.6**	**77.7**	**97.4**	**88.5**	**155.2**	**121.9**
FCF/Sales (%)	**8.6**	**15.9**	**5.2**	**10.2**	**17.5**	**11.9**	**12.9**	**9.6**	**15.1**	**10.2**

Figure 11.8 Biomet's historical free cash flow.

Profitability	93	94	95	96	97	98	99	00	01	02
Operating margin (%)	27.0	27.3	26.3	25.7	26.3	27.6	22.7	28.6	28.2	31.1
Net margin (%)	19.1	18.7	17.5	17.6	18.3	19.1	15.4	18.9	19.2	20.1
Asset turnover (avg)	1.1	1.0	1.0	0.9	1.0	0.9	0.8	0.8	0.8	0.8
Return on Assets (%)	**21.0**	**18.7**	**17.5**	**15.8**	**18.3**	**17.2**	**12.3**	**15.1**	**15.4**	**16.1**
Financial leverage (avg)	1.2	1.2	1.2	1.2	1.1	1.3	1.3	1.3	1.3	1.3
Return on Equity (%)	**25.2**	**22.4**	**21.0**	**19.0**	**20.1**	**22.4**	**16.0**	**19.6**	**20.0**	**20.9**

Figure 11.9   Biomet's profitability numbers.

has declined a bit since the early 1990s, but not to an alarming degree. The only black spot is 1999, when net margin suddenly dipped from 19 percent to about 15 percent. Even though it recovered promptly the next year, this is something we should investigate.

A quick glance at the financial results in Figure 11.10 shows that the lower margins in 1999 were likely due to the $55 million in "other" expenses that the company recorded that year. After digging into the footnotes of the 1999 10-K filing, we find that the $55 million was a charge related to a legal dispute with a competitor, which claimed that Biomet competed with it unfairly. Although this is not a great development, the medical device industry is a litigious one, and adverse legal charges are a fact of life from time to time. Because this is the only sizeable problem during the past several years—and none of the legal disputes discussed in Biomet's 2002 10-K sound particularly worrisome—it's not something I'm going to worry about too much. We should, however, make a mental note to pay extra-special attention to Biomet's balance sheet to make sure it has the resources to pay any more judgments that might come along.

Operating Expenses ($mil)	93	94	95	96	97	98	99	00	01	02
SG&A ($mil)	122.2	136.2	169.3	199.5	211.5	232.9	265.6	326.6	374.8	437.7
R&D ($mil)	18.0	20.5	21.8	24.1	23.2	36.1	35.5	40.2	43.0	50.8
Other ($mil)	0.0	0.0	0.0	0.0	0.0	0.0	55.0	11.7	26.1	0.0
Operating Income ($mil)	**90.5**	**101.8**	**119.0**	**137.3**	**159.8**	**180.1**	**171.7**	**263.7**	**290.7**	**370.7**

Figure 11.10   Biomet's historical operating expenses.

Revenue Growth	93	94	95	96	97	98	99	00	01	02
Year over year (%)	22.0	11.3	21.2	18.3	8.4	12.2	16.3	21.5	12.0	15.6
3-Year average (%)	—	21.2	18.1	16.9	15.9	12.9	12.3	16.6	16.5	16.3
10-Year average (%)	—	—	—	—	—	—	—	—	17.3	15.8

Figure 11.11 Biomet's historical revenue growth.

Overall, it looks as though Biomet has a pretty sizeable economic moat. Returns on capital and free cash flow are consistently high, and there's not much year-to-year variation. Although we'll want to make sure we dig further into Biomet's competition—to make sure that these solid financial results are likely to persist in the future—Biomet has the financial hallmarks of a solid investment so far.

Growth

Figure 11.11 indicates that revenue growth has been a little volatile, ranging from 8 percent to 20 percent, but a sales growth rate in the mid teens is about average. That's pretty good, and it's right in line with the industry growth rates we examined earlier in this section. That means Biomet is likely holding its own in terms of market share.

Now, let's see whether earnings growth is similarly solid (see Figure 11.12). Aside from 1999, which was affected by that $55 million legal charge that we mentioned earlier, earnings growth has been excellent. It's tough to increase the bottom line at 15 percent annually for a decade, but that's what Biomet has done. In addition, it looks as though long-term earnings growth of 15.7 percent is right in line with long-term sales growth of 15.8 percent, which means Biomet probably hasn't had to play any accounting games to generate such solid results. The firm increased earnings the way a great company should—by selling more products, year in and year out.

EPS Growth	93	94	95	96	97	98	99	00	01	02
Year over year (%)	21.7	8.9	13.1	18.9	14.6	18.1	-7.2	42.7	11.7	20.6
3-Year average (%)	—	20.4	14.5	13.6	15.5	17.2	7.9	16.1	14.0	24.3
10-Year average (%)	—	—	—	—	—	—	—	—	16.7	15.7

Figure 11.12 Biomet's historical EPS growth.

Profitability

We've already given very high marks to Biomet for its solid free cash flow and high returns on capital, but as we did with AMD, let's dig deeper to find out what was driving the firm's profitability. Again, we use a common size income statement as our tool (see Figure 11.13).

These are some very solid, steady results. Gross margins of 70 percent are high, and it looks as if they've been very gradually increasing over time, which means the firm has been able to maintain pricing power of the goods it sells and control costs of the materials used to make its products. Overhead (SG&A) costs have been very steady as a percentage of sales, which means Biomet isn't becoming more efficient as it grows. This is all right, though, because a big chunk of those SG&A costs are Biomet's payments to its salesforce— when salespeople sell more, they get paid more, which is as it should be.

Finally, it looks as though research and development has been declining as a percentage of sales. Although this could be positive, because it means higher overall margins as Biomet spreads R&D costs over a larger sales base, we need to be sure that Biomet hasn't pared back too far on research. Innovation is the lifeblood of a company such as Biomet, so we want to do some digging to make sure the company has plenty of new products in the pipeline. We can probably determine this by going through the company's recent press releases and annual report, and we can also compare how much Biomet is spending on research with its competitors to make sure it's in line.

Overall, though, there are few quibbles here. Biomet passes the profitability test with flying colors, and the results are as clean as can be, with very

Biomet	93	94	95	96	97	98	99	00	01	02
Revenue (%)	100.0	100.0	100.0	100.0	100.0	100.0	100.0	100.0	100.0	100.0
COGS (%)	31.2	30.8	31.4	32.6	32.0	31.0	30.3	30.2	28.7	27.9
Gross Margin %	**68.8**	**69.2**	**68.6**	**67.4**	**68.0**	**69.0**	**69.7**	**69.8**	**71.3**	**72.1**
SG&A (%)	36.4	36.5	37.4	37.3	36.5	35.8	35.1	35.5	36.4	36.7
R&D (%)	5.4	5.5	4.8	4.5	4.0	5.5	4.7	4.4	4.2	4.3
Other (%)	0.0	0.0	0.0	0.0	0.0	0.0	7.3	1.3	2.5	0.0
Operating Margin (%)	**27.0**	**27.3**	**26.3**	**25.7**	**27.5**	**27.6**	**22.7**	**28.6**	**28.2**	**31.1**

Figure 11.13 Biomet's common size income statement, representing each line item as a percentage of revenue.

few one-time charges. Most important, the charges that the company has taken truly were nonrecurring because they were the result of unpredictable legal disputes.

Financial Health

Biomet has no long-term debt, so that's one thing we won't have to worry about. The current ratio is around 4, which is high for a company with no debt to worry about, and the firm has consistently kept around 15 percent of total assets in cash.

One thing you want to watch with super-profitable companies such as Biomet is that they don't let too much cash pile up on the balance sheet. It's fine for a company to build a temporary war chest if it anticipates big investments sometime in the next few years, but cash that sits around on the balance sheet for a long time isn't being used efficiently. If you see cash as a percentage of total assets rising year after year for a firm that's already in fine financial health, try to find out why management isn't buying back stock, paying a dividend, or reinvesting it in the business. Any of the three are preferable to letting the cash account balloon.

The Bear Case

Creating a convincing bear case is especially crucial when evaluating companies like Biomet that score well on just about every front. Things that look too good to be true usually are, and every company has some warts that need to be taken into account.

First, we need to think about litigation risks. We mentioned earlier a recent $55 million charge related to an adverse legal settlement, and it's likely that the firm will be embroiled in other disputes from time to time. Therefore, we want to make sure that the firm has adequate insurance and that it's good about disclosing the status of whatever litigation it's party to. (The "commitments and contingencies" section of the 10-K will help us do this.) Legal risks are largely unpredictable, so we should be prepared for some potential headline risk from Biomet.

Another area of concern is that Biomet's foreign operations aren't in nearly as good a shape as its U.S. operations. If we look at the "segment data" section of Biomet's 2002 10-K, we find that the firm does about 25 percent of its sales outside the United States, but only 12 percent of the firm's operating income stems from its foreign units. Because the foreign segment is a big portion of the overall company and it's only half as profitable—and it's not growing as quickly—we want to find out what Biomet's plans are for its foreign operations. Why are they so much less profitable and growing so much slower? How does Biomet plan to fix them? If Biomet can't get its foreign operations on track, does it plan to exit them altogether, or is there some larger strategic reason that the firm needs an international presence? We want to try to get answers to these questions so we know just how big a risk the firm's foreign operations are likely to be.

Biomet's size is also an issue, because digging into the orthopedic devices industry reveals that Biomet is not as large as some of its competitors. Biomet has about 7 percent of the worldwide orthopedic market, whereas its competitor Stryker has 15 percent and the DePuy division of Johnson & Johnson has about 14 percent. Firms with more market share can sometimes gain greater economies of scale—which would allow them to price their products lower—and may also be able to outmuscle smaller competitors by offering customers a more diverse product lineup. Because Biomet has been growing nicely for some time and there's no evidence yet of margin pressure, it looks as though the firm is holding its own against its larger peers. However, we want to keep in mind the risk that a larger competitor will try to squeeze Biomet.

Finally, we want to look into some big-picture industry risks. Biomet's large gross margins suggest that the firm has been able to charge premium prices for its products, and highly profitable health care industries tend to attract political pressure from time to time—just ask the large drug firms. A change in the rules for Medicare reimbursements or some other arcane regulatory issue could have a big impact on the whole orthopedic device industry. Like legal risks, regulatory changes are tough to predict, so we want to mentally prepare ourselves for a potentially unpleasant shock.

Management

As with AMD, Biomet's proxy statement—which details executives' compensation—is a good first stop in assessing management. They're paid pretty reasonably: President and CEO Dane Miller pulled in less than $500,000 in salary *and* bonus, and other members of the executive team are in roughly the same range. One vice president even had a higher base salary than Miller in

2002. Salaries and bonuses have been moving up steadily over the past few years, but so have Biomet's profits. Finally, there's none of the "other compensation" frippery that executives at so many firms receive—no mention of loans, company cars, life insurance policies, special deferred retire-like-a-king accounts, and so on. Management is paid a healthy cash salary, some receive modest stock option grants, and that's that.

On the stock option front, neither Miller nor Chairman of the Board Niles Noblitt has received any stock options over the past three years, and some further digging into the proxy reveals that Miller has never received a stock option from the firm. Because Miller owns 3 percent of the outstanding shares and Noblitt owns 1.8 percent, this is entirely appropriate—both already have substantial ownership stakes that motivate them to act in shareholders' interests, and they see no need for greater ownership stakes. (Contrast this behavior with executives such as Larry Ellison of Oracle or Steve Jobs of Apple, each of whom has received substantial options grants in recent years despite already-large ownership stakes.)

For those executives who did receive option grants, the amounts look reasonable—over the past few years, no executive has received more than 1 percent of the total options granted in a given year, which means options are likely being widely distributed throughout the firm. Moreover, the total amount being granted each year is rarely above 1 percent of the total number of shares outstanding, and the firm's total number of shares has barely budged over the past decade. That tells me Biomet is using options responsibly to motivate employees and executives without diluting shareholder value, which is exactly the kind of behavior you want to see in the management team of a firm.

Valuation

For a firm as high quality as Biomet, valuation is likely to be the Achilles' heel in the investment analysis process. Companies this good are rarely cheap, so we need to tread carefully as we decide what a reasonable value would be for Biomet's shares. Even though the firm's high growth rate and strong profitability mean that we should be willing to pay up for the shares, we can't pay too much, or we'll be unlikely to receive a decent return on our investment.

Starting with the basic valuation multiples, we find that Biomet was trading at about 28 times the past year's earnings as of this writing. That's pricey—it's way above the market's price-to-earnings ratio of about 20—but it's substantially lower than the firm's average P/E of 38 over the past five years. Price-to-cash flow (P/CF) tells a similar story: The current P/CF ratio of 35 was higher than the market P/CF of 14, but lower than Biomet's historical average of 45.

Finally, Biomet's earnings yield and cash return of 3.0 percent and 2.1 percent, respectively, didn't exactly scream "undervalued." We could get better returns in risk-free treasuries, and given Biomet's higher risk than a T-bond, we should demand a *higher* cash return and earnings yield from its shares.

However, bond payments are fixed, whereas Biomet's earnings and cash flow should grow substantially over time. Moreover, Biomet's business has been consistent over the past several years, which means we can forecast the firm's future with more confidence than we could, for example, AMD's future. Sounds to me like Biomet is a perfect candidate for a discounted cash flow analysis.

Biomet's free cash flow has increased pretty steadily over the past several years, so let's use $180 million as our estimated amount for 2004. (Biomet's historical free cash flows are shown in Figure 11.8.)

If we increase free cash flow at 15 percent over the next five years and conservatively assume that Biomet starts to lose market share and grow more slowly after five years, we see that the present value of the free cash that Biomet will generate over the next 10 years is about $2 billion. (I used a relatively low discount rate of 9 percent—versus a market average of 10.5 percent—because Biomet is a very financially stable company.) Add in our perpetuity value of about $3.5 billion, and Biomet is worth $5.5 billion, or about $21 per share (Figure 11.14 runs through these calculations for you).

With the stock trading at about $28 as of this writing, Biomet doesn't look like much of a value under this set of assumptions. However, maybe we're being *too* conservative by forecasting that a competitor will start eating Biomet's lunch in just five years. Moreover, it might not be reasonable to assume that a firm in an industry as young and robust as orthopedic devices will be growing at just 3 percent after a decade. That's a really low growth rate—in line with the overall economy—and it's entirely possible that Biomet will still be growing at an above-average rate in 10 years' time. Therefore, let's try another scenario. We'll assume Biomet can grow faster starting in year six, and

Assumptions for Biomet

Current stock price:	$29.00
Shares outstanding (mil)	258.0
Next year's free cash flow (mil)	$180.00
Perpetuity growth rate (g)	3.0%
Discount rate (R)	9.0%

10-Year Valuation Model for Biomet

Step 1: Forecast free cash flow (FCF) for the next 10 years.
Assumes 15% growth rate for years 1–5; 10% growth rate for years 6–10. Free cash flows in $ millions.

		Yr 1	Yr 2	Yr 3	Yr 4	Yr 5	Yr 6	Yr 7	Yr 8	Yr 9	Yr 10
Free cash flow	→	180.0	207.0	238.1	273.8	314.8	362.0	398.3	438.1	460.0	483.0

Step 2: Discount these free cash flows to reflect the present value.
Discount Factor = $(1 + R)^N$ (where R = discount rate and N = year being discounted)

		Yr 1	Yr 2	Yr 3	Yr 4	Yr 5	Yr 6	Yr 7	Yr 8	Yr 9	Yr 10
Free cash flow		180.0	207.0	238.1	273.8	314.8	362.0	398.3	438.1	460.0	483.0
÷ Discount factor		1.09^1	1.09^2	1.09^3	1.09^4	1.09^5	1.09^6	1.09^7	1.09^8	1.09^9	1.09^{10}
= Discounted FCF	→	165.1	174.2	183.8	193.9	204.6	215.9	217.9	219.9	211.8	204.0

Step 3: Calculate the perpetuity value and discount it to the present.
Perpetuity Value = Yr 10 FCF × $(1 + g) ÷ (R − g)$ (where g = perpetuity growth rate and R = discount rate)

Perpetuity value	→	$(483.0 × 1.03) ÷ (.09−.03) = \$8,291.16$
Discounted	→	$\$8,291.16 ÷ 1.09^{10} = \$3,502.27$

Step 4: Calculate total equity value.
Add the discounted perpetuity value (above) to the sum of the 10 discounted cash flows (see step 2).

Total equity value → $1,991.13 + $3,502.27 = $5,493.40

Step 5: Calculate per share value.
Divide total equity value by shares outstanding.

Per share value → $5,493.40 ÷ 258 = $21.29

Figure 11.14 Valuing Biomet using discounted cash flow. *Source:* Morningstar, Inc.

Biomet	Yr 6	Yr 7	Yr 8	Yr 9	Yr 10	Yr 11	Yr 12	Yr 13	Yr 14	Yr 15
Free cash flow ($mil)	362	406	454	509	570	638	702	772	849	934
Growth rate (%)	12	12	12	12	12	10	10	10	10	10
Present value ($mil)	216	222	228	234	241	247	250	252	254	257

Figure 11.15   Biomet's free cash flow estimates from year 6 onward.

we'll push our forecast horizon out to 15 years, at which time we assume that Biomet's growth rate declines to a steady state of 3 percent (see Figure 11.15).

This set of assumptions results in an estimated intrinsic value per share of about $30, which is right around where the shares are trading as of this writing. Assuming this is a reasonable scenario, I'd start getting interested in the stock at around $24, which would be a 20 percent discount to my estimated intrinsic value. I'm not looking for much of a margin of safety because Biomet's strong balance sheet, excellent industry prospects, and solid profitability all make it less likely that something will go horribly wrong with my assumptions.

However, this process has taught us something very important: For us to believe that Biomet's shares are worth $30, rather than $20, we have to believe that the firm can hold off its competition and grow at an above-average rate for a long period of time. Companies that can increase free cash flow at an average annual rate of 12 percent for a lengthy period of time—which is what our second scenario assumes—are few and far between, after all.

This is the key benefit of a discounted cash flow approach to valuation. Having thought through a couple of possible scenarios for Biomet, we now know exactly what assumptions are incorporated in our estimated intrinsic value of $30 per share. Armed with that knowledge, we can make a more informed investment decision—we wouldn't know as much about the assumptions needed to believe that the stock is reasonably valued if we'd just looked at the current P/E relative to the historical average P/E. For example, we should probably pay very close attention to Biomet's competitive position relative to other firms in the industry, as well as to any signs that the long-term demand for orthopedic devices might be slowing, because those two factors are what moved our value estimate from $20 to $30.

Conclusion

There you have it—real-world application of the tools of fundamental analysis, in a simplified form, is exactly what we do at Morningstar every day.

This is some pretty painstaking stuff, and it's not reasonable to do a super-thorough analysis of every single company you investigate. In the real world, time is short, so even the pros use shortcuts to help separate the companies that really are worth a great deal of analytical time from the ones that are unlikely to be good investments. In the next chapter, I show you exactly how to separate the wheat from the chaff when you're trying to narrow down a list of investment candidates to the ones that are really worth a thorough investigation.

12

The 10-Minute Test

WITH LITERALLY THOUSANDS of companies available to invest in, one of the toughest challenges for any investor is figuring out which ones are worth detailed examination and which ones aren't. Now that you know the tools of in-depth fundamental analysis, I want to give you some tips on narrowing down the field. Apply the following tests to any stock that you think might be a worthwhile investment, and you should be able to decide in 10 minutes whether it warrants much of your time.

In fact, I'll bet that asking the questions in this chapter will allow you to eliminate at least half—if not more—of the stocks you run across from consideration. Throwing out less-promising stocks early in the process will leave you more time to investigate and value the ones that really might be great investments.

Two caveats before we start: First, these rules of thumb are starting points, no more and no less. There are exceptions to every guideline I list in this chapter. These shortcuts aren't designed to cover every possible situation—but if you apply them, they will eliminate poor investments more often than not.

Second, although the following list of questions might *seem* daunting at first, you can answer all of them using a compilation of 10 years' worth of financial data that's available on Morningstar.com.

Does the Firm Pass a Minimum Quality Hurdle?

Avoiding the junk that litters the investment landscape is the first step in our 10-minute test. Companies with miniscule market capitalizations and firms that trade on the bulletin boards (or pink sheets) are the first ones to rule out. Also avoid foreign firms that don't file regular financials with the SEC—even some large foreign firms issue only brief press releases each quarter and publish full financials only once per year.

Finally, recent initial public offerings (IPOs) are usually not worth your time. Companies sell shares to the public only when they think they're getting a high price, so IPOs are rarely bargains. Moreover, most IPOs are young, unseasoned firms with short track records. The big exception to this rule is firms that are spun off from larger parent companies. Spinoffs are often solid companies with long operating histories that the larger firm no longer wants to manage, and the stocks can often be attractively valued as well.

Has the Company Ever Made an Operating Profit?

This test sounds simple, but it'll keep you out of a lot of trouble. Very often, companies that are still in the money-losing stage sound the most exciting—they're investigating a novel treatment for some rare disease, or they're about to offer some exciting new product or service, the likes of which the world has never seen.

Unfortunately, stocks like this will also blow up your portfolio more often than not. They usually have only a single product or service in the pipeline, and the eventual viability of the product or service will make or break the company. (Going by the statistics of how many start-ups fail, *break* is a more likely occurrence than *make.*) Unless you're looking for an alternative to lottery tickets, take a pass on any firm that hasn't yet proven it can earn a buck.

Does the Company Generate Consistent Cash Flow from Operations?

Fast-growing firms can sometimes report profits before they generate cash—but every company has to generate cash eventually. Companies with negative cash flow from operations will eventually have to seek additional financing by selling bonds or issuing more shares. The former will likely increase the riskiness of the firm, whereas the latter will dilute your ownership stake as a shareholder.

Are Returns on Equity Consistently above 10 Percent, with Reasonable Leverage?

Use 10 percent as a minimum hurdle. If a nonfinancial firm can't post ROEs over 10 percent for four years out of every five, for example, odds are good that it's not worth your time. For financial firms, raise your ROE bar to 12 percent. Don't forget to check leverage to make sure that it's in line with industry norms. A 15 percent ROE generated with minimal leverage is a much higher quality result than one generated using lots of leverage.

One exception is that cyclical firms—companies whose results vary strongly with the general economy—may have wildly varying results from year to year. However, the best will make money and post decent ROEs even when times are tough.

Is Earnings Growth Consistent or Erratic?

The best companies post reasonably consistent growth rates. If a firm's earnings bounce all over the place, it's either in an extremely volatile industry or it's regularly getting shellacked by competitors. The former is not necessarily bad as long as the long-term industry outlook is good and the shares are cheap, but the latter is potentially a big problem.

How Clean Is the Balance Sheet?

Firms with a lot of debt require extra care because their capital structures are often very complicated. If a nonbank firm has a financial leverage ratio above about 4—or a debt-to-equity ratio over 1.0—ask yourself the following questions:

- ▶ *Is the firm in a stable business?* Firms in industries such as consumer products and food can withstand more leverage than economically sensitive firms with volatile earnings.
- ▶ *Has debt been going down or up as a percentage of total assets?* One thing you don't want to see in a highly leveraged firm is even more debt.

► *Do you understand the debt?* If a quick glance at the 10-K reveals questionable debt and quasi-debt instruments that you can't wrap your head around, move on. There are many fine companies out there with simpler capital structures.

Does the Firm Generate Free Cash Flow?

As we know, free cash flow is the holy grail—cash generated after capital expenditures that truly increases the value of the firm. Generally, you should prefer firms that create free cash to ones that don't and firms that create more free cash to ones that create less. As I discussed in Chapter 6, divide free cash flow by sales, and use 5 percent as a rough benchmark.

The one exception—and it's a big one—is that it's fine for a firm to be generating negative free cash flow *if* it's investing that cash wisely in projects that are likely to pay off well in the future. For example, neither Starbucks nor Home Depot generated meaningful free cash flow until 2001—yet there's no question that they had been creating economic value (and shareholder wealth) for many years before 2001. That's because they were plowing every cent they earned right back into their businesses because their management teams believed that they still had many high-return investment opportunities for the cash they were generating.

So don't automatically write off firms with negative free cash flow if they have solid ROEs and pass the other tests in this chapter. Just be sure you believe that the firm really is reinvesting the cash wisely.

How Much "Other" Is There?

Companies can hide many bad decisions in supposedly one-time charges, so if a firm is already questionable on some other front and has a history of taking big charges, take a pass. Not only are charge-happy firms more difficult to analyze because of their complicated financials, but numerous charges hint at a management team that may be trying to burnish poor results.

Has the Number of Shares Outstanding Increased Markedly over the Past Several Years?

If so, the firm is either issuing new shares to buy other companies or granting numerous options to employees and executives. The former is a red flag because most acquisitions fail, and the latter is not something you want to see because it means that your ownership stake in the firm is slowly shrinking as employees exercise their options. If shares outstanding are consistently increasing by more than around 2 percent per year—assuming no big acquisitions—think long and hard before investing in the firm.

However, if the number of shares is actually *shrinking,* the company potentially gets a big gold star. Firms that buy back many shares are returning excess cash to shareholders, which is generally a responsible thing to do. Just be careful that the company isn't going hog-wild with share repurchases even as their shares keep zooming ever upward because stock repurchases are a good use of capital only when the company's shares are trading for a reasonable valuation. You don't want to see a company buying its own overvalued stock any more than you want to invest in overvalued shares yourself.

Beyond the 10 Minutes

If the firm does pass these tests and it looks as though it's worth a detailed examination, here's how to proceed. This research process will take much longer than 10 minutes, but it's worth the effort for an idea that passes the initial hurdles:

- Look over the 10-year summary balance sheet, income statement, and statement of cash flows on Morningstar.com or another Web site. Look for trends, and make notes of anything that raises an eyebrow and deserves further investigation. This process should give you an initial road map for investigation.
- Read the most recent 10-K filing front to back. Pay special attention to the sections that describe the company and its industry, the sections about risks and competition, any mention of legal issues (sometimes labeled "commitments and contingencies"), and the "management's discussion and analysis" section. The latter is where the firm explains, in reasonably plain English, why the most recent year's financial results were what they were. Write down anything you don't understand or which you want to investigate further. You don't necessarily need to read every page of the 10-K—sometimes firms include scores of pages of mind-numbing detail about leases, for example—but you should at least skim every page

to make sure there's nothing buried in the text that you do need to know. Be on the watch for any sections that describe loans, guarantees, contractual obligations, or the like. If the firm is going to owe someone a large amount of money in a few years, you need to know about it.

▶ Read the two most recent proxies (form DEF-14A, in the SEC's jargon). Look for reasonable compensation that varies with corporate financial performance and a reasonable options-granting policy. Check to make sure the board of directors isn't packed with individuals with close ties to management.

▶ Read the most recent annual report, as well as the past two years' reports, if possible, to get a feel for the company. Is the letter to shareholders candid and frank, or does management gloss over problems with jargon? Ignoring problems won't make them go away, after all. In addition, does the firm present industry information to give you context for evaluating it? Does the report look as though the firm spent way too much money on it?

▶ Look at the two most recent quarterly earnings reports and 10-Q filings to see whether anything has changed recently. Look for signs that business is getting better—or worse—as well as for anything major that has changed since the last 10-K. If it's still available, listen to the most recent quarterly conference call. (Companies often archive these on their Web sites for some time after the quarter is over.) Does management get defensive or evasive when analysts ask tough questions, or does it respond with straightforward answers?

▶ Start valuing the stock. Look at the stock's valuation multiples relative to the market, the industry, and the stock's historical valuation ranges. If the firm has low reinvestment needs, low risk, high returns on capital, or a high growth rate, be prepared to accept a higher price-to-earnings ratio. Do at least a very rough discounted cash flow valuation—think about how much free cash flow the firm is likely to generate next year, how fast it will grow, and add the discounted value of these cash flows to a perpetuity value. If your estimated intrinsic value is very different from the market price, check your assumptions. Are you being too pessimistic or too optimistic? If you recheck your assumptions, the stock still looks undervalued, and your multiple-based analysis didn't scream "sell," you might just have uncovered a great investment.

13

A Guided Tour of the Market

IN THE PREVIOUS chapter, I discussed easy ways to home in on companies that will be worth your while. In the next section of the book, we'll focus on tools for understanding different areas of the market.

As I said in Chapter 3, it's easier for companies to make money in some industries than in others. Moreover, some industries lend themselves to the creation of economic moats more so than others, and these are the industries where you'll want to spend most of your time. Although we don't advocate a *top-down* investment strategy—in which you select areas of the market that you think will perform better than others and invest heavily in your top-rated industries—the economics of some industries are superior to others. Hence, you should spend more time learning about attractive industries than unattractive ones.

Every industry has its own unique dynamics and set of jargon—and some industries (such as financial services) even have financial statements that look very different from the ones we discussed in Chapter 5. I asked Morningstar's staff of 30 equity analysts to put together a series of chapters covering just about every corner of the market. These chapters should help you wade through the different economics of each industry and understand how companies in each industry can create economic moats—which strategies work and how you can identify companies pursuing those strategies.

Where to Look

Because you're likely as pressed for time as every other person with a day job who also manages his or her own investments, let me try to briefly steer you toward some areas of the market that are definitely worth more of your time.

Banks and Financial Services

In general, most financial services firms are in excellent economic positions as middlemen for money. Banks in particular enjoy the enviable position of paying very little to hold on to depositors' money (when you consider the low rates on checking accounts and all of the fee income that such accounts generate), which they then turn around and lend out at substantially higher interest rates than they're paying to depositors. In fact, some banks do so well at levying fees and cross-selling financial products that depositors literally pay the bank to hold their money. Moreover, because banks have somewhat confusing financial statements, many investors simply pass them by or look at only the biggest and most well-known firms. By learning what makes banks and other financial services firms tick, you'll be ahead of most investors, and because this ground is less picked-over, you'll likely find some solid investment ideas as well. (Financial services is such a broad area of the market that we've devoted two chapters to the area—one on banks and one on asset managers and insurance companies.)

Business Services

This is the ultimate catchall area of the market, so many investors pass it by. That's a shame because it contains some very attractive firms. In addition to larger industries such as data processing—which is boring but profitable as can be—business services is packed with niche firms that dominate their corner of the economy. Cintas, for example, has generated an enormous amount of shareholder wealth by convincing companies that it can design and maintain employee uniforms better than employers can. Who would have thought that renting uniforms could be so profitable? Moody's (which rates bonds) and Equifax (which maintains a credit-scoring database) are other examples of highly profitable but not-so-well-known firms with strong positions in niche industries.

Business services firms often fly beneath the market's radar because they don't fit neatly into the industry-oriented coverage lists of Wall Street analysts—there are usually only a few public companies in any one niche, so the industry specialists on Wall Street tend to pass them by. As a result, the stocks don't get hyped as much to institutional investors. (The other reason companies in this area tend to get less attention from Wall Street is that they're usually self-funding, which means they don't need many investment banking services.) Less attention from Wall Street can mean more opportunity for smart investors, so don't ignore business services.

Health Care

This area of the market is similar to financial services because the long-term demand outlook is very strong, and companies tend to be highly profitable. As our Biomet analysis in Chapter 11 showed, even smaller firms can build lasting economic moats. Tread carefully with biotechs and some managed-care firms, though. Most biotechs are single-product lottery tickets, and most managed-care firms are affected by truly arcane regulatory issues—seemingly minor changes in Medicare rules can have a huge impact.

Media

Finally, spend some time getting to know the media business. Many media companies build moats around themselves through natural oligopolies or monopolies—there's little demand for more than a couple of daily news-papers in any one city, for example. Moreover, media is one of the few indus-tries in which product vendors are paid before they have to deliver anything, because a large amount of media is sold via subscription. Can you imagine getting paid on January 1 for the coming year's work? That's how many media firms make money.

Conclusion

These aren't the only four areas of the market with worthwhile investments—I've highlighted these because they contain so many wide-moat companies. There are great firms in even the least likely areas of the stock market.

You may want to read the next 13 chapters straight through, or you might want to use them as a reference guide the next time you find yourself analyzing a company in a specific area of the market. However you use these chapters, our goal in writing this section of the book is to help you answer a few essential questions: How do companies in this industry make money? How can they create economic moats? What quirks does this industry have that an investor should know about? How can you separate successful from unsuccessful firms in each industry? What pitfalls should you watch out for?

Over the long haul, a big part of successful investing is building a mental database of companies and industries on which you can draw as the need arises. The next section of the book should give you a jumpstart in compiling that mental database, and that will make you a better investor.

14

Health Care

MOST PEOPLE COULD survive without gourmet coffee or the latest DVD player, but health care is one of the few areas of the economy that's directly linked to human survival. New medical innovations can significantly improve or extend patients' lives. The vital importance of health care—combined with the relatively free regulatory environment in the United States—gives this sector the potential for above-average financial returns. Many areas in the health care sector are dominated by a few big players that don't need to compete on price. As a result, health care companies are often highly profitable, with strong free cash flow and returns on capital.

Health care has also benefited from powerful growth trends. Between 1980 and 2002, total health care spending increased from 9 percent of the total U.S. economy to almost 15 percent. Although this growth rate may slow, the Centers for Medicare and Medicaid, which tracks health care statistics for the government, still estimates 5 percent annual growth in health spending over the next decade versus 3 percent growth for the economy. If this forecast holds true, health care will make up 18 percent of the U.S. economy in 10 years.

Jill Kiersky, Debbie Wang, and Damon Ficklin with Pat Dorsey.

Health care firms benefit from consistent demand, as well. Even when the economy is in the tank, people still get sick and need doctors and hospitals. As a result, the health care sector has traditionally been a defensive safe haven.

The health care sector includes drug companies, biotechs, medical device firms, and health care service organizations. Of all these areas, we think drug companies and medical devices firms are usually the most promising because they typically have the widest economic moats. However, investors often get swept away by these companies' heady growth rates, so valuations can be steep.

Economic Moats in Health Care

Health care companies often benefit from economic moats in the form of high start-up costs, patent protection, significant product differentiation, and economies of scale. This makes it tough for new players to enter the market, particularly for drug companies with valuable patent rights, managed care organizations with large provider networks, or medical device firms with long clinical track records. These characteristics make for great profitability: The market-weighted return on equity for health care firms has averaged 23 percent over the last five years, despite the economic recession.

For example, in big pharmaceutical companies, patent protection often prevents direct competition, so firms charge the highest price the market will bear for prescription drugs. And because most costs are paid by insurance plans, there's even less price sensitivity for the end consumer. These higher prices—combined with economies of scale—have led to gross margins often surpassing 75 percent to 85 percent.

Size is another barrier to entry for drug companies. Developing a single drug can take 15 to 20 years to get through the entire research, development, and regulatory process and can cost hundreds of millions over that time frame. Few scientists and entrepreneurs have access to that kind of capital. Even if they surmount the time and money hurdles, going head-to-head against a Pfizer or Merck when selling to physicians requires a large salesforce and lots of advertising dollars. In contrast to, say, software or restaurants, where start-up costs are low and new entrants spring up frequently, consolidation has been the trend for many health industries in the last several decades, and established players usually have an edge. Smaller firms often can't compete.

Health care's vast size and rapid expansion makes investing in the sector look like a no-brainer. But it is also fraught with complex relationships, intense controversy, and political pressures to regulate who gets what and who pays for it. Unlike clothing, computers, or consulting services, health care consumers are frequently not the ones writing the check for the products and services they use, and many times they aren't even the ones making the buying decision.

Whereas Wal-Mart shoppers can easily see which brand of paper towels is cheapest and works best on big spills, pricing is often opaque to health care consumers and irrelevant to physicians helping make the decisions. Thus, there is little incentive to shop around for the best price to keep costs lower. (This trend has shown some signs of changing, as companies have been shifting a greater percentage of the health care burden to their employees. But overall, price generally isn't the primary consideration for a patient seeking medical care or a doctor prescribing a drug.)

In the following sections, we explore the dynamics and trends of some of the major health care industries. We won't cover every corner—health care is too broad and diverse to cram everything into a couple of dozen pages—but we'll introduce you to the sector's biggest industries.

Pharmaceuticals

Big pharmaceutical companies typically have wide moats and some of the most attractive financial characteristics of any industry. Branded pharmaceutical companies (as opposed to generics, which have a lower return business model) generally boast top-notch profit margins. Most global pharmaceutical companies have returns on invested capital (ROICs) in the mid-20s. Top-notch companies such as Pfizer are often in the 30s. Drug-company margins are also worth salivating over, with gross margins often near 80 percent and operating margins between 25 percent and 35 percent. What's more, drug companies offer plentiful free cash flow and virtually debt-free balance sheets.

But innovation isn't cheap. It takes money to make money, and the average cost of taking a drug from discovery to the pharmacy shelf is $800 million. Only a third of those drugs ever return their costs of development. Plus, drugs take years to develop. The clinical testing phase (trials in humans) alone can take a decade. All the while, the company is pumping money into the research process with no guarantee of a return.

There's also budgetary pressure in the United States to reduce health care costs, specifically the dollars spent on prescription drugs. Since 1980, prescription drug costs have increased faster than every other health care cost, almost doubling as a percentage of total health care dollars, from 4.9 percent to 9.4 percent. But if political pressure leads to lower drug prices (as a Medicare prescription drug plan might), big pharma could see its margins come down.

Demystifying the Drug Development Process

Drugs are discovered in many different ways. Sometimes they're discovered by mistake, like Viagra. (Pfizer scientists noticed the "side effect" from a blood pressure drug.) Other times, they're discovered only after an exhaustive process of testing thousands of compounds in petri dishes and lab rats. This process of identifying possible targets and determining whether they should move down the development chain can take five years or more and cost in the hundreds of millions of dollars.

With new technology and supercomputers, scientists are finding ways to "virtually" test molecules against different genes to narrow the number of compounds before they start testing in live animals. But for now, drugs still go through years of initial research before being tested in mice, let alone humans.

Drugs typically take the path outlined in Figure 14.1 before they get to the pharmacy shelf.

Preclinical Testing: This animal testing phase is called *preclinical testing.* The primary objective is to evaluate potential toxic effects. Before a drug gets anywhere near a human, scientists must have a clear understanding of the possible damage it could do. It takes two to three years on average to discover a viable drug candidate and another year to find out if it is fit for human testing. For the small percentage of drugs that survive, an investigational new drug (IND) application is filed with the Food and Drug Administration (FDA). Approximately 85 percent of INDs move on to Phase I.

Human Clinical Trials (Phase I): Phase I is the first of three stages of human clinical testing. In Phase I, a drug is tested in a small group (fewer than 100) of healthy volunteers with the goal of gathering initial data on safety and efficacy—whether the drug has the ability to produce the desired

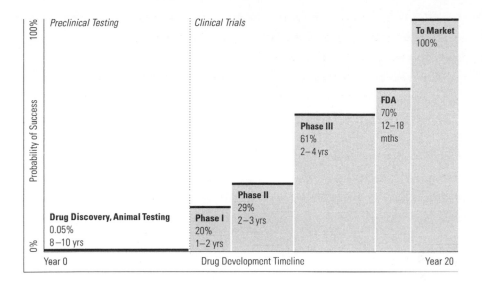

Figure 14.1 Drug development timeline and cumulative probability of success. *Source:* Professor Alicia Loffler, Kellogg School of Management and Biochem Pharma 1998 Annual Report.

effect. Safety is the number-one concern here, though scientists and physicians also evaluate the body's reaction to the drug. A drug in Phase I has only a 20 percent chance of eventual approval but can still cost a few million dollars, including the cost of development, clinical trials, and continuous communication with the FDA.

Human Clinical Trials (Phase II): In Phase II, the drug is tested in a larger population (usually 300 to 500) of patients afflicted with the targeted disease to get a more comprehensive profile of how well the drug works. The managers of these trials use them to compile additional data on safety and side effects. Here, physicians and scientists test for how much of the drug to give and how often to give it. This phase often costs more than $5 million, and more than half of all drugs in Phase II fail to move to the next phase.

Human Clinical Trials (Phase III): The final testing hurdle is Phase III. These trials involve testing the drug in a much larger group of afflicted patients over longer periods. Safety is still an issue—Phase III trials are the first trials to focus on long-term patient safety—but efficacy gets more attention. Because of the number of patients (often 5,000 patients or more), administrative needs, and time and resources involved, Phase III trials are very expensive. These trials consume the bulk of the $800 million cost of developing the average drug, and a drug in Phase III has about a 60 percent chance of eventual approval.

Role of the United States Food and Drug Administration

So far, a drug has spent two to three years in preclinical testing, 8 to 12 years in clinical testing, and still hasn't brought in dime one. And its toughest test is still to come. Once a drug clears Phase III testing, the company files a new drug application with the U.S. FDA (and other regulatory agencies around the world) to be able to place the drug on pharmacy shelves and actually market the drug. An FDA filing is a tome that may weigh more than some small cars, so preparing it can take months. According to PhRMA, the U.S. pharmaceutical industry's trade group, it takes about 17 months for the FDA to review an application, and a drug under review with the FDA still has only about a 70 percent chance of approval.

Each filing typically seeks approval in a single (and highly specific) indication. For example, Rituxan is a drug approved to treat specific types of lymphoma patients who no longer respond to other forms of treatment. Once Rituxan was approved, that particular indication was the only one for which its maker can market the drug (although physicians can prescribe it for anything they choose, often referred to as "off-label usage").

The FDA has advisory committees that meet several times per year to discuss the applications. These committees submit their opinion to the FDA, which then decides the fate of the drug. The FDA can exercise any number of judgments for a new drug application, including granting marketing approval (which means the company can market the drug for the specified indication), requesting additional data or another round of testing, or denying the application.

The last outcome is definitely bad for the company filing the application. It comes as a "not-approvable letter" and means that the information in the filing did not convince the FDA of the drug's merits. It's not always death for the compound, however. Drug applications can be re-filed, but if an application gets all the way through the FDA review process and is rejected, it's likely the company has no more information to back its claims. That means it's back to the drawing board. Another filing is probably years away, and millions more will have to be spent researching the compound. Or the company can scrap the project and move on. Either way, it's painful.

Patents, Intellectual Property Rights, and Market Exclusivity

Once a drug gets the nod from the FDA, the marketing can begin. Brand name drugs enjoy patent protection for 20 years from the date the company first completes the patent application (or 17 years from the issue date). However, because a patent application is usually filed as soon as a drug is identified and not when it hits the market, drugs rarely enjoy 20 years of monopoly profits because a significant portion of the protected period is eaten up by trials and the approval process. Many drugs enjoy only 8 to 10 years of patent protection after they are launched in the marketplace. During that period, no other company can market the same chemical compound, although competitors are still free to develop different compounds that treat the same condition.

To find out about a drug company's patent protection, look at the 10-K report, under the section titled "Patents and Intellectual Property Rights." You should find a discussion of the company's patents and when they expire, but because drug companies often engage in fierce legal battles to try to extend their patents, you'll likely need to visit the company's Web site for complete information. The 10-K also discusses any pending lawsuits, which can be a sign of trouble on the horizon.

Generic Drug Competition

After a drug goes off patent or loses market exclusivity, whichever comes later, the field is open to competition from generic medications. Generic drugs have the same chemical composition as brand name drugs but cost significantly less—usually 40 percent to 60 percent less. Generic drug makers can charge much less because they don't have to recoup the $800 million in per drug research and development costs. And for most drugs, the manufacturing costs are nominal (20 percent to 25 percent of sales), so the price can be nominal as well.

The entrance of a generic competitor in the United States can be devastating for its brand name counterpart. Drugs have been known to lose as much as 80 percent of their sales in the first six months after going off patent. Eli Lilly's famous depression drug, Prozac, is a case in point. In 2001, when Prozac lost its patent protection, the drug's quarterly revenues dropped from $575 million in the second quarter to $96 million two quarters later. So if you're considering buying shares in a drug company that depends on a specific drug for a significant percentage of its sales, don't bank on the money continuing to come in after the patent expires.

Hallmarks of Success for Pharmaceutical Companies

Branded pharmaceutical companies have historically offered high margins, little debt, and cash flow galore. To find companies that can continue to provide stellar performance, focus on these traits:

▶ *Blockbuster drugs* (typically defined as drugs with more than $1 billion in sales): Companies with blockbusters gain manufacturing efficiencies by spreading fixed costs over more products. Selling the drug at high prices, driven by strong demand, inflates a drug maker's profitability and provides more bang for the buck. Pfizer is the perfect example: In 1997, only two Pfizer drugs had annual sales greater than $1 billion, but by 2002, eight drugs surpassed the $1 billion mark, with four drugs breaking the $2 billion mark. Thanks in part to these blockbusters, Pfizer's operating margins improved from 20 percent in 1997 to 38 percent in 2002.

▶ *Patent protection:* All drugs eventually lose patent protection, but the companies that manage those losses the best will generally provide investors with a steadier stream of cash flows. Bristol-Myers Squibb showed what can happen when a drug firm loses patent protection on large products without replacement drugs waiting in the wings. Between the second quarter of 2000 and the first quarter of 2002, Bristol lost the U.S. patents on three heavy hitters, and nearly 20 percent of the firm's total revenue evaporated in less than two years. On the other hand, when AstraZeneca's Prilosec was about to lose its U.S. patent in 2001, the company had already begun switching patients from the first-generation drug to the patent-protected second-generation version. By the time a generic competitor entered the market, AstraZeneca's new drug had established itself in the market and was bringing in 35 percent of the revenue of the first-generation drug.

▶ *A full pipeline of drugs in clinical trials (and the larger the population those drugs serve, such as cancer and arthritis, the better):* Merck is a decent model for this strategy. It generally has had an abundance of products in development and has directed research efforts toward unmet medical needs with millions of potential patients. Merck's five top-selling products in 2002 had a combined potential market of 138 million Americans.

▶ *Strong sales and marketing capabilities:* Physicians rely on pharmaceutical salespeople to learn about new products, and a salesforce that has successfully penetrated the physician market in the company's core therapeutic franchises already has physicians' ears and often their trust as well. Pfizer's relationship with cardiologists, Wyeth's access to gynecologists, and Eli Lilly's close ties with psychiatrists shouldn't be ignored. This expertise is so valuable that biotech firms often partner with large drug firms and give up a sizeable chunk of their profits just to leverage the marketing resources of their drug-company partners.

▶ *Big market potential:* Drugs that treat conditions affecting a large percentage of the population (such as erectile dysfunction, high cholesterol, depression, or high blood pressure) typically have better potential than niche products. So do drugs that treat chronic conditions, because patients must continue taking the medication to stay healthy.

All of this information can be found in the company's 10-K. Specific disease Web sites (such as the National Kidney Foundation or cancer.gov) also often have information on clinical trials and drugs available to treat a disease or disorder as well as the number of patients suffering from those diseases. Being able to analyze the depth and breadth of a company's drugs and development pipeline is half the battle when looking at pharmaceutical and biotechnology stocks. So, roll up your sleeves and dig into the 10-K to get the details on the strength of the company's drug pipeline.

Generic Drug Companies

Generic drug makers don't have the extraordinary margins of branded drug makers, but they are growing much faster as generic drugs become more

Common Investing Pitfall: Too Much Single-Product Risk

It might sound strange to view megablockbuster drugs as a negative, but they can become a disadvantage. If a drug's revenues become a large enough piece of the pie, a company's fate can be linked too heavily to that drug. Because that drug will eventually lose its patent protection, we think it's wise for investors to account for the *single-product risk* by demanding a slightly larger margin of safety.

Pfizer's Lipitor brought in a staggering $8 billion in sales for 2002. By the time Lipitor loses its U.S. patent protection in 2011, annual U.S. sales could easily be more than $10 billion. That's such a huge amount that it will be nearly impossible for Pfizer to fill the gap once generic competition hits. In addition, just five drugs pull in half the company's revenue. Megablockbusters such as Lipitor not only contribute large portions of total revenue, but also are often high-margin products. When the patent expires, the maker loses a chunk of revenue and its profitability usually declines as well.

popular. These copycat companies usually have gross margins in the 40 percent to 50 percent range, with operating margins around 15 percent to 20 percent. Returns on invested capital vary dramatically depending on the company's exposure to branded drugs. (Most generic drug makers also sell nonblockbuster branded drugs.) Teva Pharmaceuticals, the closest thing to a pure-play generic company, has ROICs around 10 percent, whereas Watson Pharmaceuticals, which generates a little more than half its revenue from branded drugs, has ROICs in the low to mid teens.

Ironically, generic drug companies can still benefit from some competitive barriers. The first company to file a legitimate patent challenge against a branded drug enjoys 180 days of marketing exclusivity, which allows the generic company to cash in before others join the party. The windfall can dramatically change the company's profitability in the short term; a 10-percentage point increase in operating margins isn't uncommon. Once the multitude is allowed to join the fray, the only company that comes out ahead is the low-cost manufacturer. Given the crucial importance of manufacturing scale, you're usually better off with an established player in generic drugs.

Generic companies have benefited from some longer term trends. As of mid-2003, nearly 50 percent of all prescriptions were filled with generics, up from about 20 percent in the mid-1980s. This trend should keep moving up, thanks to the numerous drugs coming off patent each year, as well as pressure to rein in rising prescription costs. Even at lower margins, these drugs can be profitable with the right cost structure. Last, the political winds are blowing in favor of generic companies as politicians and the general public look for ways to lower health care costs.

Biotechnology

Although the best biotech companies can generate enormous free cash flow—biotech giant Amgen threw off more about $1.5 billion in free cash flow in 2002—most are too speculative for all but the most aggressive investors. Picking successful firms requires a bit of skill, some understanding of the science, and a lot of luck.

Biotechnology firms are often thought of as younger, hipper, more innovative, and faster growing than their pharmaceutical counterparts. They seek to discover new drug therapies using biologic—cellular and molecular—processes rather than the chemical processes used by big pharma. Biotech firms are also on the cutting edge of developing novel therapeutic products, using groundbreaking technology platforms such as proteomics and genomics.

However, biotech drug development is still all about probabilities, but with even more product risk because the therapies are often completely new forms of treatment. For example, Genentech has been developing a treatment that attempts to stop the body's mechanism for growing new blood vessels (a process called *angiogenesis*) on the theory that a cancerous tumor will die if it no longer receives blood. Although several companies are working on similar therapies, none have been successful to date. Even if they are successful, the true size of these markets is anyone's guess. This adds another layer of uncertainty to the drug development process—as well as volatility in stock prices.

Hallmarks of Success for Biotech Companies

Think about biotech firms in three categories: established, up and coming, and speculative.

Established: These are the bigwigs of biotech and include companies such as Amgen, Genentech, and Biogen IDEC, which each have annual product revenues of more than $1 billion and market capitalizations beginning to rival those of big drug companies. They generate positive earnings and cash flow, and their drug development pipelines are large enough to sustain decent sales and earnings growth. As these firms become larger, their future cash flows become less risky.

In this category, look for:

▶ Firms with a large number of drugs in late-stage clinical trials
▶ Plenty of cash on hand, plus cash flow to cover several years of research and development expenditures
▶ Firms that have built a salesforce of their own—so they no longer have to pay another firm to market their products and can begin to build relationships with physicians
▶ A stock price that provides a margin of safety of around 30 percent to 40 percent to its fair value

Up and Coming: Many biotech firms are on the cusp of success, either with a product on the market or within arm's length. Some are on the verge of breaking into the black, while others have already demonstrated small but positive earnings. In other words, they've got more than a cell in a petri dish, but they still have a lot to prove. All of these firms hold lots of risk and typically have a narrow economic moat or none at all, depending on competing products.

Cash is king during this stage, and these companies are often able to raise capital during the market's periodic biotech booms. But it's worth keeping an eye on how quickly they are spending that cash because the last phases of clinical trials are the most expensive, and preparing literally truckloads of documents for the FDA isn't cheap. That's why it often makes sense for up-and-comers to form partnerships with bigger pharmaceutical or biotech firms. Although a partnership agreement means giving up a chunk of the profits, getting to market faster can be worth the cost.

Investors should ask the following questions to reduce their risk:

▶ Does the company have enough cash to get through the final (and most expensive) stages of testing? Compare the amount of cash on the balance sheet to the amount of cash that the firm burns through in a typical year. Phase III trials can cost tens of millions. Can the company write a check for these trials, or will it have to go outside for capital?

▶ Have larger biotechnology firms or pharmaceutical companies been willing to join forces with the firm? Partnerships can be a double-edged sword. They often validate the viability of a biotech's technology and provide knowledge and sales expertise, but they also take a huge chunk of the profits. For example, Biogen IDEC's cancer drug Rituxan has gone gangbusters since its 1997 approval, but because of the company's partnership with Genentech, Biogen IDEC sees only about a third of the drug's sales.

▶ Because future cash flows are so difficult to predict, does the stock price trade at a big enough discount to fair value to provide a margin of safety? A 50 percent margin of safety is reasonable given the risks of biotech.

Speculative: Newer biotech companies, which make up the majority of all companies in this industry, are too risky for the vast majority of investors. Although firms in this category undoubtedly have interesting technology and could be extremely successful some day, real revenues from real drug products are many years away, and positive cash flow from operations is even further out. Compound that risk with the slim odds that most early-stage drugs will ever reach the market, and we'd classify them as high-risk, no-moat stocks—which means we'd need a gargantuan margin of safety before we'd be willing to own them. These stocks are more like lottery tickets than anything else.

If you're doing research on a biotech company, the company's 10-K is the best place to start. Here, the company typically explains in layman's terms the technology and drugs in development and explains how the company is funding its research and partnerships. Disease Web sites cancer.gov and

MedicineNet.com and science journals often have information about drug classifications, market sizes, and competing and substitute products. In addition, industry resources such as the Biotech Industry Organization and BioSpace each have drug, company, and industry information.

Medical Device Companies

Medical device companies are probably the most straightforward of the health care industries. These are the companies that make the hardware, such as pacemakers and artificial hips, for medical procedures. There are two main types of device firms—cardiovascular and orthopedic—and they're well worth getting to know, given how many firms in this industry have wide economic moats.

As with the other health care sectors, the aging population and increase in life expectancy will drive sales growth in medical devices. Both the incidence of heart disease and the need for joint replacement rise substantially among older people. Also, now that physically active Baby Boomers are suffering from a few aches and pains of aging, physicians are starting to perform more joint replacement procedures in younger patients. Because a new hip has an average life of about 10 years, this should eventually expand the market for revision surgeries when the first hip wears out.

The ongoing pressure on medical costs also helps spur demand for some medical device companies, as new surgical techniques dramatically reduce the cost of some procedures by reducing the length of the associated hospital stay.

For example, traditional cardiac bypass surgery, aimed at increasing blood flow to the heart, involves a 10- to 12-inch incision down the chest, cracking open the rib cage, and approximately eight days in the hospital, followed by two months of recuperation. Less invasive cardiac bypass surgery is performed with a three- to five-inch incision between the ribs (or several one-inch incisions) and requires a three-day hospital stay and about two weeks of recovery time. What's more, minimally invasive procedures typically cost 25 percent less than the traditional open-heart bypass.

In addition to their attractive growth characteristics, device companies also typically boast wide economic moats. Economies of scale, high switching costs, and long-term clinical histories (in excess of 30 years for some orthopedic devices) all serve as high barriers to new entrants. As a result, a few major players dominate both the cardiac and orthopedic device markets. Patent protection on devices and instrumentation used for installation also provides a measure of protection from competitors for each company.

Switching costs tend to be high for orthopedic devices because physicians are often reluctant to drop one firm's devices in favor of another's. Installing an artificial hip or knee is complicated, and the procedures require specialized tools and training. Because each company makes its own proprietary set of tools that work exclusively with its own joint replacements, a surgeon who decides to use a different company's artificial hip must squeeze in time to receive training on how to use the new instrumentation system. Given how busy surgeons generally are, that's unlikely to happen unless the new joint is significantly better than the one the surgeon is currently using. It also takes time to complete enough procedures to become comfortable with the new system.

Medical device companies hold a great deal of pricing power as well. Medicare and insurance companies have so far been reluctant to limit brand choices when it comes to joint replacements and pacemakers, which has allowed orthopedic device makers (for example) to consistently raise prices by 3 percent to 5 percent each year.

Finally, some device firms face less risk than pharmaceutical firms because product improvements tend to be evolutionary rather than revolutionary. This benefits industry players in two ways. First, it decreases regulatory risk because incremental improvements to existing devices can go through a streamlined review process at the FDA. Second, it reduces the odds that one company will leapfrog the rest by rolling out a truly revolutionary product. Although major advances in medical devices do occur, they're less common than in some other areas of health care, so industry players tend to compete by making each successive generation of any particular device just a little bit better than the previous one. (Contrast this type of competition with the winner-take-all structure of the drug industry, in which a new drug can literally wipe out the market for competing drugs in very short order.)

However, device firms are not without risk. Product cycles can be very short, so companies must spend heavily on research and development to keep up with their competitors. Especially in cardiac devices, where switching costs for surgeons are lower, market share among the major competitors can change dramatically within the space of 12 or 18 months as new products arrive on the market. The implantation procedure for a cardiac device is largely the same whether you're using this year's model or last year's, which makes it easy for physicians to switch over to the latest product very quickly.

Legal risks are also an issue. In recent years, cardiac device companies have used litigation as a defensive (and sometimes offensive) tactic against competitors. All the suits and countersuits eat up a great deal of time and money and increase risk as well because the outcomes are usually difficult to predict.

Hallmarks of Success for Medical Device Companies

Medical device firms often enjoy high margins and strong earnings. Here are the key factors we look for in a device firm:

- *Salesforce penetration:* Many firms train their sales reps to serve as consultants, with some even assisting in surgeries. For example, Biomet sales representatives attend the majority of joint replacement surgeries where the company's products are being used and often contribute their expertise on the devices and instruments to the surgeon during the procedure. This deep relationship with physicians can increase the cost to switch to a competing product.
- *Product diversification:* Firms can reduce their risk by offering a strong mix of high-margin products (such as replacement hips or pacemakers) and commodity or recurring products that often have lower margins. For example, Medtronic has been working on adapting its core electronic stimulation technology (used in pacemakers) for use in controlling tremors from Parkinson's disease. Developing this higher margin product should help offset anticipated declines in its lower margin stent business.
- *Product innovation:* Looking at new product introductions relative to research and development costs is a good way to measure a firm's ability to pump out new products. A firm's annual report will mention new products being released in a given year as well as R&D expenditures. Going back several years may take some digging into past reports.

Health Insurance/Managed Care

Insurance and managed care firms are subject to intense regulatory pressure and widespread litigation, making them somewhat less attractive than some other health care industries. They typically don't have wide economic moats. Although firms that focus on making a profit can throw off large amounts of free cash flow, we'd tread carefully and require a hefty margin of safety before investing in most companies in this industry. Most health care consumers don't spend much time thinking about how money gets from their pockets to their physician's because they're not responsible for paying the full bill at the end of the day. As a result, there's little incentive to shop around for the best prices, and insurance companies are the ones who ultimately foot the bill if they underestimate the growth in health care costs.

Starting in the 1980s, insurers tried to gain some pricing control by creating managed-care organizations (MCOs) to coordinate and consolidate providers and buyers. MCOs make money in two primary ways. One is by underwriting medical insurance. Because it's tough to predict future medical expenses, this is known as *risk-based business.* Under this model, the MCO bears the risk of rising health care costs. The other way that MCOs make money is by providing administrative services—such as claims processing or network access—for a monthly fee. In this instance, employers underwrite their employees' medical insurance, and the MCO simply administers the health plan. In this model, called *fee-based business,* the employer bears the risk of rising costs.

Companies with a greater proportion of fee-based business hold less risk because cash flows are more predictable. In risk-based accounts, each trip to the hospital takes more money out of the MCO's pocket. So the upside might be great because if nobody gets sick, the MCO keeps all the premiums. But if hospital costs or prescription drug prices increase more than expected, a company's profits can be wiped out. Because medical costs are generally increasing, we think fee-based businesses are usually more attractive.

Hallmarks of Success for Health Insurance/Managed Care Companies

Although managed care generally isn't the most rewarding place for your health care dollars, some companies manage to do well. Here's how to find them:

▶ *Effective medical cost management and underwriting:* The medical loss ratio (medical costs paid divided by premium revenue) is the best measure of a firm's effectiveness in this area. Be sure not to include fee-based revenues and investment income when calculating this ratio, though. The average medical loss ratio has been about 84 percent to 85 percent over the past several years, and this measure captures both pricing and medical cost management, reflecting a company's overall success and consistency in managing its risk-based business.

▶ *Minimal dual-option business:* Managed care organizations often give individuals the opportunity to choose from two or more types of plans (such as an HMO, PPO, or traditional indemnity plan). Watch out for companies with a large portion of this dual-option, also known as *slice,* business. These slice accounts not only often promote hypercompetition among managed care groups, but also are more susceptible to mispricing because demand for each option in a sponsoring company is difficult to predict.

▶ *Large mix of fee-based business:* Underwriting health insurance has proved to be risky business, and lower exposure to this risk is generally a positive in our book. For example, UnitedHealth Group increased its fee-based membership to 64 percent of total members at the end of 2002, up from 55 percent at the end of 1999, and its overall financial results improved over the same period.

▶ *Minimal exposure to government accounts:* Government-funded programs, such as Medicare and Medicaid, aren't increasing reimbursement rates in tandem with rising medical costs. Companies with less exposure to government accounts will outperform those that rely on government revenues.

The company's Web site will have information about products and services offered—it's also a good way of seeing how customer-friendly the company is. The 10-K will have information about underwriting, account mix if any customer is a large source of revenues (10 percent or greater), as well as product information and financial statements.

Investor's Checklist: Health Care

▶ Developing drugs is time-consuming, costly, and there are no guarantees of success. Look for companies with long patent lives and full pipelines to spread the development risk.

▶ Drug companies whose products target large patient populations or significant unmet needs have a better chance of paying off.

▶ Make sure you have a big margin of safety for pharmaceutical companies with megablockbuster drugs that make up a large percentage of sales. Any unexpected developments can send cash flow, and the stock price, reeling.

▶ Unless you have a deep understanding of the technology, don't invest in biotech startups. Payoffs could be large, but the cash flows are so far out and uncertain that it's easier to lose your shirt than win big.

▶ Don't overlook the medical device industry, which is full of firms with wide economic moats.

▶ Cash is king for firms that rely on development (pharmaceuticals, biotechnology, and medical devices). Make sure firms have enough cash or cash from operations to get through the next development cycle.

▶ Keep an eye on the government. Any drastic changes in Medicare/Medicaid spending or regulatory requirements can have a deep impact on pricing throughout the sector.

▶ Managed care organizations that spread risk—whether through a high mix of fee-based business, product diversification, strong underwriting, or minimal government accounts—will provide more sustainable returns.

15

Consumer Services

NOT SURPRISINGLY, WE generally don't find a ton of great long-term stock ideas in retail and consumer services because most economic moats for the sector are extremely narrow, if they exist at all. The only way a retailer can earn a wide economic moat is by doing something that keeps consumers shopping at its stores rather than at competitors'. It can do this by offering unique products or low prices. The former method is tough to do on a large scale because unique products rarely remain unique forever. It's rare to find a retailer or consumer service firm that maintains any kind of economic moat for more than a few years.

The few consumer service firms that have established a wide economic moat include Home Depot and Lowe's in the home improvement area, Walgreen's for prescription drugs and convenience items, and Wal-Mart for just about everything. These firms developed distinctive store prototypes that set them apart from their competitors, and they now enjoy vast economies of scale that make it tough for competitors to earn consistent profits. Identifying

Tom Goetzinger and Carl Sibilski with Pat Dorsey.

and investing in firms like these (at the right price) is the best way to make money over the long haul in this classic "buy what you know" area of the market. Although you can also do well buying high-quality specialty and clothing retailers when the industry sees one of its periodic sell-offs, very few of these kinds of firms make great long-term holdings.

Companies We See Every Day

Most of the companies in the consumer services sector are very familiar: We shop at their stores and eat their food just about every day. The sector contains discount stores such as Wal-Mart and Target, drugstores such as Walgreen and CVS, clothing stores such as Gap, home improvement shops such as Home Depot and Lowe's, restaurants such as McDonald's and Outback Steakhouse, and scores of other well-known names. Being able to peruse the aisles of these stores, interact with employees, and sample products is a huge advantage from an investment standpoint. After all, when was the last time you tinkered with a semiconductor before buying shares of Intel or spoke with a claims representative before investing in Aetna or Cigna?

The consumer services sector has seen strong growth, too. Our time-starved culture, with both parents working full time in more families, demands quick and reliable service and is willing to pay for it. Grocery stores offer more ready-to-eat or quick-to-prepare meals, discount stores now almost exclusively have centralized checkouts at the front of stores, and many drugstores stay open 24 hours a day. Companies that provide the best overall service at a competitive price survive and thrive, while those that don't fade and eventually disappear.

According to the U.S. Census Bureau, the U.S. economy increased from $6 trillion in 1991 to $10.1 trillion in 2001. During that time, consumer spending increased from 66 percent to 69 percent of the economy. Consumer service firms are becoming a bigger piece of the economy, and we expect that trend to continue. It's not surprising that these companies have outperformed the overall market over the past decade.

From 1993 through 2002, the S&P Retailing Index posted a cumulative return of 122 percent, sparked by stock price advances in bellwether names such as Wal-Mart, Home Depot, and Target, versus a 102 percent gain for the S&P

500. Because many consumer purchases other than food are discretionary (can be put off for later), it's not surprising that retail stocks generally outperform during periods of economic strength and underperform during times of economic weakness.

In the following sections, we examine some of the key characteristics and trends of the major industries in the consumer services sector.

Restaurants

For simplicity, the restaurant industry can be split into quick-service restaurants (QSR, better known as fast food) and full-service restaurants. QSR patrons visit a counter where they pay and receive their meals (e.g., McDonald's and Wendy's). Full-service customers are seated at a table and place orders with a wait staff (e.g., Outback Steakhouse or Darden's Red Lobster chain). Because there aren't many ways to reinvent food service, the industry often tries new concepts with different mixes of price, food quality, level of service, menu offerings, and atmosphere.

Demographic shifts and changes in the workforce make the long-term outlook for restaurants pretty bright. Eating food prepared by restaurants is becoming a more attractive alternative to home meal preparation—with both parents working in many households, there's little time to cook and even less for grocery shopping and cleanup. The economics of meal preparation are shifting in favor of eating out as well because families are getting smaller. Consider that it takes about the same amount of time to cook for a family of six as it does for a family of four. Economy of scale for family meals just isn't as prevalent, and for single person households, it can simply take too much time to prepare a well-balanced meal.

Investing in Restaurants: Understanding the Company Life Cycle

Restaurant chains experience the business life cycle like any other business. Most new restaurant concepts start off in a speculative growth stage where managers are trying to nail down operational details and estimate growth potential for expansion. Many concepts fail; hence the term *speculative* growth. At this stage, most investors are happy with strong sales growth, indicating that the concept is gaining traction. Chains in this stage normally report negative or, at best, inconsistent earnings. Within a short time, they either fail or they move on and become aggressive growth companies.

In the aggressive growth stage, restaurants must be profitable on a per unit basis to support the opening of new stores. For example, the successful Cheesecake Factory chain funds all of its unit growth with profits from existing units. During this growth stage, the company is earning a profit at current units, but it's spending so fast to open new units that free cash flow is typically negative. One of the dangers is that a restaurant company outgrows its funding and balance sheet.

Even though current operations are profitable, rapid expansion often requires more money than the business can generate internally. Thanks to operating leases, which are akin to renting space for a business, restaurants can usually finance their expansion on a store-by-store basis and don't need to take out a huge chunk of debt at one time. However, leases aren't a panacea. Starbucks has grown so fast over the past decade that if a number of store locations were unsuccessful, the company would be forced to pay through the nose to exit the leases—most of which have terms approaching 10 or more years.

Like all companies, restaurants can't grow aggressively forever. As expansion opportunities dry up, profits from existing operations become increasingly important and managers try to drive healthy same-store sales increases. Strong same-store sales tell us that customers like what they're getting and come back for more. To keep customers interested (and boost profits), managers look for new ways to squeeze out more money. Restaurants in the slow-growth stage typically have strong free cash flows, solid returns on capital, and usually start to pay out a dividend because they're running out of investment opportunities in the business.

Few restaurants reach the slow-growth stage—most just go straight into decline. To be a successful slow-growth restaurant chain, the concept has to be ingrained in consumers. In the United States, McDonald's, Wendy's, and Red Lobster have long passed the stage where their stores were destinations or chic places to visit. However, consumers know what to expect before they walk into the stores or cruise into the drive-thru. It's up to the restaurants to maintain that familiarity with consistent advertising and service. Failure to provide the quality of food or service that people expect can bring slow-growth firms into the realm of decline.

Hallmarks of Successful Restaurants

▶ The best restaurants have already developed a successful concept. Most restaurants fail to advance beyond the initial speculative growth stage, so those that do have already passed one of the most difficult tests of running a successful chain.

▶ Replication is key. Investors need to determine if a restaurant's concept can be repeated in other geographic areas. Outback Steakhouse and Cheesecake Factory serve menus that are popular throughout the country, but that's not the case for all chains and concepts. Darden's China Coast concept worked on a small scale in the early 1990s, but the complications of Mandarin Wok cooking resulted in inconsistent food service across the chain and led to its demise.

▶ Older chains must stay fresh, without having to reinvent themselves. Darden remodels its Red Lobster and Olive Garden chains every seven years or so. The process is expensive, but over the long term it's necessary for survival, and restaurants usually throw off enough cash to cover the remodeling costs. If a chain waits too long, it will reach a point where the locations look old and unattractive—and by then, they won't be generating sufficient profits and cash flow, and the costs to resuscitate the brand will be prohibitive.

Retail

The retail game has undergone a major facelift over the past two decades. First came the development of category killers, with specialized merchandise and service. Chains such as Home Depot and Lowe's put many smaller, regional players out of business in the home improvement area. In 1992, the two firms posted combined sales of $8 billion; in 2002, they sold more than $80 billion worth of nails, hammers, and appliances. Office Depot, Office Max, and Staples did the same thing to the office supply business in the late 1980s and 1990s.

The second major shift has been the move off the mall. Once upon a time, department stores were infallible in the world of retailing. Well-known chains such as Sears that were once destinations in their own right became the anchor tenants for malls. The stores aimed to provide customers with a one-stop shopping experience, and some even housed full-service restaurants. Customers had more time to shop and placed more value on the personal attention these stores provided.

Over the past 20 years, however, traditional department stores have become dinosaurs. Nowadays, companies such as Sears and JC Penney are struggling to remain relevant—a battle that chains such as Montgomery Ward and Woolworth have already lost. Changing consumer trends are largely, but not totally, to blame. In this era of dual-income households, shoppers want selection, quality, and reasonable prices, and they want it fast. And they've shown a willingness to shift their spending to stores that can provide this experience.

Firms such as Wal-Mart, Target, and Kohl's have stolen the thunder of the traditional department stores with innovation and efficiency. These are the firms that developed everyday low prices, pioneered centralized checkouts at the front of stores, and set up shop in freestanding locations with more convenient parking. Whereas, Sears and Penney averaged 0 percent and 1 percent annual sales growth, respectively, from 1998 to 2002, Wal-Mart, Target, and Kohl's averaged 15 percent, 10 percent, and 24 percent, respectively. Over the next several years, we expect this divergence to continue.

Investing in Retail: Understanding the Cash Conversion Cycle

One of the best ways to distinguish excellent retailers from average or below-average ones is to look at their cash conversion cycles. The cash cycle tells us how quickly a firm sells its goods (inventory), how fast it collects payments

Figure 15.1   The cash conversion cycle. *Source:* Morningstar, Inc.

from customers for the goods (receivables), and how long it can hold on to the goods itself before it has to pay suppliers (payables). Figure 15.1 illustrates the cash conversion cycle, and Figure 15.2 shows the conversion cycle for Home Depot.

Naturally, a retailer wants to sell its products as fast as possible (high inventory turns), collect payments from customers as fast as possible (high receivables turns), but pay suppliers as slowly as possible (low payables turns). The best-case scenario for a retailer is to sell its goods and collect from customers before it even has to pay the supplier. Wal-Mart is one of the best in the business at this: 70 percent of its sales are rung up and paid for before the firm even pays its suppliers.

Example: Home Depot

Balance sheet ($ billions)	2002	2001
Beginning inventory	6.7	6.6
Ending inventory	8.3	6.7
Average inventory	7.5	6.6
Accounts receivable	1.1	0.9
Accounts payable	4.6	3.4

Income statement ($ billions)	2002	2001
Sales	58.2	53.6
Cost of goods sold	40.1	37.4

2002 Cash Conversion Cycle = 34 days

365 ÷ Inventory turnover	+	365 ÷ Receivables turnover	−	365 ÷ Payables turnover
365 ÷ (40.1 ÷ 7.5)	+	365 ÷ (58.2 ÷ 1.1)	−	365 ÷ (40.1 ÷ 4.6)
68 days in inventory	**+**	**7 days in receivables**	**−**	**41 days payable outstanding**

2001 Cash Conversion Cycle = 37 days

365 ÷ Inventory turnover	+	365 ÷ Receivables turnover	−	365 ÷ Payables turnover
365 ÷ (37.4 ÷ 6.6)	+	365 ÷ (53.6 ÷ 0.9)	−	365 : (37.4 : 3.4)
64 days in inventory	**+**	**6 days in receivables**	**−**	**33 days payable outstanding**

Figure 15.2   Cash Conversion Cycle for Home Depot. *Source:* Morningstar, Inc.

Looking at the components of a retailer's cash cycle tells us a great deal. A retailer with increasing days in inventory (and decreasing inventory turns) is likely stocking its shelves with merchandise that is out of favor. This leads to excess inventory, clearance sales, and, usually, declining sales and stock prices.

Days in receivables is the least important part of the cash conversion cycle for retailers because most stores either collect cash directly from customers at the time of the sale or sell off their credit card receivables to banks and other finance companies for a price. Retailers don't really control this part of the cycle too much. However, some stores, such as Sears and Target, have brought attention to the receivables line because they've opted to offer customers credit and manage the receivables themselves. The credit card business is a profitable way to make a buck, but it's also very complicated, and it's a completely different business from retail. We're wary of retailers that try to boost profits by taking on risk in their credit card business because it's generally not something they're very good at.

If days in inventory and days in receivables illustrate how well a retailer interacts with customers, days payable outstanding shows how well a retailer negotiates with suppliers. It's also a great gauge for the strength of a retailer. Wide-moat retailers such as Wal-Mart, Home Depot, and Walgreen optimize credit terms with suppliers because they're one of the few (if not the only) games in town. For example, 17 percent of P&G's 2002 sales came from Wal-Mart. The fortunes of many consumer product firms depend on sales to Wal-Mart, so the king of retail has a huge advantage when ordering inventory: It can push for low prices and extended payment terms.

Home Depot finally started taking advantage of its competitive position by squeezing suppliers in 2001 and 2002. Days payable outstanding for the home improvement titan has historically been around 25. In 2001, the figure hit 33 days, and by 2002, it exceeded 40 days. By holding on to its cash longer and reducing short-term borrowing needs, Home Depot increased its operating cash flow from an average of $2.4 billion from 1998 to 2000 to $5.6 billion from 2002 to 2003.

Hallmarks of Successful Retailers

▶ Sometimes you never get a second chance to make a good first impression. Retail is a fickle business, and shoppers have plenty of alternatives,

Common Investing Pitfall: Are Those Same-Store Sales Growth Numbers Accurate?

Every quarter and, for most restaurants and retailers, every month, same-store sales numbers are released. Same-store sales growth measures sales at locations open for at least a year and excludes sales increases attributed to current openings. For purposes of reporting, same-store sales are also known as comparable-store sales or comps.

But, what if a new store doesn't fully mature in 12 months? The process of that new store reaching maturity in year two or year three helps boost the same-store sales figure, while sales at older stores may not be growing at all or are declining.

This is a very important consideration for companies that are transitioning from aggressive growth into slower or steadier growth. As long as they can open a greater number of stores year after year, the comps will look impressive. But every company's expansion plan reaches an inflection point—they're still growing, just not as fast. This has two effects. First, opening fewer stores obviously translates into smaller new store sales growth. Second, having fewer stores entering those productive years two and three also lowers comps.

The combination of slower new store growth and lower comps can send overall growth and the stock price plunging quickly. From 1995 to 2000, Office Depot averaged 14 percent per year in new store growth. However, the office supply store business quickly became saturated when competitors Staples and Office Max also engaged in aggressive expansion plans. In 1999 and 2000, the last two years of its rapid expansion, Office Depot's total same-store sales increased 6 percent and 7.5 percent. In 2001, new store growth stopped and same-store sales declined 2 percent; the stock price sank below $10 from a high in the mid-$20's in 1999.

so companies have to make a concerted effort to keep stores clean and fresh. Lowe's has benefited mightily in its battle with Home Depot because its stores are widely perceived to be more aesthetically pleasing and easier to navigate. Home Depot is reinvesting in its stores, but as we mentioned in the restaurant section, maintenance and renovation is easier than reinvention.

▶ Keep an eye out for store traffic. You don't want to see a traffic bottleneck at the checkout aisles, but you don't want to see empty parking lots on weekends either. This is particularly true for specialty retail companies such as clothing stores that cater to a particular demographic. Traffic to teen hot spot Abercrombie & Fitch and women's outfitter Chico's FAS has remained relatively robust even in times of lax consumer spending. These stores have carved out a brand identity and won customer loyalty, and their stock prices held up during the tough market conditions in 2001 and 2002. Remember, though, specialty retailers have a much shorter shelf life than traditional retailers do, so these investments have to be monitored much more closely.

▶ Successful retailers have a positive employee culture. After all, retail is about customer service—period. Sam Walton helped build Wal-Mart into the largest retailer (and largest company) in the world based on sales using

Common Investing Pitfall: How Healthy Is the Balance Sheet with All Those Leases?

Many retailers use operating leases to "rent" space for their stores. Because these leases aren't capitalized and are kept off the balance sheet, they understate a firm's total financial obligations and can artificially inflate financial health. The leases aren't inherently bad or sneaky; in fact, their existence is core to most retailers' expansion plans. Lease obligations can be found in the footnotes of a firm's 10-K under the heading "commitments and contingencies."

Be sure to give a retailer a thorough checkup before declaring it to be in tip-top financial shape. For example, Tommy Hilfiger appeared to have pretty good financial health going into 2002. The firm had $387 million in cash and $638 million in total debt. However, the specialty apparel firm also had $273 million of future financial obligations in the form of operating leases. If we add off-balance sheet leases to the debt on the balance sheet, the total comes to $911 million, and the coverage ratios don't look as robust. Tommy Hilfiger entered 2002 with declining sales and stagnating profits and cash flow. When Hilfiger announced that it needed to close many of its retail stores in October 2002 and pay to break the leases, the stock price was hammered.

the premise that the customer is always right. During its growth heyday in the 1990s, Home Depot's employees were always visible and customers usually walked away satisfied. In 2001 and 2002, Home Depot's service waned noticeably, largely due to an influx of part-time employees who didn't have the same connection to the company.

Conclusion

As we've mentioned numerous times in earlier chapters, great companies in attractive industries generate returns on invested capital that far exceed the cost of capital. However, retail is generally a very low-return business with low or no barriers to entry. Retail bellwethers Wal-Mart and Walgreen earn little more than 3 cents profit for every dollar of sales, so store management is critical. The problem is that many retailers don't execute as flawlessly as these two and flame out as soon as trouble hits.

The sector is rampant with competition. Think of all the specialty apparel shops that try to imitate Abercrombie & Fitch and Gap. A few succeed; most fail, but the point is that nothing exists to prevent new concepts and stores from being launched. There are few, if any, barriers to entry. Customers may be swayed to buy a cool $50 sweater, but they'll quickly go to the store next door if the same sweater can be had for $40.

The primary way a firm can build an economic moat in the sector is to be the low-cost leader. Wal-Mart sells items that can be purchased just about anywhere, but it sells it all for less than the competition, and consumers keep coming back for the bargains. Others may try to imitate Wal-Mart's strategy in the short run but lack the economies of scale to remain profitable employing the strategy in the long run.

Investor's Checklist: Consumer Services

▶ Most consumer services concepts fail in the long run, so any investment in a company in the speculative or aggressive growth stage of the business life cycle needs to be monitored more closely than the average stock investment.

▶ Beware of stocks that have already priced in lofty growth expectations. You can make money if you get in early enough, but you can also lose your shirt on the stock's rapid downslide.

▶ The sector is rife with low switching costs. Companies that establish store loyalty or store dependence are very attractive. Tiffany's is a good example; it faces limited competition in the retail jewelry market.

▶ Make sure to compare inventory and payables turns to determine which retailers are superior operators. Companies that know what their customers want and how to exploit their negotiating power are more likely to make solid bets in the sector.

▶ Keep an eye on those off-balance sheet obligations. Many retailers have little or no debt on the books, but their overall financial health might not be that good.

▶ Look for a buying opportunity when a solid company releases poor monthly or quarterly sales numbers. Many investors overreact to one month's worth of bad same-store sales results, and the reason might just be bad weather or an overly difficult comparison to the prior-year period. Focus on the fundamentals of the business and not the emotion of the stock.

▶ Companies also tend to move in tandem when news comes out about the economy. Look for a chance to pick up shares of a great retailer when the entire sector falls—keep that watch list handy.

16

Business Services

WHILE THE COMPANIES in our business services sector operate in relative obscurity, the sector deserves more attention. Here, we can find a large number of firms running wonderful, wide-moat businesses—just the kind we like to buy at the right price and hold as long-term investors.

Companies in the business services sector are almost as varied as the businesses they serve. After all, the group includes firms such as Fiserv (financial institution data processing), Waste Management (waste hauling), Omnicom (advertising), and even United Airlines (air transportation). Because the business services sector is so varied, we divide it into three major subsectors based on how companies set up their businesses to make money. Specifically, we look at technology-based, people-based, and hard-asset-based subsectors. Although not all companies within the industry fit perfectly into just one of these categories, it's a useful distinction to make when you're analyzing a potential investment in business services. Despite being such a diverse group of businesses, a few major themes impact the majority of business services companies.

Todd Lukasik, Fritz Kaegi, and Sanjay Ayer with Pat Dorsey.

Outsourcing Trend

Business-to-business services have grown significantly, increasing as a percentage of GDP from 3.5 percent in 1990 to 5.4 percent in 2001. Fueling the growth has been the popularity of outsourcing—the practice of offloading noncore tasks to third parties.

Many business services providers have essentially created markets for themselves based on this trend. Cintas, for example, has successfully convinced companies that it's better to pay Cintas to service employees' uniforms than to leave the responsibility to each individual employee or to handle it themselves. Other industries developed to fill needs that would be difficult or impossible for companies to handle internally. It is impractical, for example, for every mom-and-pop retailer to develop its own infrastructure to facilitate its acceptance of credit and debit card payments. Instead, companies such as First Data and National Processing allow retailers to tap into larger systems, the fixed costs of which can be leveraged across many clients.

Outsourcing makes sense to many business owners because it usually saves time and money, removes the hassle of dealing with noncore tasks, and allows management to focus on what's really important to the success of their company.

Economic Moats in Business Services

In business services, size does indeed matter. Companies can leverage size to boost both their top and bottom lines. By expanding the range of services offered, companies can increase total revenue per customer. By handling more volume—especially over fixed-cost networks—companies can lower unit costs and achieve greater profitability.

To capitalize on this, many business services firms have attempted to acquire their way to critical mass and achieve scale economies by consolidating the operations of multiple businesses. For example, data processing firms such as Fiserv, First Data, and ADP have all made acquisitions an important part of their overall strategies.

Size impacts the industry through branding as well. Often, brands play a major role in a business outsourcing purchase decision. Companies may be hesitant to outsource payroll processing (and the related handling of employee pay and tax funds) to Fly-By-Night Upstart, Inc., but are comfortable entrusting the responsibility to ADP, founded in 1949 and currently the biggest payroll processor. Even in business services, brands count, and it's usually the biggest companies that have the most recognizable brands.

Many industries in business services have significant barriers to entry, making it tough for new players to enter the field. For example, a company that wanted to process credit card transactions for banks and retailers would have to build a processing infrastructure to support its business, including hardware, the software development to manage the data, and a sales network to sign customers. Such a company would have to go through considerable trouble and expense just to try to compete against a company such as First Data, which already handles billions of transactions each year.

Despite the relatively high barriers to entry in the electronic transaction processing industry, there's little protection against competition from other industry participants. For example, in 2001, Concord EFS lost Bank of America's electronic funds transfer switching business to a very aggressive bid from competitor Visa. Thus, although most business services industries have wide moats, companies still need to differentiate themselves further to fend off potentially intense competition from established industry players.

Technology-Based Businesses

Technology-based companies include data processors (ADP, First Data), database providers (IMS Health, Equifax, Getty Images), and other companies that leverage technology to deliver their services. When technology-based companies get cheap, they can be a great opportunity for investors. Due to the sizable and defensible competitive advantages most companies in this subsector enjoy, they've often generated better-than-average long-term returns. For example, the 10-year average total return for a group of data processors was 14.2 percent through May 2003, which was above the 9.7 percent average total return for the S&P 500.

Industry Structure

Technology-based businesses often offer the strongest cases for outsourcing. For example, a bank looking to implement electronic check imaging could spend the money to develop and maintain its own proprietary system, or it could contract with Fiserv. Because Fiserv spreads its system's development and maintenance costs across many banks, the cost of Fiserv's system to any one bank is relatively low. And with input from all its clients feeding feature development, it's likely that Fiserv's product would be superior to something just one bank could develop on its own.

In general, technology-based businesses like Fiserv and its check imaging system require huge initial investments to set up an infrastructure that can be leveraged across many customers. These huge investments are a barrier to entry for new competitors.

Although the current participants in the various technology-based industries compete vigorously against one another, their markets generally have so much potential that price competition tends to be less intense than you might otherwise expect. For example, in 2002, Paychex and ADP—by far the two largest companies in payroll processing—had fewer than 900,000 U.S. clients between them, which represented only about 12 percent of the 7.2 million employers believed to be operating in the United States. Similarly, the use of card payments (such as credit and debit transactions) is expected to grow from about 28 percent of all consumer expenditures in 1999 to almost 50 percent by 2010 (based on dollar volume of transactions in the United States),[1] which should benefit firms such as First Data and National Processing. Faced with markets like these, companies are less inclined to compete vigorously on price, instead counting on enough growth to go around for all companies to benefit.

Another desirable characteristic of technology-based businesses is the low ongoing capital investment required to maintain their systems. For firms already in the industry, the huge upfront technology investments have already taken place. And the cost of technology tends to drop over time, so upkeep expenditures are minimal. First Data's Western Union franchise, for example, spends only about 5 percent of revenue each year to maintain and build its fixed assets in the business.

Companies in this subsector often benefit from both economies of scale and operating leverage. *Economies of scale* refers to a company's ability to leverage its fixed cost infrastructure across more and more clients, as demonstrated

---

[1] The Nilson Report, Number 753, December 2001.

by Cintas washing loads upon loads of uniforms in a single plant and First Data processing billions of transactions via one network. The result of scale economies should be operating leverage, whereby profits are able to grow faster than sales.

The combination of operating leverage and low ongoing capital requirements suggests that technology-based firms should have plenty of free cash to throw around. Telltale signs of good cash generation are dividends, share buybacks, and an accumulation of cash on the balance sheet.

Another characteristic to look for when evaluating investments in this subsector is predictable sales and profits. Because 5- to 10-year customer contracts can be the norm for technology-based businesses, 80 percent to 90 percent of a company's revenue may be booked before the year even begins. That makes financial results more stable and predictable.

As a result of the high barriers to entry into technology-based businesses and long-term customer contracts, firms in this subsector tend to have wide, defensible moats. For this reason, when a technology-based business services stock is cheap, it's usually worth a good look.

Hallmarks of Success for Technology-Based Businesses

Investors interested in technology-based companies should look for businesses that:

► *Throw off cash:* With big market opportunities, operating leverage, and minimal ongoing investment requirements, technology-based businesses have no excuse for not generating loads of cash. Technology-based businesses often have free cash flow margins in the mid-teens or higher.

► *Enjoy economies of scale:* Because bigger is better in this industry, the market leaders benefit from cost advantages relative to small competitors. This usually translates into better financial performance, either by retaining cost advantages or sharing them with clients and gaining even more market share.

► *Report stable financial performance:* Because customers usually sign contracts that last 5 to 10 years, the majority of technology-based companies' revenue should be recurring and predictable year in and year out.

▶ *Are exposed to fast-growing or underpenetrated markets:* Given the operating leverage of most technology-based firms, exposure to markets with lots of growth potential should translate into impressive profit expansion.

▶ *Offer a complete range of services:* Many outsourcing buyers look to consolidate their purchases, so they have fewer relationships to manage. Companies with a one-stop collection of services should benefit from this trend. Furthermore, getting existing clients to sign up for more services is generally easier than signing up a new client, and cross sales can also increase customer switching costs, binding customers ever tighter to the firm.

▶ *Have strong sales capabilities and access to distribution channels:* Business services don't sell by themselves, so it's no surprise that the most successful companies have strong salesforces.

People-Based Businesses

The people-based subsector includes companies that rely heavily on people to deliver their services, such as consultants and professional advisors (Accenture, Moody's), temporary staffing companies (Manpower, Robert Half), and advertising agencies (Omnicom, Interpublic). Investments can be attractive at the right price, but the model is generally less attractive than that of our technology-based subsector.

Industry Structure

People-based businesses make their money by leveraging an investment in their employees' time. The classic example of this model is the consulting industry. An analyst who is paid $50 per hour by the consulting firm may actually be hired out to clients at a rate of $250 per hour. Thus, the consulting firm makes a spread on the analyst's billed time. That spread has to cover other costs, such as overhead and partners' bonuses, so it's not pure profit for the firm. But marking up the cost of peoples' time is the basic way consulting firms make money.

As a result of this business model, growth for people-based companies comes mainly from finding and hiring more skilled workers to deploy. Training (or some might say, indoctrinating) new hires is important because it helps to ensure a somewhat standard level of service quality. Salary expense is essentially a big, fixed cost that must be covered for profits to be made. But when the economy slows and companies become more careful with spending, these firms' services (such as consulting and advertising) are normally popular places for cutbacks.

While most companies in this subsector operate in very fragmented industries, there are definite advantages to businesses with national and international scale. Manpower, for example, has an advantage relative to smaller players when competing for the largest companies' business because Manpower can staff workers around the globe wherever they're needed. Scale also fosters efficiencies in advertising and brand development that smaller competitors don't enjoy. For example, in 2001, Accenture spent about $150 million on image development to bolster its brand after splitting away from Arthur Andersen.

Relationships are also very important in this subsector. The very nature of the business—with a somewhat unique product for every client—makes it difficult to clearly differentiate one company's offering from the next. As such, relationships play a key role in driving business. Purchase decisions may be made because the project buyer went to school with the consulting partner or another division at the buyer's firm has used a particular advertising agency for years with success.

Although some people-based businesses, such as Moody's, have wide moats, economic moats for companies operating people-based models are usually narrow at best. Brands, longstanding relationships with customers, and geographic scope can provide some advantages relative to competitors. But within most people-based industries, there are usually multiple competitors with similar strengths in these areas, and they tend to compete aggressively with one another.

Hallmarks of Success for People-Based Businesses

- *Differentiation of offering:* Differentiation can give companies an advantage and lead to superior financial results. Robert Half has successfully differentiated itself in the staffing business by focusing on professional labor for smaller employers and developing different brands for the different markets it serves.
- *Providing a necessary and/or low-cost service:* When customers feel compelled to purchase the service and when the cost of the service is relatively

low, customers are less likely to spend time trying to negotiate a better price. Firms view Moody's, for example, as an important component of debt issuance because investors are familiar and comfortable with Moody's debt ratings. Furthermore, the cost of a Moody's rating is a fraction of the total value of the money raised through the debt issue.

▶ *Organic growth:* Look for internally generated growth instead of growth generated by acquisitions because it signals healthy demand for the firm's service. In addition, acquisitions don't always integrate as smoothly as planned, subjecting the business to integration risks.

Hard-Asset-Based Businesses

Companies in the hard-asset-based subsector depend on big investments in fixed assets to grow their businesses. Airlines, waste haulers (Waste Management, Allied Waste, Republic Services), and expedited delivery companies (FedEx, UPS) all fall into this subsector. In general, these companies aren't as attractive as technology-based businesses, but investors can still find some wide-moat stocks and good investments in this area.

Industry Structure

Growth for hard-asset-based businesses inevitably requires large incremental outlays for fixed assets. After all, once an airline is flying full planes, the only way to get more passengers from point A to point B is to acquire an additional aircraft, which can cost $35 million or more.

Because the incremental fixed investment occurs before asset deployment, companies in this sector generally finance their growth with external funding. Debt can be used to finance almost all of the asset's cost, so lenders generally require the asset to provide collateral against the loan. With this model, high leverage is not necessarily a bad thing, provided that the company can make enough money deploying the asset to cover the cost of debt financing and earn a reasonable return for shareholders.

With this in mind, airlines are generally the least attractive investment of all the companies in this subsector. Airlines must bear enormous fixed costs to maintain their fleets and meet the demands of expensive labor contracts, yet they sell a commodity service that's difficult to differentiate. As a result,

Common Investing Pitfall: Off Balance-Sheet Financing

FedEx reported $1.8 billion in debt in fiscal 2002. Given its market cap of about $16 billion at fiscal year end 2002, the implied leverage of 11 percent (i.e., $1.8 billion/$16 billion) seems reasonable, if not low. Further scrutiny, however, reveals large lease obligations that would have added almost $12 billion in debt to FedEx's balance sheet, had FedEx chosen to purchase the assets outright instead of leasing them. Including this off-balance sheet obligation as part of debt financing pushes FedEx's leverage much higher. (A good rule of thumb for getting a handle on leases is to find a footnote to the 10-K labeled "lease commitments," and look for a discussion of "future minimum lease payments" related to "operating leases." Find the minimum lease payment for next year, multiply it by eight, and you'll have a good rough estimate of how much debt the leases represent.)

price competition is intense, profit margins are razor-thin—and often non-existent—and operating leverage is so high that the firms can swing from being wildly profitable to nearly bankrupt in a short time. If you don't think this sounds like a recipe for good long-term investments, you're right—airlines have lost a collective $11 billion (excluding the impact of recent government handouts) between deregulation in 1978 and 2002. Over the same time period, 125 airlines had filed for Chapter 11 bankruptcy protection, and 12 of them filed for Chapter 7 liquidation.

But despite the terrible performance for airlines in general, a few carriers have fared very well. Southwest, for one, has been profitable for 30 consecutive years—an amazing achievement considering the cyclicality of its business and the dismal operating environment for the industry in 2002. Southwest's superior financial performance is largely because of its main strategic advantage: a low cost structure driven by its practice of flying one type of aircraft for all of its no frills, point-to-point routes. In an industry with less-than-desirable fundamentals, Southwest has achieved superior financial results by deploying a different, and dominant, business strategy.

Other characteristics of hard-asset-based businesses make this segment worth watching. The idea of limited or shrinking assets, for example, can go a long way to providing stability in the competitive landscape for these companies. Because of the NIMBY (not in my back yard) principle, it is very difficult to get approval for new landfill sites. As a result, it is highly unlikely that new competitors will enter the landfill side of the waste management business. That puts a company such as Waste Management, which owns 40 percent of the total U.S. disposal capacity via its 300 landfills, at an advantage.

The majority of hard-asset-based companies fall into the narrow- or no-moat buckets. With few, if any, competitive advantages for many of these companies, investors should look for a pretty steep discount to a fair value estimate before buying shares.

Hallmarks of Success for Hard-Asset-Based Businesses

▶ *Cost leadership:* Because hard-asset-based companies have large fixed costs, those that deliver their products most efficiently have a strong advantage and can achieve superior financial performance, such as Southwest in the airline industry. Firms don't usually advertise their cost structures per se, so to get an idea about how efficiently a company operates, look at its fixed asset turnover, operating margins, and ROIC—and compare its numbers to industry peers.

▶ *Unique assets:* When limited assets are required to fulfill the delivery of a particular service, ownership of those assets is key. For example, Waste Management's numerous, well-located landfill assets represent a significant competitive advantage and barrier to entry in the waste management market because it's unlikely that enough new landfill locations will get government approval to diminish its share of this business.

▶ *Prudent financing:* Remember, having a load of debt is not itself a bad thing. Having a load of debt that cannot be easily financed by the cash flow of the business is a recipe for disaster. When analyzing companies with high debt, always be sure that the debt can be serviced from free cash flow, even under a downside scenario.

Investor's Checklist: Business Services

▶ Understand the business model. Knowing if a company leverages technology, people, or hard assets will provide insight as to the kind of financial results the company may produce.

▶ Look for scale and operating leverage. These characteristics can provide significant barriers to entry and lead to impressive financial performance.

▶ Look for recurring revenue. Long-term customer contracts can guarantee certain levels of revenue for years into the future. This can provide a degree of stability in financial results.

▶ Focus on cash flow. Investors ultimately earn returns based on a company's cash-generating ability. Avoid investments that aren't expected to generate adequate cash flow.

▶ Size the market opportunity. Industries with big, untapped market opportunities provide an attractive environment for high growth. In addition, companies chasing markets perceived to be big enough to accommodate growth for all industry participants are less likely to compete on price alone.

▶ Examine growth expectations. Understand what kind of growth rates are incorporated into the share price. If the rates of growth are unrealistic, avoid the stock.

17

Banks

Banks possess an enviable spot in the global economy. They're the funnel in the capital formation process and the engine that keeps the car humming. Without banks, corporations would struggle to scrounge up money to expand, and consumers would face a near-insurmountable obstacle in their quest to buy a home or to profitably save and invest. Because the service that banks provide is so vital to long-term economic growth, the banking industry is almost certain to grow in line with the world's total output, no matter which sector generates the greatest need for capital. Whether the demand for money comes from an industry such as technology or pharmaceuticals or consumers' incessant demand for housing, banks will benefit.

The banking business model is simple. Banks receive money from depositors and the capital markets and lend to borrowers, profiting from the difference, or *spread.* If a bank borrows money from a depositor at 4 percent and lends it out at 6 percent, the bank has earned a 2 percent spread, which is called *net interest income.* Most banks also make money from basic fees and other services, which is usually referred to as *noninterest income.* Combine net

---

Craig Woker and Richard McCaffery with Pat Dorsey.

interest income and noninterest income to get *net revenues,* a view of the bank's top line. That's the banking model.

Banks have a number of inherent strengths that help create a competitive advantage. By assembling large, diverse portfolios of loans, banks reduce their risks and pass some of the resulting savings along to all borrowers, thus lowering the cost of capital in the marketplace compared with what it would be if borrowers and lenders worked directly with one another.[1] This unique advantage forms one of the bases for a strong and lasting economic moat for the banking industry.

In addition, the federal government has all but given the keys to the liquidity kingdom to banks by essentially subsidizing the banking industry. The federal government guarantees well over half of the banking industry's liabilities (via FDIC insurance), and banks can turn to the Federal Reserve as a lender of last resort if they're caught in a short-term liquidity crunch. These implicit subsidies, which other corporations don't have, allow banks to effectively borrow at below-market rates. They also make the banking industry the lowest cost, safest producer of liquidity in the world. The low cost of borrowing—combined with the advantage banks have on the lending side—allows banks to earn attractive returns on their spread.

That said, because many banks enjoy these advantages, we think there are few that truly have wide economic moats. Money is a commodity, after all, and financial products are generic. So what makes one bank better than another? There isn't a formula, but throughout this chapter, we'll show you what to look for. Here are a few examples of wide-moat banks with different strategies:

▸ Citigroup uses its worldwide geographic reach and deep product bench to increase revenues and diversify its risk exposure, which allows it to perform well in even difficult environments.

▸ Wells Fargo is an expert at attracting deposits, which are a key source of lower cost funds, and it has a deeply ingrained sales culture that drives revenues.

---

[1] *Investing: The Collected Works of Martin L. Leibowitz,* edited by Frank J. Fabozzi (McGraw-Hill, 1991).

▶ Fifth Third has an aggressive sales culture, a low-risk loan philosophy, and a sharp focus on costs.

It's All about Risk

Whether a financial institution specializes in making commercial loans or consumer loans, the heart and soul of banking is centered on one thing: risk management. Banks accept three types of risk: (1) credit, (2) liquidity, and (3) interest rate, and they get paid to take on this risk. Borrowers and lenders pay banks through interest or fees because they are unwilling to manage the risk on their own, or because banks can do it more cheaply.

But just as their advantage lies in mitigating others' risk, banks' greatest strength—the ability to earn a premium for managing credit and interest rate risk—can quickly become their greatest weakness if, for example, loan losses grow faster than expected.

Managing Credit Risk

Credit risk is a core part of the lending business. Investors can get a sense of a bank's credit quality by examining its balance sheet, loan categories, trends in nonperforming loans and charge-off rates, as well as management's lending philosophy. (Nonperforming loans are those on which borrowers aren't paying, and charge-off rates measure the percentage of loans the bank doesn't think will ever be repaid.) The problem is that these measures are historical, which is the problem with many financial measures: They tell you where a company has been, not necessarily where it's going. Almost everything we know about the credit quality of a lending institution is learned after the fact.

This risk often rears its ugly head in the form of delinquent loans or outright defaults and could potentially be borne by anyone, not just banks.

Consider a commercial loan with a 7 percent interest rate. Banks know that some of their clients will default, so they build this cost into the price of every loan. But if you made a similar loan as an individual, chances are you wouldn't have enough capital to diversify. As a result, you'd either earn a 7 percent return or lose everything. Banks' giant balance sheets provide three major shields to insulate them against risk in ways that others can't achieve:

1. Portfolio diversity
2. Conservative underwriting and account management
3. Aggressive collections procedures

Here's how these techniques work in practice. The most straightforward way banks manage risk is to divvy up the amount they lend among many companies, industries, or geographies. In the words of oil tycoon J. Paul Getty, "If you owe the bank $100, that's your problem. If you owe the bank $100 million, that's the bank's problem." To manage this risk, banks can either originate a wide variety of loans themselves or buy and sell loan portfolios. By assembling diverse portfolios, banks reduce their risks.

Within the industry, banks can also distinguish themselves through solid underwriting and collections procedures. In other words, they figure out ways to avoid writing bad loans, and if a loan is in trouble, banks can chase down the deadbeats. Banks that develop these specialized skills better than others have an edge over their competitors. In contrast, large nonbank companies often lack the sophisticated credit approval systems and processes to reduce default risk. History is littered with giant corporations that at one time or another tried to make money by providing credit and ran into trouble because of their inexperience (e.g., AT&T and Sears).

One of the biggest challenges to investing in banks is spotting credit quality problems before they blow up in investors' faces. To help avoid getting stuck with a bank that blows up, investors should pay close attention to charge-off rates and delinquency rates, which are seen as an indicator of future charge-offs. Look for trends, not just absolute levels. The best regional banks saw their charge-off rates rise quickly in the latest economic downturn, but they remained fairly low—less than 1 percent of loans. (This measure is higher, for example, for a credit card company and lower for a savings and loan.)

Unfortunately, there's no absolute measure that can be considered good or bad, so investors must compare a bank's charge-off rates with those of its competitors and see how they have trended over time. Charge-offs, nonperforming loans, and delinquency rates are reported in press releases and can be found in annual and quarterly reports to the Securities and Exchange Commission. In addition, listen carefully to management. No manager knows exactly where charge-offs are headed, but a good management team should be able to accurately outline trends.

Finally, beware of super-fast growth. It's an axiom in the financial services industry that fast growth can lead to big troubles. Fast growth is not always bad—many of the best players have above-average growth rates—but any financial services company that's growing significantly faster than competitors should be eyed with skepticism.

Look for clear evidence that the credit culture is sound, is conservative, and has been tested. You can do this by examining charge-offs and delinquency rates, becoming familiar with the type of lending a bank does from reading the annual reports, and considering the economic environment in which the company operates. Five years of fast growth in perfect economic conditions doesn't really tell you much about credit quality, after all. If you invest in fast-growing lenders, watch them carefully.

Selling Liquidity

There's no doubt that a top-notch credit culture—along with the subsequent borrower/lender relationships that banks establish—can create a competitive advantage for firms in the industry. Less intuitive, but equally attractive from a business perspective, is the role that liquidity management plays. This is the second main type of risk that a bank has to deal with.

Suppose in a friction-free world that there were no banks and that lenders (depositors) worked directly with borrowers. That's perfectly acceptable as long as lenders know exactly when they'll need their money back. But, if something unexpected happened and the lender suddenly needed cash sooner rather than later, the lender might have to sell the loan for a big discount. In a bank-filled world, however, they can just run to the nearest branch and make a withdrawal.

Banks offer liquidity management services in many forms. For instance, many businesses pay banks a standing fee to maintain a back-up line of credit. Essentially, the bank has sold nothing but a promise. Some firms also sell their receivables to financial services firms at a discount in a service known as *factoring,* because the business wants or needs cash as soon as possible.

Less obvious to many consumers is that they are actually paying for liquidity services, as well. Consider the case of Wells Fargo, one of the nation's largest retail banks. In 2002, depositors paid the bank $2.2 billion in fees on their accounts. The bank paid depositors about $1.9 billion in interest on deposits. Netting these two numbers, account-holders at Wells paid the bank nearly $300 million to hold on to their money. Then the bank turned around, lent the money out, and made more money on it.

There is no other business in the world where you can take money from people and effectively charge them to take it off their hands. Can you imagine walking up to someone on the street and offering to hold on to his $100 bill if he pays you a few bucks? It's ludicrous. Yet, that's what banks do every day. In this sense, liabilities in the form of deposits are truly assets for banks. Low-cost core deposits (e.g., checking accounts) are very stable and cheap.

This is why it's important to track deposit levels. For example, check to see whether deposits are increasing or decreasing. In particular, check to see if low-cost deposit categories such as checking and savings accounts are growing. Most banks provide a breakout of deposit categories in their annual reports. If management has been talking about the importance of a strong deposit base and deposits have been declining over the last five years, they aren't getting the job done.

Investors must also pay close attention to a bank's balance sheet. Seek out firms with a diverse stable of loans to prevent rising defaults in any one sector from causing the bank to get into trouble. The annual report shows details about the type of loans a bank holds, and investors should track how it has changed over time. Has a bank that has traditionally been a mortgage lender expanded into indirect auto loans, a much riskier type of lending? It takes time to become familiar with the characteristics of different types of loans, and you shouldn't invest in any financial services company without a feel for the types of loans it makes and without confidence that the firm has plenty of experience in making those types of loans.

Managing Interest Rate Risk

This is the third main type of risk faced by banks. If there's a reservation that investors frequently harbor about investing in banks, it's that earnings can be squeezed by interest rates, which are completely outside banks' control.

The impact of rates on banks is often oversimplified to "Higher rates, good; Lower rates, bad." But there are more nuances to interest rate management than this. For instance, at any point, banks can be either asset sensitive or liability sensitive. Asset sensitivity means that the interest rate on assets (like loans) will change more quickly than the interest rate on liabilities. In this situation, rising rates will be profitable—at least for a while. But when banks are liability sensitive and rates start to rise, the interest rate on liabilities will change faster than the interest rate on assets, pinching margins.

However, banks aren't nearly as interest rate sensitive as they used to be. Banks try to closely match the life of their assets to their liabilities. And big banks have additional risk management tools at their disposal that small banks don't.

To understand why banks aren't entirely at the mercy of prevailing interest rates, consider how banks report their revenue and income. Unlike traditional firms, there is no explicit "revenue" or "sales" line. Instead, there are four major components to examine: (1) interest income, (2) interest expense, (3) noninterest (or fee) income, and (4) provisions for loan losses. Here's an example of how the top of a bank income statement will look:

$1,000	Interest income
−500	Interest expense
$ 500	Net interest income
−100	Provisions for loan losses
+500	Noninterest income
$ 900	

For now, let's ignore the noninterest income component because this is generally steadier than interest income and interest expense. When we do this, we see that banks have a natural hedge built into their business. Consider the following as a base case for a bank operating in a strong economy:

$1,000	Interest income
−500	Interest expense
$ 500	Net interest income
−100	Provisions for loan losses
$ 400	

Suppose now that the Federal Reserve cuts rates. Because the Fed understands the benefit of maintaining a strong banking system, subtle cues are generally communicated before any cuts. In the meantime, banks reposition their balance sheets so that they're liability sensitive, thus allowing net interest income to widen. However, if a cut happens, it's for a good reason. A recession might be causing unemployment to rise and bankruptcies to increase. That, in turn, leads to higher provisions for loan losses for banks. Here's what might happen in a weak economy:

$1,000	Interest income
−400	Interest expense
$600	Net interest income
−200	Provisions
$ 400	

Have interest rates impacted the bank? Yes and no. Sure, net interest income widened, but this number is meaningless in isolation. After all, the weak economy caused provisioning to double, thereby wiping out the wider interest spread. In the real world, this relationship doesn't come out to the perfect round numbers laid out here, but it can be close. From 2000 to 2001, for example, FDIC data shows that net interest income grew $16.1 billion for the banking industry, mostly because of lower rates. However, the weakening economy caused banks to give most of that benefit back in the form of $13.8 billion of increased provisioning.[2]

Virtually all banks can benefit in this type of scenario. However, big banks also have additional tools at their disposal. For starters, the breadth of their business lines makes it easier for them to reposition their balance sheet to focus on one sector versus another, depending on the operating environment. Perhaps most importantly, big banks have the ability to access the capital markets to pass the buck by letting investors purchase the loans (much like a bond) and assume the interest rate risk. Then banks—which still service the loans and collect a fee doing so—can focus on their strengths: credit and liquidity risk management.

---

[2] "Historical Statistics on Banking," FDIC, Annual report.

At the end of 2002, for example, Bank One owned just $11.6 billion of credit card loans—those it held on its balance sheet—yet it managed a total card portfolio of $74 billion. This has happened industrywide and highlights the strength of larger lenders. For instance, although commercial banks and savings banks held 56 percent of all U.S. consumer loans on their balance sheets in 1990, that number had fallen to 37 percent by the end of 2002. Why? Because securitized assets—those that are sold off to investors and that banks continue to service—had risen from 6 percent of loans outstanding to 35 percent, according to the Federal Reserve.

Thus, while margins can be impacted by interest rates, large financial institutions are making progress toward managing the interest rate cycle. As you're thinking about interest rate risk, remember that the impact it has on a bank's balance sheet is complex, dynamic, and varies from institution to institution.

Economic Moats in Banks

Banks have taken considerable advantage of their birthright as leaders in risk management. But several other factors have also led to deeper and wider economic moats. These deterrents to competition include:

1. Huge balance sheet requirements
2. Large economies of scale
3. A regional oligopoly type industry structure
4. Customer switching costs

Balance Sheet

There likely is no industry more capital-intensive than banking or, more generally, financial services. Of the 20 largest corporations by asset size in early 2003, 19 were financial conglomerates, according to Morningstar data. The only nonfinancial name to crack the top 20 was General Electric, and even General Electric generates a big chunk of its earnings from its finance arm. Heavy capital requirement is one of the primary competitive deterrents. In 2001, Citigroup, for instance, passed the $1 trillion mark of assets on its balance sheet. It is very difficult to raise an asset base that is larger than the economies of all but a handful of countries.

Economies of Scale

Hand in hand with the capital requirements is the fact that banking offers huge economies of scale. This has been a driving factor behind the industry's pervasive consolidation, with the number of U.S. banks declining by 44 percent from 1980 through 2001. Large banks (defined as those with more than $10 billion of assets) generated $264,000 of revenue per employee in 2002, according to the FDIC. This was 2.2 times higher than the per-employee revenue generated by small community banks, defined as those with less than $100 million of assets. Part of this advantage stems from the fact that large bank employees were responsible for nearly double the assets on average, but big banks were also better at squeezing their customers' assets for more revenue (primarily through fees). On this front, big banks generated 23 percent more revenues per dollar of asset than small banks.

Market Oligopolies

Even though the top U.S. retail bank in 2002—Bank of America—still controlled a bit less than 10 percent of the country's deposits, the industry has become very concentrated on a regional level, with the biggest banks in individual cities often operating as difficult-to-penetrate oligopolies. For instance, in the 10 largest U.S. metro areas in 2002, the top three banks on average had 50 percent deposit market share, with the remainder often fragmented among hundreds of small community banks with no pricing power. Even in banking endeavors that have gone national, a handful of players often dominate. For instance, in corporate syndicated lending, the top three loan arrangers—J.P. Morgan Chase, Bank of America, and Citigroup—controlled 70 percent of the underwriting market in 2002. In the credit card industry, Citigroup, MBNA, and Bank One carve up about half of the market share, thanks to their low-cost advantage.

Customer Switching

Another key advantage is that banks tend to have very loyal customers. U.S. Bancorp, Wells Fargo, and other large retail banks estimate that attrition runs at about 15 percent per year. In other words, 85 percent of accounts—and, therefore, revenues—recur every year, a pretty sticky business. This is partially due to branding and the desire to stick with a firm you trust.

Equally important is inertia. Most people don't switch banks, even if they feel that they're being nickeled and dimed by their current bank. For instance, a 2001 study found that 38 percent of checking account customers didn't recall the last time that the price was raised on their account. Of the remaining 62 percent, only 4 percent of those people moved banks because of the higher fees.[3]

Hallmarks of Success for Banks

What should investors look for when investing in banks and other financiers? Because their entire business—their strengths and their opportunities—is built on risk, it's a good idea to focus on conservatively managed institutions that consistently deliver solid—but not knockout—profits. Here's a list of some major metrics to consider.

Strong Capital Base

A strong capital base is the number one issue to consider before investing in a lender. Investors can look at several metrics. The simplest is the equity-to-assets ratio; the higher, the better. It's difficult to give a rule of thumb because the level of capital should vary with each institution based on a number of factors including the riskiness of its loans, but most of the bigger banks we analyze have capital ratios in the 8 percent to 9 percent range. Also, look for a high level of loan loss reserves relative to nonperforming assets.

These ratios vary depending on the type of lending an institution does, as well as the point of the business cycle in which they are taken. All of these metrics are found in banks' financial reports, and they can be compared to industry averages by logging on to the FDIC Web site, www.fdic.gov.

Return on Equity and Return on Assets

These metrics are the de facto standards for gauging bank profitability. Generally, investors should look for banks that can consistently generate mid- to high-teen returns on equity. Ironically, investors should be concerned if a bank earns a level not only too far below this industry benchmark, but also

---

[3] "Bank deposits get interesting," *The McKinsey Quarterly*, 2 (2002).

Understanding Leverage

Given the size of the average bank's asset base relative to equity, it's not difficult to imagine a doomsday scenario. Earnings serve as the first layer of protection against credit losses. If losses in a given period exceed earnings, a reserve account on the balance sheet serves as a second layer of protection. Banks must have a pool of reserves to protect shareholders, who hold only a small stake in the company because of the leverage employed.

If losses in a period exceed reserves, the difference comes directly from shareholders' equity. *Equity* is an accounting-based expression of a company's net worth, and it's critical for banks. Go back to the basic balance sheet equation: Assets = Liabilities + Equity. Liquidate the company and equity represents anything that's left over. Eliminate equity, and the only party left with any claim on the assets is creditors. When losses at a bank start destroying equity, turn out the lights.

Leverage is easily expressed as a ratio: assets/equity. The average bank has a leverage ratio in the range of 12 to 1 or so, compared to 2 to 1 or 3 to 1 for the average company. Leverage isn't evil. It can enhance returns, but there are inherent dangers. For example, if you buy a $100,000 home with $8,000 down, your equity is 8 percent. In other words, you're leveraged 12.5 to 1, which is pretty typical for a bank. Now, if something atypical happens and the value of your home suddenly drops to $90,000 (just 10 percent), your equity is gone. You still owe the lender $92,000, but the house isn't worth that much. You could walk away from the house $8,000 poorer and still owe $2,000. Highly leveraged businesses put themselves in a similar situation.

This doesn't mean all leverage is bad. As a rule, the more liquid a company's balance sheet, the more the company can be leveraged because its assets can be quickly converted to cash at a fair price.

too far above it. After all, many fast-growing lenders have thrown off 30 percent or more ROEs just by provisioning too little for loan losses. Remember, it can be very easy to boost bank's earnings in the short term by underprovisioning or leveraging up the balance sheet, but this can be unduly risky over the long term. For this reason, it's good to see a high level of return on assets, as well. For banks, a top ROA would be in the 1.2 percent to 1.4 percent range.

Efficiency Ratios

The efficiency ratio measures noninterest expense, or operating costs, as a percentage of net revenues. Basically, it tells you how efficiently the bank is managed. Many good banks have efficiency ratios under 55 percent (lower is better). For comparison, the average efficiency ratio of all insured institutions in the fourth quarter of 2002 was 58.4 percent, according to the FDIC. Look for banks with strong efficiency ratios as evidence that costs are being kept in check.

Net Interest Margins

Another simple measure to watch is net interest margin, which looks at net interest income as a percentage of average earning assets. Virtually all banks report net interest margins because it measures lending profitability. You'll see a wide variety of net interest margins depending on the type of lending a bank engages in, but most banks' margins fall into the 3 percent to 4 percent range. Track margins over time to get a feel for the trend—if margins are rising, check to see what's been happening with interest rates. (Falling rates generally push up net interest margins.) In addition, examine the bank's loan categories to see whether the bank has been moving into different lending areas. For example, credit card loans typically carry much higher interest rates than residential mortgages, but credit card lending is also riskier than lending money secured by a house.

Strong Revenues

Historically, many of the best-performing bank investments have been those that have proven capable of above-average revenue growth. Wide margins have generally been elusive in a commodity industry that competes on service quality. But, some of the most successful banks have been able to cross-sell new services, which adds to fee income, or pay a slightly lower rate on deposits and charge a slightly higher rate on loans.

Keep an eye on three major metrics: (1) net interest margin, (2) fee income as a percent of total revenues, and (3) fee income growth. The net interest margin can vary widely depending on economic factors, the interest rate environment, and the type of business the lender focuses on, so it's best to compare the bank you're interested in to other similar institutions. Fee income made up

42 percent of bank industry revenue in 2001 and has grown at an 11.6 percent compound annual rate over the past two decades. A large and diversified company such as Fifth Third generates more than 40 percent of its net revenues from fee income, whereas smaller, less diversified companies such as thrifts (e.g., Golden West) get just 10 percent to 12 percent of income from fees. Make sure, therefore, that you're comparing similar companies and that you understand the company's strategy. As always, examine the number over a period of time to get a sense of the trend.

Price-to-Book

Because banks' balance sheets consist mostly of financial assets with varying degrees of liquidity, book value is a good proxy for the value of a banking stock. Assuming the assets and liabilities closely approximate their reported value, the base value for a bank should be book value. For any premium above that, investors are paying for future growth and excess earnings. Seldom do banks trade for less than book, but if they do, the bank's assets could be distressed. Typically, big banks have traded in the two or three times book range over the past decade; regionals have often traded for less than that.

A solid bank trading at less than two times book value is often worth a closer look. Remember, there is almost always a reason the bank is selling at a discount, so be sure you understand the risks. On the other hand, some banks are worth three times book value or more, but we would exercise caution before paying that much. Bank stocks are volatile creatures, and you can find good values if you're patient—especially because even the best banks will generally be hit hard when any high-profile blowup occurs in the financial services sector. Lining up several banks for a relative P/B valuation isn't as good as putting together a discounted cash flow model, but for this industry, it can be a reasonable approximation of the value of the business.

These metrics should serve as a starting point for seeking out quality bank stocks. Overall, we think the best defense for investors who want to pick their own financial services stocks is patience and a healthy sense of skepticism. Build a paper portfolio of core companies that look promising and learn the businesses over time. Get a feel for the kind of lending they do, the way that risk is managed, the quality of management, and the amount of equity capital the bank holds. When an opportunity presents itself—and one always does—you'll be in a much better position to act.

Investor's Checklist: Banks

▶ The business model of banks can be summed up as the management of three types of risk: credit, liquidity, and interest rate.

▶ Investors should focus on conservatively run institutions. They should seek out firms that hold large equity bases relative to competitors and provision conservatively for future loan losses.

▶ Different components of banks' income statements can show volatile swings depending on a number of factors such as the interest rate and credit environment. However, well-run banks should generally show steady net income growth through varying environments. Investors are well served to seek out firms with a good track record.

▶ Well-run banks focus heavily on matching the duration of assets with the duration of liabilities. For instance, banks should fund long-term loans with liabilities such as long-term debt or deposits, not short-term funding. Avoid lenders that don't.

▶ Banks have numerous competitive advantages. They can borrow money at rates lower than even the federal government. There are large economies of scale in this business derived from having an established distribution network. The capital-intensive nature of banking deters new competitors. Customer-switching costs are high, and there are limited barriers to exit money-losing endeavors.

▶ Investors should seek out banks with a strong equity base, consistently solid ROEs and ROAs, and an ability to grow revenues at a steady pace.

▶ Comparing similar banks on a price-to-book measure can be a good way to make sure you're not overpaying for a bank stock.

18

Asset Management and Insurance

LIKE BANKS, ASSET managers and insurance companies make profits from other people's money. Asset managers charge a fee for investing clients' money in stocks or bonds, and insurance firms invest the money they receive from customers' insurance premiums to generate additional earnings on top of their core underwriting businesses. However, the basic economics, and hence the economic moats, of these two groups of firms couldn't be more different. Asset management is incredibly lucrative, and even a poorly managed asset manager is likely to post stellar financial results. Historically, asset managers have been excellent investments, and they're well worth getting to know. By contrast, the insurance industry is extremely competitive, making it tough to build a lasting economic moat. In this chapter, we'll dig into the nuts and bolts of how these firms make money and highlight what you should look for when examining asset managers and insurers.

Asset Management
With huge margins and constant streams of fee income, asset managers are perennial profit machines. However, these companies are so tied to the

Rachel Barnard, Dreyfus Neenan, and Matthew Scholz with Pat Dorsey.

markets that their stock prices often reflect oversized doses of the current optimism or pessimism prevailing in the economy, which means it pays off to take a contrarian approach when you're thinking about when to invest. The best asset managers can present truly outstanding investment opportunities when they are selling at the right price.

What Makes Asset Managers Tick

Most people are familiar with mutual funds, but what about the companies that manage them? Asset management firms run money for their customers and demand a small chunk of the assets as a fee in return. This is lucrative work and requires very little capital investment. The real assets of the firm are its investment managers, so typically compensation is the firm's main expense. Even better, it doesn't take twice as many people to run twice as much money, so economies of scale are excellent. This means that increases in assets under management—and, therefore, in advisory fees—will drop almost completely to the bottom line. All this adds up to stellar operating margins, which are usually in the 30 percent to 40 percent range—something you won't see in many industries.

The majority of asset managers we cover have economic moats, especially if money management is the company's main business segment. Attaining scale in this industry is evidence of a solid moat. Beyond the favorable economics mentioned previously, asset managers also benefit from reaching a level of maturity and scale that is almost impossible for upstart firms to duplicate. Gathering assets takes time, and gaining significant scale (at least $10 billion in assets under management) takes a track record. Most funds toil in obscurity until their third birthday, and even then, it takes years to build up an asset base. This puts large, established asset managers at a huge advantage.

Asset managers create wide economic moats by establishing a dominant presence in a profitable segment of the industry. The most important competitive advantages we look for are diversification (both in products and customers) and stickiness of assets (money that stays with the firm even when times are tough).

Diversification: Because of their close ties to the market itself, asset management stocks tend to move in tandem with the broader equity indexes.

Many investors think that selling investment products in a bear market is like selling popsicles at the North Pole. But in truth, the correlation to any particular market is more difficult to pin down because many asset managers now sell a broad array of products, from money markets to bonds to equities to hedge funds, all of which thrive under different conditions.

Diversity of products is one way asset managers overcome market fluctuations. Bonds and money markets, which may look as dull as ditch water in a great equity market, can be an oasis in a bear market. Even better, having a large stable of diverse funds can ensure that assets stay with the company.

Asset Stickiness: If customers bailed out at the first sign of trouble, fund firms would have a volatile time of it. But the most desirable assets tend to be sticky. Institutions and pension funds, in particular, like to stick with a manager once they have a relationship. Wealthy investors often enjoy the red-carpet treatment too much to dump their wealth management firm, even when their investments haven't performed well. Assets that are held in tax-deferred portfolios, such as 401(k)s and IRAs, also tend to move around less than assets in taxable accounts. Government regulations discourage cashing out early, and a long-term horizon helps to keep many retirement customers invested for long periods.

Direct-sold retail funds can be great for investors, but sometimes they can work against the fund companies that market them. Throughout the recent bear market, advisor-sold funds did a better job in retaining their assets because financial advisors were able to prevent clients from selling in a panic. A little handholding goes a long way in convincing clients to ride out the turbulent markets.

Asset Management Accounting 101

The single biggest metric to watch for any company in this industry is assets under management (AUM), the sum of all the money that customers have entrusted to the firm. Because an asset manager derives its revenue as a percentage of assets under management, AUM is a good indication of how well—or how badly—a firm is doing.

Unlike a bank or insurer, where big losses can cause the firm to become insolvent, big losses in asset management portfolios are borne by customers.

Big losses will affect fee income by reducing AUM, but an asset manager could lose well over half the value of its assets under management and still remain in business. In a worst-case scenario, customers could withdraw their remaining dollars and the firm could fold if its fee income became inadequate to support its operations. But because asset management requires almost no capital investment, these companies can pare back to the bone to remain in business.

Key Drivers of Asset Management Companies

The level of assets under management is the biggest driver of revenue for an asset manager, but not all assets are created equal. Money managers typically charge higher fees to manage stock portfolios than to manage bonds or money market funds. More specialized funds, such as foreign-stock funds, real estate, or high-yield bond funds, often carry the highest fees. Institutions and large investors can count on volume discounts if they place multiple millions or billions with one firm, whereas retail investors pay steeper fees for small accounts. This means that an asset manager may see a 10 percent increase in overall AUM, but only an 8 percent increase in revenue if, for example, sales of bond funds outpaced sales of equity funds.

Beyond tracking the ups and downs of particular asset classes, we like to keep a close eye on just where changes in AUM come from. Market movements—appreciation or depreciation of securities prices—can have a huge effect, so much so that many asset managers can almost be considered as leveraged bets on the market. Firms with a heavy concentration in equities, such as Janus or London-based Amvescap, have seen their stocks soar during bull markets and market rallies. These market movements lift AUM without any new money moving in or out of funds, and this increases revenue from investment management fees.

But the best asset managers are not simple bets on the market. Investors should look for asset management companies that are able to consistently bring in new money and don't rely only on the market to increase their AUM. Look for net inflows (inflows higher than outflows) in a variety of market conditions. This is a signal that the asset manager is offering products that new investors want and that existing investors are happy with the products they have.

Inside the Back Office

Custody and asset services are the lesser known sidekick of asset management. Like many sidekicks out there, this one does much of the boring work and doesn't garner much glory or recognition. (Think of Tonto feeding the horses day in and day out while the Lone Ranger gets to do the more exciting stuff.) However, custody operations are essential to many pension plans, insurance companies, asset managers, and even wealthy individuals who need someone to keep track of their investments and perform the back office accounting work every day.

The custody and asset servicing business works on a principle similar to the asset management business, but with lower fees and more economies of scale. Many trust banks such as State Street and Bank of New York have huge custody operations that manage trillions of dollars in assets. Custodians don't invest the money they are entrusted with; they just keep track of it. Mutual fund companies frequently outsource their back offices to custodians because they don't want the hassle of record keeping. Custodians keep track of the securities that their customers buy and sell, collect dividends, and calculate an accurate value at the end of the day. Many offer a huge array of additional services, such as performance analytics, risk management, and pension consulting.

This business requires a hefty investment in technology and a penchant for absolute accuracy. It isn't particularly profitable, however, until you collect well over a billion dollars in custodial assets. Fees for custody typically come in below .05 percent of assets under custody, making scale essential to support the necessary technology investment.

Key Drivers of Custody Companies

Revenues in this industry are primarily driven by the level of assets under custody. Because economies of scale are so significant here, higher levels of assets under custody are a sign of competitive advantage. Bigger operations can pay for leading-edge technology and make a larger profit from each additional dollar of custody fees. This bigger-is-better model has fueled increasing consolidation, with smaller players exiting and custodial assets being concentrated with the largest players. As a result, barriers to entry have risen, and small operations have little chance of attaining competitive scale. This gives the largest players, such as State Street and Bank of New York, wide economic moats.

Watch out for custody firms' loan portfolios, though. Most custodians also lend money to their clients as part of their overall service relationship. As with any bank, these loans can become too concentrated in one company, one industry, or one sector. Many of these loans are not very profitable for the banks, but they can be one of the largest risk factors. Bad loans can easily eat into a profitable custody operation. For example, during the tech and telecom bubble of the 1990s, Bank of New York loaned billions of dollars to cable and telecom companies, forcing it to write off the bad loans when many of these firms collapsed. This ate into the profits from its lucrative global custody business, which was then the largest in the world.

Hallmarks of Success for Asset Management Companies

Asset managers can be great investments, but it's important to buy into the right ones. We recommend seeking the following qualities:

- *Diversity of products and investors:* Asset managers and custodians benefit from having a diverse pool of managed assets. Swings in the markets can take a grinding toll on one-trick ponies. Janus Capital is a good example of an asset manager with all its eggs in one basket. Because its assets were mostly in growth stock funds, the firm's shares were killed when the stock market fell in 2001 and 2002. Diversified firms such as Franklin Resources have enjoyed much greater stability.
- *Sticky assets:* Firms that are revolving doors can be extremely volatile. Asset managers who attract the buy-and-hold crowd, including institutional investors and retirement savers, can count on a steadier stream of fees in varying market conditions. With its large retirement savings business, for example, T. Rowe Price enjoys relative stability in its equity assets under management.
- *Niche market:* Asset management is an increasingly crowded field, as attractive profits have lured many firms into the industry. Those companies with unique products and capabilities have more control over pricing and less competition for investor assets. Eaton Vance is a good example of an asset

management boutique. The firm specializes in tax-managed products—both stocks and bonds—and has had success in attracting and keeping tax-conscious investors.

▶ *Market leadership:* High barriers to entry and economies of scale in the custody industry make size a formidable competitive advantage. With the biggest custodians overseeing trillions in assets, smaller competitors face overwhelming challenges. Established asset managers also enjoy the advantages of long-term performance records and name recognition. Privately held Fidelity Investments is the largest asset manager in the world. It is also one of the most widely known and trusted names in the industry, a virtue which helps it gather assets and manage them profitably.

Life Insurance

The economic characteristics of the life insurance industry don't get our blood racing. From time to time, the very best life insurance companies might provide good investment value, but in general, the investment opportunities in the sector are rarely compelling. To explain why, we look into how the industry works.

The challenging economics of the life insurance business are reflected in the industry's stock performance. Over the 10 years ending August 31, 2003, the S&P Life and Health insurance index has returned 3.6 percent on an annual basis, versus 10.1 percent annually for the S&P 500 index.

Life insurance companies offer products that allow people to protect themselves or their loved ones from catastrophic events such as death or disability or to provide greater financial protection and flexibility for situations such as retirement. A life insurer pools the individual risks of many policyholders. The life insurer then strives to earn a profit by taking in and/or earning more money than it is required to eventually pay out to its policyholders.

Life Insurance Accounting 101

The life insurance business is chronically blighted by the complexity of its products and financial statements. A bizarre fact of the industry is that when an insurer sells a policy, it doesn't really know how to effectively price that policy because it doesn't really know how much it will eventually cost.

Despite the best efforts of a life insurer's actuaries to estimate variables such as future investment returns, policy persistency rates (the length of time that customers keep their policies), and life expectancy, it can take years before the insurance company knows whether it made money on the policy.

Financial statements for life insurers are very different from the statements of other businesses. Although the topic of how to read a life insurer's financial statements could fill its own book, for the sake of brevity (and the reader's sanity) let's stick to a conceptual overview.

On the asset side of the balance sheet are two major items: investments (the accumulated premiums and fees that an insurer builds up before having to pay out benefits to its policyholders) and deferred acquisition costs, which is the capitalized value of selling insurance or annuities policies. For firms that sell variable annuities, *separate account assets,* which represent the funds that variable annuity owners have invested, constitute a third important asset type. Because variable annuity owners manage their own investments, these assets are segregated and the separate account assets are offset by an equivalent amount of *separate account liabilities* on the opposite side of the balance sheet.

A life insurer's other liabilities basically consist of the actuarially estimated future benefits that need to be paid to the insurer's policyholders. The two main sources of revenue are (1) recurring premiums and fees and (2) any earned investment income. The two main expenses are (1) benefits and dividends paid to policyholders and (2) amortization of the deferred acquisition costs. Given how few revenue and expense lines there are, it is vital to keep track of their growth trends.

Key Drivers of Life Insurance Companies

Life insurance is a mature, slow-growth business that offers commodity products, which are easily substituted. Beyond certain regulatory and capital requirements, the barriers to entry are modest. But once a firm has entered the life insurance business, it can be difficult to exit. The firm owes life insurance benefits to its customers, who may still have many years to live.

Only a few of the very largest life insurers, such as MetLife, Prudential, and John Hancock, have economic moats because of their well-recognized brands, extensive distribution systems, diverse product offerings, and established relationships with numerous corporate consumers, but these are still tenuous competitive advantages. Otherwise, this is a classic no-moat business.

Given the commodity-like products of the life insurance industry, it is next to impossible for one insurer to successfully grow—without acquisitions—above the industry's long-term annual revenue growth rate (which is little more than the nominal growth in GDP). The concept of reversion to the mean is incredibly important to such a slow-growing business. For example, the net income of a life insurer might be above or below the trend in one period, thanks to some short-term event, such as outstanding investment returns. But over time, the investment returns—hence, net income—will likely return to the mean.

Examining the mix of insurance products a company offers is critical for getting a handle on what revenue and profit growth, as well as the risk level, is likely to be. It is especially important to be aware of how much and what types of annuity businesses a life insurer has. Annuities produce greater exposure to the equity markets, which means that life insurers with big annuity business are riskier investments.

Life insurers operate on a thin margin between their cost of equity and their return on equity. Look for firms that consistently generate ROEs above their costs of capital. We estimate that most life insurers have costs of equity of about 10 percent to 11 percent, whereas the average ROE has historically been around 12 percent. The strongest performing company in the industry—specialty firm AFLAC—has generated a long-term ROE of about 15 percent.

Tangible book value is the other key metric in U.S. life insurer valuation, though you'll need to adjust it by excluding marked-to-market gains or losses on available-for-sale securities from shareholders' equity. This adjustment is pretty straightforward. In the 10-K, a life insurer should have a footnote that details the amount of unrealized gain or loss on its available-for-sale securities portfolio, which is included in other comprehensive income. All you need to do is subtract the gain or add the loss to shareholders' equity to arrive at a measure of tangible book value.

Tangible book value is the safest and most practical way to think about valuation for life insurers for two fundamental reasons. First, there is very little detail available on life insurers' fundamental actuarial assumptions, and it's impossible to predict the insurers' future investment returns. Second, many major life insurers have only recently become publicly traded firms, which means there is minimal historical financial data on these companies.

Hallmarks of Success for Life Insurance Companies

Life insurers can occasionally make good investments, but it's important to avoid buying into trouble. Here's what we recommend looking for:

► *Prudent premium growth rates:* Generally, the best life insurers exhibit premium growth that isn't significantly above the industry average. According to the American Council of Life Insurers, between 1991 and 2001, the average annual increase in life insurers' premium receipts was 6.2 percent. Underpricing risk to win sales in insurance is a dangerous game.

► *ROE consistently above the cost of equity:* Given the high degree of financial leverage used in life insurance, a reliably positive spread between ROE and cost of capital is the crucial determinant of firm success in the long run. ROE for life insurers has historically been around 10 percent to 11 percent.

► *High credit rating:* Most first-rate insurers sport AA ratings. Understandably, consumers want to buy policies from firms that they expect to be around when it comes time to collect. High-quality life insurers also have risk-based capital levels that are generally around twice the minimum level set by the insurer's state regulator.

► *A diverse investment portfolio and a proven risk management culture:* About 90 percent of U.S. life insurance industry assets are invested in fixed income securities such as corporate bonds, private placements, and mortgage securities. The composition and quality of the fixed income portfolio is crucial in determining the financial strength and future earnings prospects of a life insurer. The best insurers control their exposure to riskier asset classes, such as below investment grade (i.e., junk) bonds. Compare an insurer's exposure to junk bonds to that of its competitors by looking at a ratio such as junk bonds to tangible equity or junk bonds to total assets.

Property/Casualty Insurance

Property/casualty insurance provides enormous benefits to the U.S. economy by transferring financial risks that could otherwise impede profitable transactions and raise living costs.

Unfortunately, for investors, the value that property/casualty (PC) insurance products provide the U.S. economy rarely corresponds to large investment returns. Indeed, returns are often exceedingly poor. Net margins are often razor-thin, often less than 5 percent. Returns on capital are equally poor. The average PC insurance company earns a return on equity (ROE) of less than 9 percent, and over time, most insurers achieve ROEs that are half that earned by S&P 500 companies.

These poor results often make for poor long-term performance. Over the 10 years ending in 2003, PC insurers trailed the market, often significantly. However, there are a few diamonds in the rough—consistent performers that produce attractive returns over long periods. Studious investors, armed with the keys to identifying better performing insurers, can earn solid returns in this sector.

How Property/Casualty Insurers Make Money

When an insurer sells a policy, it accepts financial risk in exchange for a premium payment. By transferring many individual risks to a common pool, an insurer is able to create a diversified risk portfolio. Because most risks aren't realized (you don't crash your car every year), insurers expect to earn a small profit margin.

Insurers also enjoy a peculiar business advantage—premiums are received well in advance of the firm's requirement to pay claims. This money is often referred to as *float,* and an insurer enjoys the use of this money between the time it receives a premium and the time it has to pay a claim. PC insurers exploit this by investing these premiums and keeping the money they make from the investments.

How much money they can make this way depends on market performance, the insurer's asset allocation, and how long the insurer holds premiums before making claim payments. Insurers writing *long-tail* insurance hold premiums longer and, hence, can invest more in equities. (The length of an insurance policy's *tail* refers to the time it takes for damages to become apparent. *Short-tail policies* are those where damages incurred during the insured period become known quickly, such as a car accident, whereas long-tail policies cover damages that may not become apparent for many years, such as an asbestos injury.)

Property/Casualty Insurance Accounting 101

Let's investigate how the PC insurance business works on an income statement and balance sheet. Premium revenue (also known as earned premium) is used to fund claim payments (loss expense), sales commissions for insurance agents (commission expense), and operating expenses (OPEX). Insurers typically express each of these expenses as ratios to earned premiums. Claim expenses, for example, typically consume 75 percent of an insurer's net revenues.

Adding together these three ratios produces the combined ratio—an insurance company's key underwriting profit measure. A combined ratio under 100 indicates an underwriting profit. For example, a combined ratio of 95 means that the insurer paid out 95 percent of its premium revenue for losses. The 5 percent remaining is the underwriting profit. A combined ratio exceeding 100 indicates an underwriting loss. For example, an insurer with a combined ratio of 105 paid out 105 percent of its premium revenue to cover losses, meaning that it had an underwriting loss equal to 5 percent of revenues.

Companies with combined ratios exceeding 105 for more than a short time have a difficult time recouping their losses via investment earnings, and this type of poor underwriting track record suggests that an insurer's competitive position is unusually weak. Insurers unable to earn even the occasional underwriting profit will produce the industry's poorest returns and may be tempted to accept large investment risks to boost profitability.

Insurers also make money from investment income, which they often report as a ratio of premiums. Adding the investment ratio to the combined ratio yields the operating profit ratio. In many instances, investment income is a key profit determinant because it offsets underwriting losses.

On the balance sheet, the key asset for most insurers is investments. In addition to float, most insurers invest a large portion of their own retained earnings as well. The investments account reveals the size of an insurer's investments relative to its asset base and details the asset allocation employed.

As a starting point, look for insurers with no more than 30 percent invested in equities (unless the company is run by Warren Buffett).

Finally, unearned premiums represent premiums received but not yet considered revenue. This oddity reflects an accounting convention. When an insurer receives a premium, it is deemed to earn it gradually across the year. After all, if a customer cancels a policy, the insurer must refund that portion of the coverage not consumed. After six months, an annual auto policy would be 50 percent *earned,* and half the premium would be considered revenue. Before this occurs, the premiums are held in the unearned premium account, and the insurer is free to invest them.

Nirvana for an insurer is being able to consistently earn underwriting profits on a large, growing customer base. In effect, this insurer would be getting paid to profit from investing other people's money and could retain this float indefinitely (as long as it grows). Unfortunately, for investors, these situations rarely occur.

Key Drivers for Property/Casualty Companies

Property/casualty insurers confront difficult economics. In most instances, pricing power is low or nonexistent, for two important reasons. Entry barriers are low, enabling competitors to quickly swoop in on profitable markets. And insurance products are often difficult to distinguish, except by price. Although insurers attempt to distinguish their products using tactics such as better customer service, bundling, and policy terms, these features are easily replicated by competitors.

Unpredictable Costs: The absence of pricing power exacerbates a more significant problem: An insurer's most important costs are mostly uncontrollable and unpredictable. Claims expense generally consumes more than 70 percent of an insurer's premiums. This encompasses cost items such as judicial awards, medical expenses, and repair parts over which an insurer has little or no control. These costs not only are difficult to control, but also are unpredictable and often grow faster than insurers are able to raise premium rates.

For example, social inflation is a particular challenge. This is the tendency of juries and judges to increase benefits and expand contract coverage, often well beyond the terms of the original insurance policy. This can make claims much larger than an insurance company could have anticipated. One study estimated that the average jury award increased 19 percent annually over the 1990s.[1] Insurers also face considerable expenses from growing insurance fraud rates. The estimated annual cost of insurance fraud is $80 billion.[2]

Unpredictable cost inflation is especially troublesome for insurers because they must estimate their costs well before the costs are incurred. Insurers lack the pricing power to incorporate a margin of safety into their pricing, so variations in loss expenses can quickly wipe out profits and cause large reserving charges. Because there are few positive cost surprises, insurers are often at the whim of the forces outlined previously.

Insurers also face contamination. If one insurer prices too low—mistakenly or otherwise—profits for all insurers can be wiped out as other industry players offer low prices in response to the perceived competitive threat. This is an especially acute problem for insurers who compete with mutual firms. (A mutual insurer is an insurance company owned solely by the people it insures, rather than by shareholders.) Mutual insurers, such as State Farm, are exceptionally dangerous competitors because they lack the profit motive of most other insurers, and they can compete on price and incur losses for long periods to build market share. For example, State Farm's enormous balance sheet— which can throw off plenty of investment income—could enable it to price below cost for many years, which would eliminate profits for listed insurers.

Cyclicality in the Insurance Business: Insurance is a mature business. We generally expect mature businesses to grow with GDP over the long term, but the insurance industry also exhibits considerable cyclicality.

This cyclicality results from pricing decisions and investment returns. When market returns are high, such as in the late 1990s, insurers face less pressure to underwrite profitably because underwriting losses are easily offset by investment income. Consequently, premium rates decline over a period of time. This is referred to as a *soft market.*

---

[1] "The Legend of the Price-Gouging Insurer," Insurance Information Institute (November 2002) and Morningstar Analysis.
[2] Coalition Against Insurance Fraud, "Insurance Fraud: The Crime you Pay For," http://www .insurancefraud.org/downloads/Backgrounder.pdf.

However, after many years of price decreases, insurers are often unprepared for a decrease in market returns or for severe losses from a large event like the terrorist attacks of September 11, 2001. Because these losses cannot be offset by investment returns, premium rates must rise to restore profitability. At this point, prices have been too low for too long, so insurers must raise rates and reduce contract terms considerably to restore profitability. This is referred to as a *hard market,* and 100 percent price increases aren't uncommon.

Hard markets aren't sustained as long as soft markets, though. Once profitability is restored and investment market returns normalize, the stronger insurers will start to lower prices again to attract customers and deter rivals, knowing they can once again start to offset losses with investment returns.

Regulation: Finally, insurers face considerable regulation. Insurance rates must often be approved on a state-by-state basis, meaning that insurers are at the mercy of the regulators in each state. In many instances, insurers are required to insure less profitable customers without being able to charge them higher prices to compensate. Furthermore, in many states, insurers are required to fund the losses of competitors who become insolvent.

Insurers are also highly susceptible to consumer lobbying, which can influence regulators to keep prices low or mandate price changes. A key example is California's Proposition 103, which mandated an immediate 20 percent cut in insurance premium prices and caused the transfer of more than $1.2 billion from insurers to customers.[3] This was good for customers but bad for insurance investors.

Hallmarks of Success for Property/Casualty Insurance Companies

Economic moats are scarce in property/casualty insurance. The industry's dismal economics condemns most insurers to perpetually poor returns and ongoing price competition. However, the news isn't all bad. Intelligent strategies and management teams can create a narrow economic moat, thereby allowing for the opportunity of decent investment returns. Five qualities we recommend seeking in a PC insurer are:

---

[3] The Foundation for Taxpayer and Consumer Rights, "Background on Insurance Reform—A Detailed Analysis of California Proposition 103." Excerpted from "Auto Insurance Crisis & Reform," by Harvey Rosenfield, published Fall 1998 in University of Memphis Law Review.

1. *Low-cost operator:* In a commodity business where firms compete on price, the lowest cost provider usually enjoys the highest profits. Insurers who can minimize their costs are most likely to earn high returns, and insurers who refuse to sell unprofitable insurance enjoy a special advantage in cost containment. Two of our favorite insurers, Progressive and Berkshire Hathaway subsidiary GEICO, employ this approach by marketing directly to consumers, avoiding sales commission expense, and underwriting strictly for profit. It's no surprise that their returns consistently lead the industry.

2. *Strategic acquirer:* Profitable insurers who can continually acquire underperforming insurers and return their operations to profitability can often earn attractive returns with an above-average growth rate. Although acquisition-driven growth can be a risky strategy, experienced management teams can often play the insurance cycle to acquire companies at bargain prices. White Mountains is a good example of a company that has done this successfully.

3. *Specialty insurer:* Insurers who specialize in niche markets can often develop relationships and underwriting expertise that can give them reasonable returns. If the markets are relatively small and nonstrategic, other insurers may not be attracted. Left to themselves, specialty insurers have more leeway to set prices. Markel has made specialty insurance pay by insuring niche markets such as summer camps, yachts, and sports organizations.

4. *A record of financial strength:* Insurance is worthless if the insurer won't survive a disaster to be able to pay the resultant claims. Insurance customers usually prefer insurers who possess the financial strength to survive a disaster (such as September 11, 2001, or Hurricane Andrew) and still be able to pay claims. Berkshire Hathaway increasingly wins catastrophe reinsurance (insuring other insurers against large claims) business because the company is renowned for possessing the capital strength to be able to pay large claims on losses such as Florida hurricanes or an earthquake in California.

5. *A rational management team with a significant portion of its personal wealth invested in the business:* Poor underwriting can quickly destroy profits. Many management teams slash prices to bring in customers, but if prices

are not high enough to cover losses, the company loses money. Management teams who are also large shareholders are more exposed to the potential pain that large underwriting losses can inflict, and teams like this usually set reasonable prices and produce better profits over the long term.

Investor's Checklist: Asset Management and Insurance

▶ Look for diversity in asset management companies. Firms that manage a number of asset classes—such as stocks, bonds, and hedge funds—are more stable during market gyrations. One-hit wonders are much more volatile and are subject to wild swings.

▶ Keep an eye on asset growth. Make sure an asset manager is successful in consistently bringing in inflows greater than outflows.

▶ Look for money managers with attractive niche markets, such as tax-managed funds or international investing.

▶ Sticky assets add stability. Look for firms with a high percentage of stable assets, such as institutional money managers or fund firms who specialize in retirement savings.

▶ Bigger is often better. Firms with more assets, longer track records, and multiple asset classes have much more to offer finicky customers.

▶ Be wary of any insurance firm that grows faster than the industry average (unless the growth can be explained by acquisitions).

▶ One of the best ways to protect against investment risk in the life insurance world is to consider companies with diversified revenue bases. Some products, such as variable annuities, have exhibited a good degree of cyclicality.

▶ Look for life insurers with high credit ratings (AA) and a consistent ability to realize ROEs above their cost of capital.

▶ Seek out property/casualty insurers who consistently achieve ROEs above 15 percent. This is a good indication of underwriting discipline and cost control.

▶ Avoid insurers who take repeated reserving charges. This often indicates pricing below cost or deteriorating cost inflation.

▶ Look for management teams committed to building shareholder value. These teams often have significant personal wealth invested in the businesses they run.

19

Software

THE SOFTWARE INDUSTRY is intensely competitive, but it has economics few industries can match. Although the up-front costs for creating software are huge, production costs are not largely because software can be burned on a compact disc or delivered over the Internet for almost nothing. When a company such as Microsoft hits a home run with a product like Windows, it can generate operating margins in excess of 40 percent.

Established software companies are cash cows, too. Working capital management is typically good because software can be stored and shipped electronically. This leads to low inventory and accounts receivable balances. And because little capital is required to build software, successful software companies generate tons of free cash flow.

Finally, software companies have excellent growth prospects. Companies will continue to buy technology that makes business run more smoothly. Software can automate tasks, such as accounting, and improve relationships with customers. High labor costs encourage the use of software because time-consuming tasks, such as budgeting, can be reduced and increase

Michael Trigg with Pat Dorsey.

productivity. And when firms face tough times with falling revenues, software can help cut costs.

Segments of the Software Industry

There are many nooks and crannies in the software industry. But a common theme is that most are oligopolies, with only a few controlling the majority of sales. Because technology buyers are inherently conservative and loath to buy products from a vendor that might go out of business and leave them stranded for basic service, companies are increasingly buying only from industry leaders. Here are some of the bigger segments of the software industry.

Operating System

An operating system runs all the other programs on a computer. Tasks include sharing memory between applications and handling directions from external hardware such as printers. There are few opportunities in this market, with Microsoft's Windows operating system running more than 90 percent of the world's PCs. However, the Linux operating system has slowly become a respectable alternative for servers. (A server is a large computer running programs that serve an entire company rather than a single user.) However, Linux specialists such as Red Hat have struggled to make money because the software can be downloaded free over the Internet.

Database

Database software collects data so it can be easily accessed and updated. High switching costs make this market attractive because it's tough to move data from one database to another. But it's also mature, with growth unlikely to exceed the high single digits over the long haul because most firms already have databases in place. Oracle, IBM, and Microsoft dominate the market: Oracle tends to have superior technology, while IBM and Microsoft offer cheaper prices.

Enterprise Resource Planning (ERP)

Enterprise resource planning aims to improve back-office business tasks, such as accounting and human resources. For instance, an accounting application makes it easier to perform basic tasks such as budgeting and billing; human resources software can keep track of employee performance. Like database software, the ERP market isn't growing very fast because most large companies already have some type of ERP system installed. SAP, PeopleSoft, and Oracle are the big names in this segment.

Customer Relationship Management (CRM)

Customer relationship management software keeps track of client data, such as purchasing histories, so salespeople and customer service employees can tailor specific product offerings to customers. This creates selling opportunities and improves customer satisfaction. Unlike ERP, however, which can automate a finite number of back-office tasks, there's no necessary limit to how companies can interact more effectively with customers. Siebel Systems is the 800-pound gorilla in the industry, but traditional ERP vendors such as SAP and PeopleSoft have been catching up.

Security

With more products and services being sold online, sensitive data is more available to employees and customers, but also to harmful hackers. The damage caused by viruses and stolen credit card numbers alone has created tremendous demand. Growing products include firewalls, virtual private networks, antivirus, and intrusion detection. Check Point Software and Symantec have been two of the biggest benefactors thus far.

Video Game

This segment of the sector is dominated by Electronic Arts. It's costly to support the numerous hardware platforms, such as Microsoft's Xbox and Sony's PlayStation, and the industry is also cyclical, with new platforms emerging every few years. Numerous platforms (e.g., Atari) are no longer viable. Last, low barriers to entry make it easy for an upstart with a popular game to achieve success.

Miscellaneous

Not all software companies compete in industries with several established players. For example, Intuit dominates tax preparation and small business software with very little competition. Likewise, Adobe dominates graphic design software; products such as Photoshop and Illustrator have near monopolies on their respective niches. Often, companies that dominate a smaller niche are more attractive investments than household names that serve larger markets.

Economic Moats in the Software Industry

Given the rapid pace of technological change, wide moats are tough to build in the software industry. Because barriers to entry are low, today's winner can quickly become tomorrow's loser if a competitor can develop a more innovative product and the industry leader can't successfully keep up. This is what makes investing in software companies difficult. Not only is it tough for investors to assess how successful a product will be, but knowing how long that technology will remain is virtually impossible for technology novices.

The trick is to look for companies that have gone beyond superior technology in creating their competitive advantages. Look for the following characteristics.

High Customer Switching Costs

High switching costs make it tough for customers to use a competitor's product without significant hassle. For example, Autodesk has a lock on the architecture and construction design software market because architects and engineers are trained to use the software early in their careers. Switching to a competing program isn't very attractive to folks who have been working with Autodesk for years. For the most part, software companies that benefit from this moat have products that are either too expensive or too time-consuming for customers to stop using.

Network Effect

Adobe is an excellent example of this economic moat at work in the software industry. With more than 500 million copies of Acrobat Reader downloaded, Acrobat has become the standard for creating and viewing documents electronically. People are more likely to create documents using Acrobat because they know the majority of personal computer users already have the Acrobat

Reader installed. Likewise, people download Acrobat Reader because it's the most popular way to share and view documents online.

Brand Names

Some software firms have managed to create strong brands that deter competitors. For example, Intuit's QuickBooks and TurboTax are two of the most well-known names in retail software. When people think of small business or tax software, they think of Intuit. Despite the fact that people come into contact with software every day, this moat is rare because the majority of software has very little consumer appeal.

Software Accounting 101

In general, software companies have fairly clean financial statements with minimal debt and fairly simple capital structures. However, there is some jargon you should understand to help you dig into the industry, as well as some metrics that are more common to the software industry than to others.

License Revenue

License revenue is the best indication of current demand because it represents how much new software was sold during a given time. It's a very profitable source of revenue because software can be produced for almost nothing after it has been developed. Service revenue, which is the other major type of revenue that many software firms report, is less profitable because it's expensive to employ consultants to install software. Keep an eye on trends: Increasing license revenue indicates healthy demand, whereas declining license revenue may indicate that growth is slowing because licenses drive future service revenue.

Deferred Revenue

Although it's recorded as a liability on the balance sheet, deferred revenue is a good liability to have—it represents cash the company has received before some services have been performed. It's common for software companies to get paid for consulting and maintenance work up front, so tracking deferred revenue can give you a good estimate of the potential trend in future revenues.

Rising deferred revenue indicates a healthy backlog of business, whereas declining deferred revenue may suggest business has started to slow because fewer sales will be recognized in the future.

Days Sales Outstanding (DSO)

Days sales outstanding indicates the number of days that it takes a company to collect its outstanding receivables. Refer to the balance sheet and income statement and calculate this formula: accounts receivable/(revenues/number of days in the reporting period). The absolute DSO number is less important than the trend in DSOs. Falling DSOs indicate a company is collecting its outstanding accounts faster than before, whereas rising DSOs may indicate that the company has extended easier credit terms to customers to close deals and boost revenues. However, this practice merely steals revenue from future periods and may lead to revenue shortfalls. In an industry where demand can change quickly, rising DSOs are often the first signal that a firm's products are no longer as hot as they once were.

Red Flags

Like many companies, software firms sometime try to make themselves look better than they are. Here are a couple of accounting issues to watch out for when you're analyzing software firms.

Revenue Recognition Changes

According to the Securities and Exchange Commission, improper revenue recognition is the biggest issue involved in the restatement of financial results, and the corporate graveyard is scattered with software companies that illegally recognized revenues. Going by the book, revenues should not be recognized until they're actually earned, which takes place when products have been delivered or services have been performed, a price has been agreed on, and there's reasonable assurance that payment will be collected.

Watch out when management changes the rules for recognizing revenue. In 2001, for example, RSA Security began booking some sales after products were shipped to distributors, whereas it had previously recognized sales only after end users had purchased products. Even though management felt that relationships with certain distributors were strong enough that the eventual sale of products to customers was guaranteed, RSA was able to boost sales artificially by stuffing its distribution channels with more inventory than could be sold in a normal amount of time. This practice stole revenue from future quarters and ultimately led to massive sales shortfalls.

Questionable Transactions

Shady deals that boost sales are notorious in the software industry. One of the most prevalent occurs when an organization both sells to and invests in another company. Another questionable transaction—called a swap deal—takes place when a vendor and customer simultaneously buy the other's products. Although engaging in these back-scratching techniques is legal, these transactions give a false picture of the overall health of business.

Hallmarks of Success for Software Companies

In addition to a wide economic moat, there are five hallmarks of success that we look for in successful software companies: increasing sales, long track records, expanding profit margins, large installed customer bases, and great management. If you can find companies that possess all five characteristics, you've probably identified the crème de la crème of the software industry.

Increasing Sales

Unlike mature industries such as consumer goods, software is relatively new and should grow faster than the economy. Successful software companies should increase revenue at least 10 percent annually in stable economic conditions. Steady growth indicates a company has either a growing demand for its software, loyal customers, or the ability to raise prices without losing business. In addition, successful companies typically have large amounts of recurring service revenue locked in.

Long Track Record

The low barriers to entry of the software industry contrast with high barriers to success—it's easy to start up a software firm, but it's much more difficult to create one that's still around after several years. Thus, look for software companies that have thrived during multiple business cycles and have solid results during both the peaks and valleys of IT spending. Sticking with firms with at least five years' worth of historical financial data will keep you from getting burned by the flashes in the pan.

Expanding Profit Margins

Successful software companies should be able to expand margins over time through economies of scale. Once software is developed, the marginal cost of producing additional copies is virtually nil, which means that each new dollar of sales should fall straight to the bottom line. Also, look for companies with high-margin license revenue increasing as a percentage of total sales.

Large Installed Customer Bases

Successful software companies typically have large customer bases that remain loyal to their products and services. Because technology buyers are inherently conservative and loath to buy products from a vendor that might go out of business, they are more prone to continue buying software from companies they trust. In the lousy IT spending conditions of the past few years, many established firms have performed well by relying on their large customer bases.

Great Management

The saying "buy the jockey, not the horse" has even more relevance in the software industry because a company's most important assets are the people (i.e., the programmers, salesforce, and management) who come to work every day. One negative characteristic of management in the software industry, however, is the egregious use of stock options. Because there's a shortage of top-notch programmers, it's not uncommon for management to give away big chunks of the company at the expense of shareholders to lure talented employees. If you can find a management team in the software industry that has resisted the temptation to give out huge option grants every year, you've definitely found a team that's willing to go against the grain.

What's Not to Like about Software?

The software industry is highly cyclical, with sales hinging on economic conditions and IT spending. The problem is that in good times software companies thrive, and in bad times they're some of the hardest hit. The primary reason for this cyclicality is that many corporations view software as a discretionary purchase that can be deferred in tough times. In other words, when the economy and business suffer, cutting IT spending is a quick way to buffer profit declines.

Software companies that cater to corporations have back-end loaded quarters in which the majority of deals are closed in the final days of the reporting period. This makes it difficult to monitor how business is performing until the quarter has ended, which increases the risk of a big disappointment. In addition, buyers know that if they wait until near the end of the quarter, a software salesman is likely to slash prices to get a deal done and meet the company's sales quota. But heavy discounting can hurt profitability.

Finally, software companies are rarely cheap. The average price-to-earnings ratio of the three largest software companies by market capitalization—Microsoft, Oracle, and SAP—was 56 between 1998 and 2002. This compares to an average price-to-earnings ratio of the S&P 500 of 25 times during that time span. Investors often bid up software stocks because of their excellent growth prospects, high returns on invested capital, and tons of cash flow. But even compared with other IT-related industries, such as hardware, software firms are typically rewarded with premium valuations because most have clean balance sheets with tons of cash and virtually no debt.

Conclusion

Software companies have impressive financial characteristics, including excellent growth prospects, high returns on invested capital, and pristine financial health. The improvements that software provides—increasing revenues, cutting costs, improved productivity—should outweigh any temporary lull in IT spending. But investors will most likely experience disappointing returns by investing in the industry blindly. Our advice is to pick stocks with economic moats that create barriers to entry, as well as ones that trade at discounts to intrinsic value. Don't get seduced by great technology alone.

Investor's Checklist: Software

▶ The software industry has economics few industries can match. Successful companies should have excellent growth prospects, expanding profit margins, and pristine financial health.

▶ Companies with wide moats are more likely to produce above-average returns. But superior technology is one of the least sustainable competitive advantages in the software industry.

▶ Look for software companies that have maintained good economics throughout multiple business cycles. We prefer companies that have been around at least several years.

▶ License revenue is one of the best indicators of current demand because it represents how much new software was sold at a given time. Watch for any license revenue trends.

▶ Rising days sales outstanding (DSOs) may indicate a company has extended easier credit terms to customers to close deals. This steals revenues from future quarters and may lead to revenue shortfalls.

▶ If deferred revenue growth slows or the deferred revenue balance begins to decline, it may signal that the company's business has started to slow down.

▶ The pace of change makes it tough to predict what software companies will look like in the future. For this reason, it's best to look for a big discount to intrinsic value before buying.

20

Hardware

THE FORCES THAT make it difficult for companies to create economic moats are magnified many times over in the hardware sector. Although other areas of the economy are also subject to product cycles, price competition, and technological advances, these factors are particularly intense in industries such as semiconductors, PCs, and telecom equipment. In fact, the environment in the hardware sector makes it fiendishly difficult to build a sustainable competitive advantage because technological advances and price competition mean that the lion's share of hardware's benefits are passed to consumers, not the company creating the products.

Investors often spend a great amount of time delving into the vast trove of technical minutiae for hardware companies. But we don't believe the hardware sector behaves by its own special rules. Rather, the sector's dynamics simply elevate the importance of the factors we look for in every area: solid management, a focused economic model, and an economic moat.

Jeremy Lopez, Fritz Kaegi, and Joseph Beaulieu with Pat Dorsey.

What Drives the Hardware Industry

Even the casual computer user has experienced the factors that drive the technology hardware sector. If you've ever bought a PC, you already know that it won't take long before one twice as fast is on sale for less money. While the average PC cost more than $1,500 in 1998 (perhaps with a Pentium II chip), you could buy a much more powerful PC for less than $1,000 in 2002.

But it's worth remembering that even goods that deliver a big benefit to society—either through increased productivity or leisure—won't necessarily make their producers a cent, much less make money for investors. In the next section, we'll examine how the most successful companies in the industry manage to keep their heads above water and how you can identify them.

The hardware sector's central driver is its ability to innovate so that computing power increases while costs of that computing power rapidly decrease. The basis for this driver is Moore's Law, which was initially observed by Intel founder Gordon Moore in 1965. (Moore's Law basically states that the number of transistors that can be crammed on to a given piece of semiconductor real estate doubles every couple of years.) Conversely, chip industry economics means that the price per transistor also tends to plummet at an inverse rate. In other words, although technology innovation happens at a rapid pace, most of the benefits of that innovation are passed on to the end user.

Moore's Law helps spread the productivity and leisure benefits of information technology (IT) to an ever-wider range of activities. Decades ago, IT processing power (software plus hardware) was economically feasible for only a few large military, communications, and financial applications. Today, however, the average person can afford a very powerful computer, and IT has countless applications in everyday life—whether in snapping photos with digital cameras or scribbling notes in a Palm Pilot.

A second driver is that advanced economies are progressively shifting their focus away from manufacturing and toward services. Most manufacturing can be performed in countries with lower costs, but services are much more difficult to import. By the very nature of their activity, services require a much larger investment in IT (directly or indirectly) than manufacturing. Both Moore's Law and the changing structure of advanced economies suggest that demand for hardware should grow faster than the economy as a whole.

A third driver is the symbiotic relationship between technology hardware and software. After all, if a person didn't have software applications to run on his or her PC, what good would it be? Advances in hardware allow software to do more in less time, whereas new software applications help create demand for more capable hardware.

Hardware Industry Dynamics

Cyclicality is the crucial dynamic in this industry, given that corporate spending on technology makes up the bulk of total hardware sales. In times of financial prosperity, firms often have the flexibility and financial health to allocate capital to IT spending. But when times are tough and business dries up, companies tend to conserve cash and try to squeeze more out of what they already have (see Figure 20.1).

Consumer spending on technology is even more prone to dramatic swings. The average person doesn't buy gadgets out of necessity, but rather for entertainment or convenience. A person who earns minimum wage or loses a job usually doesn't *need* to buy a new digital camera or Palm Pilot. During

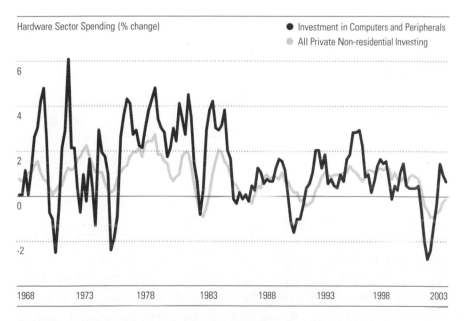

Figure 20.1 Spending on technology is even more cyclical than the overall business spending.
Source: Morningstar, Inc.

Common Investing Pitfall: Betting on New Technology

In hindsight, it's also easy to recognize the success stories—the Ciscos and Intels of the world. But for every Intel, there is an AMD, which has had very limited success competing against Intel. Or worse yet, there are companies such as Transmeta and Cyrix, which barely had a chance to get both feet on the ground. The story is the same in the PC industry. It's easy to see the success stories of Dell and Hewlett-Packard. But recalling the litany of companies that fell victim to competition over the years is like watching a VH1 "Behind the Music" special on one-hit wonders. Remember Commodore, AST, or Packard Bell? No? Exactly. Competition even derailed the efforts of stalwart companies that pioneered the PC, such as IBM, which stopped selling desktop PCs in retail stores in 1999, and Texas Instruments, which exited the PC industry altogether.

recessions, therefore, factors such as high unemployment and low consumer confidence often deter consumers from spending their money on high-tech goods and services.

A key implication of this cyclicality is that demand is volatile even over short periods of time—and this volatility worsens the farther away each firm is from the final consumer.

For example, most economic upturns catch hardware vendors and their component suppliers off guard. Because equipment makers want to get as much product out the door as quickly as possible, they often place orders for more orders than they really need. Prices and unit demand rise: boom. Chipmakers, thinking that their demand will be sustainable over a long period, spend billions on additional capacity. All is well until the demand bubble bursts and customers stop ordering. Chipmakers are usually caught with excess capacity and chip prices drop rapidly.

Economic Moats in Hardware

Given the hype that often surrounds them, evaluating the economic moats of technology companies can be especially tricky. During the tech-spending boom of the late 1990s, the rising tide was lifting all boats, and it was easy to mistakenly assume that some companies had a sustainable economic moat when in fact they were merely at the right place at the right time.

Common Investing Pitfall: Inventory Bubbles

Technology hardware companies often face periods of inventory imbalances. Either they accumulate too much inventory, or customers suddenly demand more than they can readily supply. The risk is that products or components that sit on the shelf for a long time may have to be heavily discounted, or worse, not sold at all. We saw the fall-out of this soon after the Internet bubble burst in 2000, with Cisco and a host of others writing down billions in excess inventories.

A warning sign for investors is when a company's inventories grow faster than sales over several quarters. But even this trend is obscured by the complexity of the supply chain. Component suppliers, distributors, and contract manufacturers all hold inventories above and beyond the levels of the end product producer, even though the end producer often bears the economic risk for these inventories. Look in the "risk factors" section of the 10-K for these kinds of situations. If they exist, the inventory number shown on the balance sheet may not reflect true inventory.

Although most hardware companies differentiate themselves based on technological advantages, technology itself does not constitute an economic moat. Companies with superior technology can easily fail, just as companies selling commonplace technology can dominate an industry. Companies such as Intel and IBM have built moats not with superior technology, but by focusing on distribution channels, dominant scale, and broad product lines. What's more, technological leads in the hardware industry rarely last long. For example, Palm pioneered the personal digital assistant (PDA), but it wasn't long before Sony, Microsoft, Handspring, and others all eroded the firm's early lead.

Economic moats in hardware are rare, but let's look at some real-world examples of the four key economic moats we covered in Chapter 3.

High Customer Switching Costs

Telecom equipment manufacturers such as Nortel, Alcatel, and Lucent each benefit from high switching costs. Their bread-and-butter customers, former telephone monopolies such as AT&T and the Baby Bells, are extremely conservative in their buying habits. They run extremely large, complicated networks, and they have to be 100 percent sure that any new equipment they purchase will work seamlessly within their existing networks and that their suppliers are actually going to be around 10 years from now. When buying habits are that entrenched, it is unlikely that buyers will risk their jobs by changing vendors.

Low-Cost Producer

Dell Computer is a textbook example of a company that benefits from being the low-cost producer. Part of the reason Dell has been able to achieve this status is the scale it enjoys as one of the world's largest PC vendors. Because the company purchases chips and disk drives in large volumes, it has leverage with its suppliers and can, therefore, negotiate lower component costs than its rivals. Dell is also the low-cost producer because its direct sales method is far more efficient than those used by rivals such as Hewlett-Packard. Dell not only avoids paying commissions to a third-party reseller when it sells products via the Web, but also can keep close reins on its inventories and receivables. This means Dell can pass on lower component costs to its customers more quickly than its competitors can.

A more obscure advantage that Dell gets from being the largest PC vendor is that its suppliers are more willing to wait longer for payment and are more flexible about getting Dell the components it needs exactly when it wants them. This allows Dell to keep its inventories low. Combined with Dell's direct sales business model, this creates a big competitive advantage because Dell receives payment for its products before it has to pay suppliers. With little money being tied up in inventories, Dell has low working capital requirements, thus allowing it to generate enormous returns on invested capital.

Intangible Assets

Companies often use intangible assets, such as patents and brand names, to help sustain excess returns on investment over an extended period of time. Chip companies Linear Technology and Maxim Integrated Products don't often get recognition for their performance, but both of these chipmakers have outstanding fundamental track records because of their intangible assets. Over the 10 years ending in 2002, for example, Linear posted an average sales growth of 16 percent, average gross margins of more than 70 percent, and average returns on invested capital of 90 percent—all far better than the industry average. Maxim posted similar results.

What is it that has allowed both firms to sustain such great results over an extended period of time? A key part of these companies' success is due to their niche as suppliers of high-performance analog semiconductors. Analog chips are highly proprietary, so they lack direct substitutes, and the engineers who design these products face a set of unique design challenges. Digital circuits process information in binary fashion—that is, 1's and 0's—whereas analog chips primarily process real-world signals—that is, temperature, pressure, weight, and sound. Firms like Linear, which have years of R&D and manufacturing experience, have a strong competitive edge over newer rivals. A scarcity of analog engineers also widens these companies' economic moats because it would take a long time for a potential rival to hire an experienced staff to compete with Linear and Maxim. The knowledge and experience of these firms' engineers is an intangible asset that allows both of them to earn significant excess profits.

The Network Effect

In the hardware industry, network effects can arise because hardware often needs (1) to operate with other hardware and (2) to be maintained by people. The more a certain product becomes prevalent, the more other hardware needs to take heed of the product's characteristics and the more people (and time) are invested in learning to operate the product.

Cisco Systems' routers are a great example. Routers are basically advanced computers that decide the best route for a piece of data to follow in a network. No matter who manufactures them, routers have to know how to "talk" to each other. A router that cannot communicate with the rest of a network is useless. This means that router manufacturers have to use a common set of standards when developing new products. Therefore, the vendor with the largest market share is in the driver's seat when it comes to development and evolution of standards.

Cisco was the first company to make a wide market in routers in the 1980s and gradually built code and protocols to function with more and more generations of its equipment. When others tried to enter the market, they began to realize how difficult it was to get routers to consistently operate with one another. Cisco's only other major rival in the market for high-end routers, Juniper Networks, was eventually successful, but it took over a year's time and an expensive effort to hire Cisco programmers who knew where the proverbial bodies were buried.

By becoming the de facto standard for routers, Cisco also created a secondary network effect. It takes time and extensive training to become familiar with the language and instructions for maintaining Cisco routers. The engineers who maintain networks take courses and often earn certifications to aid in their work. By being first, Cisco was able to become the first certification that most network engineers obtain—and often that's good enough, because these are the folks who also decide which equipment to buy. Cisco certification and training essentially helped to sustain the pervasiveness of Cisco's hardware.

Hallmarks of Success for Hardware Companies

Here's what to look for when you're analyzing hardware companies.

Durable Market Share and Consistent Profitability

Strong profitability and a stable market share are evidence that a wide economic moat is allowing the firm to fend off competition. Linear and Maxim, two of the chip companies discussed earlier in this chapter, are great examples of this. Although neither one dominates the high-performance analog chip market, they've both maintained steady shares of this fast-growing market, and they've both generated solid returns on capital during even the worst chip industry downturns.

Keen Operational and Marketing Focus

These companies don't spend much time in businesses where they don't have a particular advantage or those that don't fit their strategic focus. Cisco is a classic example on the operations end. Cisco has made the strategic decision not to manufacture things itself; instead, it permits contract manufacturers to make its routers. This focus helps guide decisions about what new kinds of products it wants to make, how it wants to budget its money, or whether it wants to buy a business. Likewise, Dell benefits from this discipline in terms of marketing. It knows that its business is built on directly marketed, built-to-order hardware with an upfront payment model. Ideas or projects that deviate from this model simply don't get funded. Watch out when you see hardware companies dabbling in areas that seem to be outside their strengths.

Flexible Economics

The best hardware businesses have revenues and costs with well-matched timing and levels that can be changed fairly easily. Because demand is so unpredictable and volatile in the hardware industry, the more flexibility companies have over costs and capacity, the less risk they face. Good signs of flexible economics include outsourced manufacturing, low capital expenditure requirements, and workforces that are on variable schedules or in low-cost markets.

But even in situations where the company does its own manufacturing, you can look for signs of flexibility or less risk. One of the reasons we think Jabil Circuit is the best contract manufacturing company is that it's the most disciplined in specifying that customers commit to a certain level of volume. Locking in volumes means that Jabil can make more informed decisions about what costs it takes on. Other contract manufacturers are more likely to accept any deal that comes their way, even though it makes revenues more unpredictable and creates the risk of building expensive capacity and overhead that revenues won't be able to cover.

Investor's Checklist: Hardware

▶ Information technology is an increasingly important source of productivity in advanced economies. In 2002, IT accounted for nearly 50 percent of total U.S. investment in capital equipment, up from 20 percent three decades ago.

▶ Technology innovation means that hardware firms can offer more computing power at an increasingly cheap price; thus, IT can be applied to more and more tasks.

▶ Because of rapid innovation, technology hardware companies tend to generate rapid revenue and earnings growth.

▶ At the same time, competitive rivalry is often strong in tech hardware. Moreover, demand for technology hardware is very cyclical.

▶ Technology, by itself, does not constitute a sustainable competitive advantage. Hardware companies that develop economic moats are more likely to succeed over the long term than companies that rely on a lead in technology.

► Examples of moats among technology hardware firms include low-cost producer (Dell), intangible assets (Linear and Maxim), switching costs (Nortel and Lucent), and network effect (Cisco).

► A company with a sustainable competitive advantage should be able to effectively fend off its rivals and maintain significant market share and/or sustain above-average margins over an extended period of time.

21

Media

COMPANIES IN THE media sector offer ample opportunity for great long-term investment gains, but successful investing in media stocks takes more than picking the next hit TV show, predicting the next blockbuster movie, or finding a new best-selling book. Of the two dozen media companies that we follow, all but one have some economic moat associated with their business, and five have wide economic moats. The key is identifying those companies that will continue to grow consistently and churn out lots of cash for years to come. Many companies in this sector benefit from competitive advantages, such as economies of scale and monopolies, which make it easier to sustain excess profits for long periods of time.

Overall, the media sector has been rewarding over the past decade. According to Morningstar's historical performance data, the annualized total return of the media sector was just above 16 percent between 1993 and 2002, whereas the S&P 500 returned a little more than 9 percent per year during the same period. The strong showing in the media sector can be traced to a number of factors, but we'd argue that the two most important factors are

Jonathan Schrader and T. K. MacKay with Pat Dorsey.

appealing economics and significant competitive advantages. Differentiated and focused products give media firms competitive advantages within unique geographic areas (newspapers and radio stations) or niche categories (technical books). Dominating one of these areas normally translates into strong and sustainable free cash flow for these firms.

Media is a broad term, so it helps to divide the sector into three different groups: publishing, broadcast and cable television, and entertainment production. After we review the general economics of the media sector, we'll dig into the specific characteristics of each of these three areas.

How Media Companies Make Money

Media companies generate cash by producing or delivering a message to the public. The message, or content, can take several shapes, including video, audio, or print. The method of delivery is even more varied. Television, movies, radio, the Internet, books, magazines, and newspapers are the most popular means of distributing content, but there is no real limit on how a message can be delivered.

User Fees

Business models in the media sector can vary significantly depending on a firm's primary source of revenue. We're all familiar with one-time fees that we must dole out to see the current hit movie, read the best-selling novel, or buy the hot new CD. Film studios such as Disney and Paramount, publishers such as Simon & Schuster, and music labels such as Warner Bros. are highly dependent on these one-time fees.

Companies that rely on one-time user fees sometimes suffer volatile cash flows because they're heavily affected by the success of numerous individual products, such as newly released films or novels. While having a string of hits can result in a bonanza for the firm, the converse is also true: Several flops in a row can lead to disaster. This uncertainty can make it difficult to forecast future cash flows.

Because the success of this type of business model relies so much on big hits, the big-name stars tend to reap most of the profits, which makes for narrow profit margins for the company. For example, a top box office draw such as Tom Cruise commands $25 million for each film plus a cut of the box office receipts, and studios are willing to pay this staggering amount because Cruise is an actor who attracts both interest and dollars. The situation is similar in the music and book publishing businesses, where successful bands and authors often gain a big slice of the profit pie.

Subscriptions

Subscription-based businesses (such as cable and magazine publishing) are generally more attractive than one-time user fee businesses because subscription revenue tends to be predictable, which makes forecasting and planning easier and reduces the risk of the business. There is another advantage to subscriptions: Subscribers pay upfront for services that are delivered at a later date. Although firms can't recognize this cash as revenue right away, they can use it to fund operations, thus decreasing their reliance on outside sources of capital.

Because of the ongoing customer relationship and the cash received upfront, subscription-based business models usually are less sensitive to economic downturns. Moreover, there aren't many other businesses in which you can get paid upfront before you have to spend the money to create a product.

Many subscription-based companies have heavy fixed costs, giving them significant operating leverage. Thus, swings in revenue have a large impact on earnings and cash flow. Magazines and newspapers are good examples. The most important variable cost for these businesses is paper; other than this expense, almost all other costs are fixed, regardless of the number of magazines or newspapers that are sold. Thus, as these companies gain market share, profit margins should increase dramatically.

The exception is in companies that need to make large, ongoing capital expenditures to stay in business, such as those found in the cable and satellite-television industries. For these companies, system upgrades often eat up the vast majority of operating cash flow, with little cash left over. In theory, once these upgrades are complete, these businesses should throw off loads of cash. The problem is that the upgrade cycles seem to be never ending.

Advertising Revenue

Companies with advertising-based models can enjoy decent profit margins, which are often enhanced by high operating leverage. The reason for the high operating leverage is that most of the cost in an advertising-based model is fixed. The cost of generating programming for a television or radio station or hiring a news staff for a newspaper or magazine publisher doesn't go up with more subscribers. However, advertising revenue streams can be somewhat volatile—advertising is one of the first costs that company executives cut when the economy turns south, which is why advertising revenue growth tends to move with the business cycle. Media firms that rely on advertising are fairly sensitive to the state of the overall economy.

Economic Moats in Media

Media firms enjoy a number of competitive advantages that help them generate consistent free cash flows, with economies of scale, monopolies, and unique intangible assets being the most prevalent. Economies of scale are especially important in publishing and broadcasting, whereas monopolies come into play in the cable and newspaper industries. Unique intangible assets such as licenses, trademarks, copyrights, and brand names are important across the sector.

Monopolies, Licenses, and Deregulation

Look for companies that hold monopolies in their respective markets. These companies tend to have very strong pricing power and excellent economic profits. One of the bigger risks with monopoly power is running afoul of regulators, but as long as this relationship is well maintained, media firms with monopolies should be able to increase profits for a long time. And as profits grow, so should the value of the firm. Newspapers are the best example of this competitive advantage—few cities can support more than one large daily newspaper, which means the incumbent paper in any market generally has a relatively easy time holding off competitors.

Licenses can also lead to strong profits, especially in the television and radio broadcasting industries. Even though the participants in these industries don't necessarily enjoy monopolies, it's tough for new entrants to break into the field. That's because a business must have a license from the Federal Communications Commission (FCC) to transmit a signal in a certain geographic area. Licenses protect media firms from competition because only a limited number are available in a given market. In addition, the FCC usually renews licenses for the maximum eight years for the broadcasters who own them.

Deregulation is also a key factor. Thanks to deregulation, companies such as Fox, Viacom, and Clear Channel have been able to buy multiple stations in the same market. This serves to further reduce competition and typically leads to higher profits because these companies can spread out their programming and back-office costs. Some parts of the media sector remain at least partially regulated; any future deregulation could spur even greater consolidation and, consequently, higher profitability. Newspaper, television, and radio companies with strong balance sheets would be the most likely to benefit from any future deregulation.

Publishing Profits

The publishing area is a great place to find investment opportunities. Many of these companies, especially those in the newspaper business, enjoy monopolies in their respective markets. This monopoly status gives these companies the power to raise prices without the fear of large customer defections. The companies can then use these monopoly profits to move into other geographical areas, expanding their profits and increasing the value of their shareholders' investments. At the beginning of 2003, for example, Gannett published almost 100 newspapers, and as the company's 2002 annual report stated, "most of the company's newspapers do not have daily newspaper competitors that are published in the same city." Gannett's free cash flow margins (free cash flow as a percentage of revenue) are consistently above 10 percent, which makes it an extremely profitable business.

Companies in the publishing business also benefit from economies of scale, which result from the largely fixed nature of the industry's cost structure. As more volume gets pushed through an existing production system, profitability will naturally improve. The publishing business relies on very expensive production equipment (presses) and distribution systems. It doesn't cost much more to print 1,000,001 books than it does to print 1,000,000, so most of the revenue from that 1,000,001st book turns into profit, increasing the company's profit margins.

Because of this characteristic, most of the companies in the publishing arena are continually looking for acquisitions that will increase market share and boost profitability. The larger the scale, the greater the advantage over rivals. Companies that build scale in a conservative and deliberate manner tend to do very well over time, both in terms of profits and shareholder returns. McGraw-Hill, for example, has become one of the most important players in the publishing industry by slowly acquiring competitors, boosting profitability along the way. Between 1993 and 2002, McGraw-Hill acquired about 60 companies, most of them in publishing. During this same period, the company's operating profit margins increased from 16 percent to 21 percent, largely due to a huge jump in the profitability of the publishing business from 7 percent to 14 percent.

Broadcasting and Cable

Companies in the radio, broadcast television, and cable television industries also tend to have some solid competitive advantages, which often lead to above-average and sustainable profitability.

Previously, we discussed one of the most important: FCC licenses. Recent deregulation in the broadcasting industry has led to less competition, as companies own more broadcasting licenses in a specific market. Although some media activists argue that this is a negative development for consumers, there's no denying that increased concentration has been a positive development for the broadcasting companies that have chosen to take advantage of it.

Broadcasters make most of their money from advertising, which they attract by offering programming to as many people as possible. The programming that broadcasters show is one of the their largest expenses, and the cost is basically fixed—a broadcaster pays essentially the same amount for the right to show a program regardless of how large its audience is. However, the bigger the audience, the more ad dollars the broadcaster attracts, which means that incremental increases in advertising revenue fall directly to the bottom line as profit. And as broadcasters increase the number of stations they own—which deregulation has spurred—much of the fixed programming costs can be shared among the stations.

Overall, broadcasters have a solid business model, so investing in this segment is mostly a matter of valuation. If you can buy these companies at a discount to fair value, your long-term returns should be pretty good. Make sure, though, that the company isn't involved in another business that could potentially be a drain on cash.

Finally, there's the cable industry, which has typically enjoyed the luxury of having a monopoly in many of its individual markets. Rarely have two cable companies operated in the same market, which has historically allowed for aggressive increases in monthly fees. Over the past decade, though, satellite television providers have become a force in this market, forcing cable companies to step up their efforts to differentiate themselves through high-speed Internet access. The cable companies have also tried to compete on price in some areas.

These two moves have led to diminished profitability and free cash flow. Indeed, the cable industry is highly capital intensive, which has traditionally led to paltry free cash flow. That's a big negative. Although many cable companies claim that capital spending will finally start declining as they upgrade their networks to offer advanced services such as digital cable, video-on-demand, and high-speed Internet service, they've been making similar claims for years. With the relatively recent advent of satellite as a competitive force, the cable industry may have less attractive economics in the future.

Investing in the Entertainment Industry

As we mentioned previously, companies that depend on one-time user fees often have some shortcomings, including cash flow volatility and low profit margins. In the film, television, and music industries, which largely revolve around creating and distributing feature films, television series, and musical recordings, there aren't many positives to offset these negative characteristics. We're generally not fans of companies that operate in this area of the media industry.

On the positive side, most of these businesses have large libraries of films, television series, and music recordings, which are legally protected from duplication. Revenue from these libraries tends to be lucrative because the costs of production were recorded in the past. Also, the barriers to entry are high in most cases. It takes a significant amount of capital to develop television series on an ongoing basis and create multiple feature films.

Barriers to entry in distribution also have historically been high. Over the past few years, though, the Internet has weakened this barrier, especially in the music industry. Peer-to-peer distribution of recorded music has meant hundreds of millions of dollars in lost profits for the large record labels. As

Common Investing Pitfall: Buying Big Hits

Some investors look to invest in a media company that is responsible for the current blockbuster movie, the latest triple-platinum album, or the hot new television drama. Don't! In all likelihood, the current hit is making up for the flops that no one even heard about. The media conglomerates that bring these hits to market are big, complex entities that need much more than one hit to spur long-term profit growth. Unless they are trading at deep discounts to their intrinsic value (which is not always easy to determine because of volatile cash flows), we'd look elsewhere.

technology improves, this phenomenon will become an increasingly significant problem for the movie industry as well.

Few entertainment-oriented media firms have been able to create significant shareholder value over the long haul. For example, movie and entertainment firms within the S&P 500 returned only about 3 percent annually during the 1990s, whereas publishing and printing posted average annual gains that were many times higher. The reasons for the long-term underperformance of entertainment firms is clear: The bulk of the industry's profits go to high-profile actors, directors, and executives, which leaves little for shareholders. Moreover, this is at heart a hit-driven business, and consistently predicting consumer tastes is difficult to do over a long time period.

Hallmarks of Success in the Media Sector

In general, the media sector is a great hunting ground for solid investment ideas. Here's how to find the best of the best.

Free Cash Flow

In general, we like to see free cash flow margins of at least 8 percent to 10 percent in this sector. This level of free cash flow indicates one of three things: the company has a product or service for which customers are willing to pay a premium, the company is very efficient, or the business doesn't require much ongoing capital investment. All three are attractive characteristics.

As always, use this as a general rule rather than an absolute one—if a media firm is investing heavily in a new business with excellent prospects, a low current free cash flow margin may be a worthwhile tradeoff for the prospect of faster growth in the future. For example, the Washington Post Company showed weak free cash flow in the late 1990s as the company plowed money into its Kaplan educational services business and into some of its cable properties. In 2002, this investment started to pay off, as free cash flow soared to 13 percent of sales. If you're looking at a media company with temporarily weak free cash flow, just make sure that the core business is still performing well and that you trust management's choice of where the excess cash is being invested.

Sensible Acquisitions

One of the characteristics that we look for in a media investment is a willingness and ability to make sensible acquisitions that lead to greater scale. We emphasize the word *sensible* because we're talking about smaller acquisitions that can be easily integrated into the acquiring firm's operations. We're not interested in companies that are always chasing after large firms in the quest to build an empire. And we also don't want to invest in media firms that are looking to make a transforming merger. More often than not, these fail. The AOL/Time Warner merger is the classic example of a case where promised merger synergy didn't pay off for investors.

In general, beware of companies that are attempting large mergers predicated on *synergies* between unrelated businesses. These "growth" acquisitions rarely succeed, especially in the media business. Look for firms that stick to their knitting and make digestible purchases. Publishers Reed Elsevier and McGraw-Hill are examples of firms that have historically made many small, profitable acquisitions over time.

In addition, look for companies that can fund these acquisitions without causing too much damage to their balance sheets. This is another reason that strong free cash flow is so important, because the cash can be used to make acquisitions, reducing the need for outside capital.

Risks in the Media Sector

- ▶ Many media companies are still controlled by the families of the founders, which can sometimes lead to corporate decisions that are more beneficial to the family than outside shareholders. No matter how well-managed these firms may be, shareholders as a group simply do not have the voting power that they would with a company whose majority ownership resided with the public.

▶ Media firms are also known for extensive cross-ownership holdings, which means that another media firm could potentially have much more say in your company's decision making than individual shareholders. For example, Liberty Media owns chunks of many different companies, as does News Corp.

▶ The entertainment industry revolves around glitz, glamour, and cash, and sometimes industry executives get caught up in the scene. Be wary of firms that reward executives with ridiculous compensation packages and excessive perks. Michael Eisner at Disney comes to mind immediately, and the old guard at Warner Brothers was known for this, as well.

Investor's Checklist: Media

▶ Look for media companies that consistently generate strong free cash flow. We like to see free cash flow margins around 10 percent.

▶ Seek out companies that have high market share in their primary markets—monopolies are often great for profits. Licenses, especially in broadcasting, also serve to reduce competition and keep profit margins high.

▶ Seek out companies with a history of well-executed acquisitions that have been followed by higher margins.

▶ A strong balance sheet enables media companies to make selective acquisitions without increasing the risk for shareholders or diluting the shareholders' ownership stake.

▶ Look for candid management teams, a history of sensible acquisitions, and either conservative reinvestment of shareholders' capital or the return of capital to shareholders through dividends and stock repurchases.

▶ Don't chase hits. Buying a stock because there's a lot of buzz about a hit movie or TV show rarely pays off.

22

Telecom

THE TELECOM SECTOR is filled with the kinds of companies we love to hate: They earn mediocre (and declining) returns on capital, economic moats are nonexistent or deteriorating, their future depends on the whims of regulators, and they constantly spend boatloads of money just to stay in place. Even companies that once boasted wide moats, such as those that control the local phone network, face increasing competition from newer players, such as cable and wireless networks. Because telecom is fraught with risk, we typically look for a large margin of safety before considering any telecom stock.

Before 1984, AT&T was one of the world's most reliable companies. Ma Bell essentially ruled the U.S. telecom world, owning the vast majority of networks needed to provide local and long-distance phone service. The majority of households and businesses had little choice but to send cash monthly, making AT&T shares the proverbial safe haven stock for a generation of investors.

But following years of legal challenges, the industry was split in two and divided between those that connect cities to one another and those that

Michael Hodel and Todd Bernier with Pat Dorsey.

provide network access to customers. AT&T retained the intercity, or long-distance, business, which has been increasingly competitive ever since.

The access, or local, side of the business maintained its virtual monopoly for several years because regulators decided this business was too capital-intensive for competitors to have much influence and, thus, still in need of strict oversight. AT&T's local phone networks were divided among seven companies, now known as the regional Bells. These firms have consolidated over the years, leaving the majority of the nation's local phone network in the hands of four companies: Verizon, SBC, BellSouth, and Qwest.

Local phone companies, by virtue of their control of a major access point to the phone network, retain some remnant of the old Ma Bell moat because most customers have access to only one or two fixed-line networks. But even this area of the industry has come under increasing attack as changing regulations and improving technology have fostered tremendous growth in the number of ways people connect with one another. The local phone companies are being threatened by wireless carriers and cable companies on the technological front and by their fixed-line peers on the regulatory front.

Unfortunately, the firms trying to dethrone traditional phone companies are no more attractive as investments. The wireless industry, for example, is excruciatingly competitive, with little opportunity to develop a moat. Wireless phone service is a commodity—a minute of airtime on one carrier's network is virtually identical to that on another's. There are six nationwide carriers slugging it out, while several smaller regional players carve up areas not reached by more than one or two of the majors. The presence of several large carriers has resulted in near-ubiquitous network coverage. Roughly 95 percent of the total U.S. population has access to three or more different wireless carriers, and 80 percent has access to at least five carriers. With little opportunity to differentiate their services, the wireless carriers have resorted to cutthroat pricing: The price per minute of wireless airtime has fallen more than 80 percent over the past decade.

Wireless isn't the only threat to the Baby Bells' fixed-line business. Twelve years after the breakup of AT&T, the federal government decided the time was ripe to deregulate the local business and open it up to competition. Congress passed the Telecom Act of 1996, forcing the regional Bells to lease access to their networks to competitors at discounted rates. Would-be local phone competitors, known as competitive local exchange carriers (CLECs), can build a "virtual" network to service their customers. AT&T and WorldCom/MCI have been the biggest users of this regulation, adding local service options to their traditional long-distance phone services. The result has been a loss of revenue for the Bells and greater control of customers for their competitors.

As a result of this regulatory framework, the Bells and the competitors endlessly debate which elements should be made available and how prices should be determined. State regulators individually set line-lease rates under the direction of the FCC, which directly impacts the attractiveness of each state to competitors.

However, there has been one consolation for the Bells in all this regulatory upheaval: Once a state is deemed open to competition, the local phone giants are allowed to enter the long-distance business. This isn't a huge moneymaking proposition for the Bells, but it can help them hold on to customers.

The desire of lawmakers and regulators to push fixed-line phone service to a more competitive model has further eroded the competitive advantage of the local phone companies. For example, the number of phone lines in service declined in 2001 and 2002 for the first time since the Great Depression. With local phone service generating the vast majority of the regional Bells' cash flow, declining lines in service threatens to diminish their ability to invest in network upgrades and pay out dividends.

One niche of the industry hasn't been as affected by regulatory changes—rural carriers such as Citizens, Alltel, and CenturyTel, which primarily operate local phone networks in areas ignored by the old AT&T. These less densely populated areas don't attract the level of competition seen in urban markets. Moreover, the rural carriers actually benefit from regulations, receiving subsidies to help cover the relatively higher cost of serving these areas and in many cases guaranteeing a certain return on investment.

A favorable regulatory environment, combined with the natural benefits of owning the only local phone network in town, gives these companies the strongest competitive advantages in the industry. These companies will never earn huge excess returns on capital, though, so we still wouldn't consider the moats wide. In addition, their financial stability means that the shares of rural carriers rarely trade at cheap valuations.

Telecom Economics

Building and maintaining a telecom network, whether fixed line or wireless, is an extremely expensive endeavor that requires truckloads of upfront capital. This requirement provides a substantial barrier to entry and usually protects the established players. To raise capital, a new entrant must have a great story to tell investors. The emergence of the Internet, the opening of local networks to competition, and rapid wireless growth during the 1990s gave numerous new players the yarns they needed, which is why the usual barrier provided by huge capital requirements came crumbling down as investors lined up to grab a piece of the action.

While the effects of this massive infusion of capital are still being felt in the industry, ongoing capital needs have sunk many new entrants. Even a mature telecom firm will need to invest significant capital to maintain its network, meet changing customer demands, and respond to competitive pressures. The Bells, for example, spent nearly 30 percent of their annual sales on new equipment during the late 1990s, though a spending rate of 20 percent of sales is more normal. Despite sluggish growth and sharp reductions in capital budgets in telecom, the Bells still spent a combined $30 billion on their networks in 2002.

Common Investing Pitfall: Revenues Here Today but Not Tomorrow

Telecom companies can't expect to recoup the cost of a piece of equipment in any one year, so developing recurring revenue streams is important to earning a sustained return on investment. Sometimes firms seek out nonrecurring sources of revenue to boost growth and profits, but these sources of revenue can't be counted on to deliver future returns. Qwest, for example, spent billions building a long-distance network and reported fantastic revenue growth as the network was placed into service. Unfortunately, much of this growth came from one-time sales of basic network capacity, rather than ongoing service contracts. Revenue from these capacity sales, which generated high margins, was booked upfront, giving the appearance of rapid growth. Once demand for this type of capacity dried up, revenues began to fall and margins shrank. The firm was left with a business too small to support its debt load and was forced to sell off assets.

Because of the enormous cost to build a network, carriers typically have very low ratios of sales to assets (asset turnover ratios). Even a mature carrier typically generates only around $1 per year in sales for each $1 of assets invested. But building a business of ample size to support interest payments and ongoing capital needs is very important. Because fixed costs are so high, it's imperative for carriers to have enough customers over which to spread the costs.

Squeezing as much profit from the sale as possible is also crucial. While size again plays a role here, a telecom company must be able to send bills, provide customer service, maintain the network, and market services efficiently. A mature company, either fixed line or wireless, should expect to earn operating margins between 20 percent and 30 percent. Short of this level, it is extremely difficult to earn an attractive return on invested capital, given the slow pace at which assets turn over.

With so many companies raising money and building networks in the late-1990s, the volume of business needed to support all these huge investments never materialized. Nowhere was this more true than in the long-distance industry. New entrants such as Williams Communications and 360 Networks filed for bankruptcy despite rapid revenue growth because they were never able to generate the level of sales needed to justify the enormous expense of building the networks, nor were they able to boost margins anywhere near the levels needed to support their borrowing costs. Investors eventually refused to give

Common Investing Pitfall: Margins Falling? Look Out Below

Telecom investors must pay particularly close attention to profitability. One measure commonly used in the industry is earnings before interest, taxes, depreciation, and amortization (EBITDA), which gives a sense of how well operations are generating cash to support capital spending needs and debt service. To calculate EBITDA, take operating income and add back depreciation and amortization expenses. Falling EBITDA margins may be an early indicator of competitive pressures or operating inefficiencies. EBITDA is a blunt tool, however, and should not be mistaken for operating cash flow, as reported on the cash flow statement. Focusing on EBITDA can obscure problems such as growing accounts receivable that would be readily apparent on the cash flow statement.

the firms more cash when they figured out that the field was so crowded that the odds of success were low.

Economic Moats in Telecom

Long-distance carriers have extremely small or, in most cases, no economic moats. There are numerous long-distance networks connecting most major cities, and competition remains fierce. Companies with strong reputations—notably AT&T—enjoy a small competitive advantage as business customers look for carriers with financial strength. And because switching long-distance service can be a hassle for a large business, companies with large customer bases often have the upper hand. But the threat of competition has made it tough for long-distance carriers to raise prices. A rebound in demand could bring some pricing power, but given the industry's state, we doubt long-distance firms will earn returns on invested capital equal to their cost of capital, which makes it unlikely that they'll be worthwhile investments.

Compared with the long-distance carriers, local phone companies enjoy stronger competitive advantages, though we'd still put them in the narrow-moat category. These firms still control the majority of the local phone market and are able to earn very healthy margins on this service and generate enormous cash flows. As customers' demands on the local network grow, the ability to keep networks up to snuff should increasingly offer an advantage. Regional

Common Investing Pitfall: Bloated Debt Loads

Companies that take on massive debt in the hopes of building a large business are extremely risky. Mature firms that take on massive debt to expand their businesses are similarly asking for trouble. AT&T borrowed heavily to fund its push into the cable TV business. Left with a huge debt load and large capital spending needs to upgrade its networks, the firm ended up selling the cable business for far less than the purchase price. The regional Bells, particularly SBC, have been selling assets to pay down debt and reduce the risk that declining revenues could cause financial distress. A measure of indebtedness commonly used in the telecom industry is debt divided by EBITDA; a ratio much higher than 3 should be approached with caution.

Bells might upgrade their networks to offer a whole host of services, including TV, numerous phone lines, and high-speed Internet access, over a single connection. However, the Bells have traditionally moved very slowly into new technologies, and basing an investment decision on the basis of the Bells' potential for new product offerings requires a large margin of safety.

Rural carriers (sometimes called *rural local exchange carriers* [RLECs]) benefit from a relative dearth of competition. The RLEC advantage can be seen in the number of phone lines lost—about 1 percent on average during 2002 versus about 5 percent at the Bells. Moreover, most of the decline in phone lines caused by a weak economy has been offset by an increase in broadband Internet-access services. Rural firms have also maintained even stronger margins than their Bell brethren, with operating margins exceeding 30 percent in many cases, which is roughly 10 percentage points higher than the Bells.

Wireless, meanwhile, is almost a textbook case of perfect competition, with near-zero pricing power and easily substituted services. Only Nextel has been able to meaningfully differentiate itself with its unique Direct Connect feature, and even that competitive advantage will likely be eroded away in the future as competing carriers promote similar push-to-talk capabilities. With that small—and likely temporary—exception, no wireless carrier has a sustainable competitive advantage. To most consumers, the carriers look identical from the outside, which forces them to compete almost solely on price. Like the long-distance industry, wireless providers offer calling plans that are nearly indistinguishable: a finite number of minutes during peak calling hours and plenty of cheap—or free—airtime on nights and weekends.

Without economic moats, investment opportunities are few and far between in the wireless industry. The six national carriers continue to scratch and claw for new subscribers, hoping to benefit from better economies of scale. But subscriber growth is weakening as the industry rapidly matures, intensifying cutthroat price competition.

Hallmarks of Success in Telecom

With the long-distance business struggling to survive in its current form, firms with local operations typically make the best investments. Even on the local side, though, growth is typically very slow and the future regulatory and competitive environments are uncertain. In addition, bankrupt telecom firms, including WilTel and WorldCom/MCI, are starting to emerge with much smaller debt loads, making them more able competitors. To weather what storms may come, it is vital that a telecom carrier be in strong financial health.

Even with a dearth of growth opportunities today, capital spending needs in the industry are likely to remain high. That makes a strong balance sheet and solid free cash flows even more important. Healthy and consistent margins are also vital to success because they mean that free cash flow can remain strong. Rural carriers, such as CenturyTel and Citizens Communications, have maintained the best margins in the business. Regional Bell SBC has seen its margins pressured, but as of mid-2003, the firm had arguably the best balance sheet in the entire sector, with cash flow covering interest expenses about a phenomenal 12 times over.

The biggest difficulty for wireless carriers will be differentiating their services. For a while, Nextel Communications escaped the commodity trap by offering a unique product and by focusing on business customers, who tend to be heavy cell phone users and who are more concerned with quality and features than price. As a result, Nextel has had the highest average revenue per user and lowest rate of customer disconnection among nationwide wireless carriers. Nextel's strong performance was due primarily to its Direct Connect feature; because until recently, no other operator offered a similar push-to-talk service. Unlike rivals that competed mainly on price, Nextel wasn't forced to promote cheap calling plans to win customers. However, rival carriers have already rolled out services similar to Direct Connect, which will substantially erode Nextel's competitive advantage. As in most industries, technological superiority can keep the competition at bay only for so long.

Conclusion

The telecom sector of tomorrow will look nothing like the sector of the past. Competition is far greater throughout the industry and economic moats exceedingly difficult to come by. The future of the industry will be shaped by regulatory and technological changes, which means that financial strength and flexibility are likely to be what separate successful firms from unsuccessful ones over the next few years.

Investor's Checklist: Telecom

► Shifting regulations and new technologies have made the telecom industry far more competitive. Though some areas are more stable than others, look for a wide margin of safety to any estimate of value before investing.

► Telecom is a capital-intensive business. Having the resources to maintain and improve the network is critical to success.

► Telecom is high fixed-cost business. Keeping an eye on margins is very important.

► Watching debt is also important. Firms can easily overextend themselves as they build networks.

► The price of wireless airtime is plummeting. Carriers continue to compete primarily on price.

23

Consumer Goods

IF YOU'RE LOOKING for some new investments, consider checking your refrigerator, broom closet, or bathroom drawers for plenty of consumer goods ideas. Many familiar household brands, such as Tide laundry detergent and Oreo cookies, are made and marketed by companies that can be worthwhile investments. These companies can be good defensive havens during economic downturns because people still use toothpaste and shampoo even if the economy is in recession.

The consumer goods sector is composed of industries such as food, beverages, household and personal products, and tobacco. Like anything large and old, it also moves slowly: Consumer goods markets typically grow no faster than the gross domestic product and sometimes even slower. (Domestic beer consumption has been growing at a paltry 1 percent annually, for example.) Despite this slow growth, consumer goods stocks tend to be solidly profitable, fairly steady performers, which can make them excellent long-term holdings for your portfolio.

Debbie Wang and Carl Sibilski with Pat Dorsey.

How Companies Make Money in Consumer Goods

Consumer goods companies generate profits the old-fashioned way: They make products and sell them to customers, usually supermarkets, mass merchandisers, warehouse clubs, and convenience stores. Kimberly-Clark makes diapers and sells them to Wal-Mart and Target. Smucker's cooks up jams, jellies, and preserves for Safeway and Kroger.

The beverage companies offer a slight twist in the equation by selling their products to their distribution channels: bottlers and beer distributors. For example, nonalcoholic beverage firms such as Coca-Cola and PepsiCo manufacture the concentrate and syrups for the finished soft drink products and sell them to their bottling partners, who mix them with other ingredients, package the finished product, and sell it to retailers. In the case of alcoholic beverage manufacturers, companies such as Coors and Allied Domecq make and market spirits that are then sold to their network of distributors, who resell and distribute the finished product to the retail customers.

Key Strategies for Growth

Because of their maturity, most consumer goods industries have already gone through periods of consolidation. As a result, most industries are dominated by a handful of huge companies that account for the majority of category volume and sales. For instance, in 2002 Anheuser-Busch, Coors, and SAB Miller, the three largest brewers, controlled more than an 80 percent share of the domestic beer market. Wrigley owns close to a 60 percent share of the domestic gum market.

The sector's maturity also means that firms have only a few basic strategies for growth available, and most companies rely on some combination of these approaches.

Steal Market Share from Competitors, Usually by Introducing New Products

This approach can be a fairly costly proposition. PepsiCo (which makes both beverages and salty snacks through its Frito-Lay division) spends an estimated $1.6 million, on average, to develop a new product. That doesn't include the cost of consumer marketing support and sales allowances to retailers critical to the success of any product in the crowded consumer markets. Since PepsiCo launched 456 new products between 1998 and 2000 (many of which were in the Frito-Lay division), the bill for all that innovation was a whopping $729.6 million.

Unfortunately, the road to a successful new product is littered with many failures. Of the thousands of new food and beverage products launched in 2002, only 130 generated more than $7.5 million in revenue during the first year.[1] If sales of a new product do not show signs of positive momentum in the initial 6- to 12-month trial-building window, store managers are often reluctant to leave it sitting on valuable shelf or freezer space.

For companies as large as many of the consumer goods firms, even a strong lineup of new products can lift revenue by only so much—usually just slightly above GDP growth. Thus, on the whole, leading firms post no better than mid-single-digit revenue growth.

Grow by Acquiring Other Consumer Goods Companies

Some companies opt to enter new product lines by purchasing other firms. For example, Gillette acquired the Duracell Battery business from Ralston-Purina in 1996 to establish a presence in that market. In 2001, PepsiCo purchased Quaker Oats primarily for the Gatorade franchise. Unfortunately, this strategy can be hit-or-miss, depending on the companies and price paid. Following some initial bumps in the first year after acquiring Quaker, PepsiCo managed to iron out problems and was ahead of schedule to achieve operating efficiencies in mid-2003. There was a high level of synergy in this particular case because both companies were mainly in the food and beverage businesses. The distribution systems and retail customers of the firms overlapped, and both companies were strong marketing organizations.

On the other hand, Gillette's acquisitions have not turned out as well. Gillette is famous for dominating the razor and blades market with nearly an 80 percent share. It's also a category where product innovation leads to increased pricing power, as customers paid 15 percent to 20 percent more for each successive product from Sensor to Mach3 and Mach3 Turbo. Gillette thought it could apply this model to batteries when it bought Duracell in the mid-1990s. However, several important characteristics of the battery business were

---

[1] *Times and Trends,* IRI, Inc., p. 6 (May 2003).

not the same, and Gillette's Duracell battery unit failed to produce the intended results. The Duracell division performed poorly from 1999 through 2002 and took up a great deal of top management's time.

Reduce Operating Costs

Because top-line growth for consumer goods companies, whether it comes from innovation or acquisition, is not much greater than that of the overall economy, earnings growth must rely more on a streamlined operating structure than on revenue growth. With large retail customers such as Wal-Mart dedicated to keeping inventories tight and prices low, a consumer product maker must have a lean and flexible manufacturing structure. One tried and true method of becoming leaner has been large-scale restructuring, which is often very expensive in the short term, but can pay off in longer term efficiency gains. Procter & Gamble, Gillette, and Coca-Cola have consolidated manufacturing and laid off thousands of workers to reduce administrative overlap. It is not uncommon to see these companies undergo a substantial restructuring over a five-year period. For instance, Colgate-Palmolive racked up more than $500 million in restructuring charges in 1995, nearly wiping out net income for that year.

Starting in the mid-1990s, for example, Colgate-Palmolive took several steps to increase earnings by cutting costs as opposed to boosting top-line sales. This increased its operating profit margin from about 14 percent in 1997 to 20 percent in 2002. And the company thinks it can squeeze out more costs by using SAP's integrated enterprise software to search out inefficiencies in international supply lines and operations.

The danger of this strategy is that the firm focuses too much on trying to achieve earnings growth through cost-cutting and too little on looking for ways to grow or at least maintain revenue growth. Colgate, which has an innovative history, has lagged Procter & Gamble's new product launches in recent years, and Colgate has also launched less effective products that suggest a "me too" approach to product innovation. Moreover, Colgate's focus on cost-cutting led to reduced media exposure at a time when Procter & Gamble increased spending because P&G saw low advertising prices as a good opportunity to invest in its brands. Cost-cutting is important, but it can damage long-term business performance when taken to extremes.

Sell Products Overseas

Facing slow top-line growth in a mature domestic market, many consumer product makers have chosen to expand internationally to supplement domestic growth. This allows a firm such as Procter & Gamble to launch Pepto-Bismol in Argentina and Brazil, where stomach remedy medication is still a new category experiencing accelerated growth, even though the same product has been in the United States for more than a century and hasn't seen double-digit growth in years. Consequently, many multinational consumer products companies derive a substantial portion of their business from overseas. For example, Coca-Cola gets 77 percent of its operating profits from abroad, and Avon earns 65 percent of the same from overseas markets.

Selling overseas can lead to currency risk (for example, if the euro declines relative to the dollar, reported sales for U.S.–based companies selling products in Europe will suffer). But most consumer goods companies use hedging instruments to mitigate this risk.

What's Not to Like in Consumer Products

At first blush, it might seem a company that has racked up a century-old track record, survived industry consolidation, and can look forward to steady (albeit relatively slow) growth would be a good investment choice. However, investors should also carefully consider some of the potential risks that consumer goods companies face before jumping into a stock.

Increasing Power of Retailers

As Wal-Mart has increasingly come to dominate the U.S. retail landscape, consumer goods manufacturers have lost much of the pricing power they used to enjoy. Everybody wants their products in Wal-Mart's stores, which means that Wal-Mart is able to dictate many of the terms under which it will sell these products, including price. Other retailers have also been squeezed. They've had to improve their cost structures to compete with Wal-Mart, but haven't been able to pass along price increases to consumers.

Litigation Risk

This risk mainly concerns tobacco companies, but it's a big one. After successfully defending itself in court for years, Big Tobacco has suffered a number of legal setbacks, which raise the specter of a bankrupting settlement down the road. The industry has lost a handful of lawsuits filed by individual smokers and been ordered to pay amounts it can easily afford; the fear is that such outcomes will unleash a torrent of costly new lawsuits.

Foreign Currency Exchange Risk

As mentioned earlier, many consumer goods companies conduct a considerable portion of their businesses internationally. For these multinational firms, a strong American dollar can depress overseas sales. American goods become relatively more expensive in foreign markets, and foreign currencies are translated back into fewer dollars for the same number of euros, pesos, or yen (because it takes more foreign currency to buy a strong dollar). On the other hand, when the American dollar weakens, the process works in reverse, and these companies can benefit from an earnings tailwind.

Expensive Stocks

Strong brands and reliable financial performance mean that well-known consumer goods stocks often sell at premium valuations. Especially during periods of weak economic growth, consumer goods shares may be bid up to levels that imply unrealistic growth rates. Remember that growth will always be a challenge for these mature companies, and approach them with the same valuation discipline that you would any other stock.

Economic Moats in Consumer Goods

Despite the risks, one very attractive feature of this competitive sector is that consumer goods companies often have wide economic moats or at least a narrow moat—and this helps preserve pricing power.

Economies of Scale

The handful of giant firms that dominate each consumer goods industry enjoy such massive economies of scale that it would be virtually impossible for a small new entrant to catch up. Anheuser-Busch, the largest brewer in the world with 12 breweries in the United States, consistently invests in upgrading its plants with new technology that makes it possible to brew and package vast quantities of beer at lower costs.

Case Study: Chewing up the Gum Market

The Wm. Wrigley Jr. Company is a good example of a strong and steady consumer goods company that has built up a wide economic moat over many years. Its Juicy Fruit and Spearmint brands have been around since the early 1890s, and it's been the world's leading gum maker for most of the past century. It has a nearly 60 percent share of the U.S. gum market, more than twice as much as second-place Cadbury Schweppes. Its products are sold in 140 countries, making it number one in world gum market share as well. This dominance has helped Wrigley to become very profitable, with net margins around 15 percent and returns on equity consistently in the 25 percent to 30 percent range.

Wrigley has traditionally been a very conservative company, but it has also done a good job of innovating to stay ahead of the competition. When Bill Wrigley Jr. took over the company in 1999, increased competition from breath mints such as Altoids had threatened Wrigley's market dominance and caused its growth to slow. The youthful CEO stepped up the pace of innovation in response to these threats, and Wrigley has come out with a plethora of new products focused on breath freshening, including Orbit gum and Eclipse Flash Strips. Sales grew at a strong double-digit rate in 2001 and 2002, and the company is looking more energized than it has been in years.

Big, Powerful Brands

Consumer product companies often invest a great deal of time and money in building up strong relationships with end users in the form of brands. Brands were born in the late nineteenth century when these consumer goods firms sought to provide consumers with assurance of consistent quality—so you'd know what you were getting for your money. Since then, brands have evolved into a host of meanings, including expressions of aspiration and affirmation of self-image. By imbuing a product with a meaning that extends beyond functionality, companies create a higher level of perceived value.

For instance, for years, Heinz Ketchup built up a reputation for top quality—the thickest, richest ketchup that premier food establishments preferred. By the time Hunt's Ketchup finally matched the Heinz product with comparable thickness, it was too late. Hunt's didn't gain much share, and Heinz continued to command a premium price over its competition.

Not all brands are created equal, however. Simply putting a trade-marked name or logo on the product does not turn it into a brand that can command higher prices or greater share. The most powerful brands have nurtured a connection with consumers that can last for years, creating a significant challenge to new entrants, but this takes time, money, and marketing savvy.

Distribution Channels and Relationships

The networks that manufacturers use to get their products on to shelves in the stores can be another competitive advantage that is very difficult for competitors to replicate. For instance, beverage manufacturers rely on their wholesalers and bottlers, each of whom retains exclusive control over a certain geographic area, to cultivate close relationships with retail customers.

Large beverage firms can leverage extensive distribution networks that span the map. On the other hand, a small company often finds it prohibitively expensive to build a network from scratch and must rely on creating an alliance with a large firm to distribute its products, usually by demonstrating how its products can fill a niche in the bigger firm's product portfolio. For example, 7Up did not have its own bottler network that provided full coverage of the entire United States and had agreed that some of PepsiCo's bottlers would distribute 7Up products. This approach, however, leaves the smaller firm at the mercy of the large one. Once PepsiCo formulated its own lemon-lime soft drink to compete with 7Up, PepsiCo applied pressure to make its bottlers drop 7Up and distribute Sierra Mist instead.

Exclusivity is another aspect of the distribution system that can enhance a company's economic moat. For instance, 60 percent of Anheuser-Busch's distributors sell only Anheuser-Busch products. This arrangement leads to wholesalers with focus and incentive to sell harder. In contrast, the vast majority of Coors and Miller distributors are not exclusive and, thus, sell a variety of competitive brands. This means that a Miller wholesaler who tries to sell Miller products unsuccessfully can pull a competitive product out of his portfolio to sell instead. In the end, Miller's distribution system may not be as dedicated to Miller products as Anheuser-Busch's are to its products.

Hallmarks of Success in Consumer Goods

When you're checking out a potential investment in consumer goods, look for several characteristics.

Market Share

Companies with brands that hold dominant market share are likely to stay in that position because shifts in share tend to be fairly small from year to year. Thus, whoever is number one right now is likely to remain in that position over the next several years (barring any truly extraordinary events such as product contamination). For example, Tide has been the market leader in laundry detergent for about as long as anyone can remember. It's not always easy to find specific numbers on market share, but you'll sometimes see this discussed in the company's annual report. General business publications such as *BusinessWeek* and *The Wall Street Journal* can also be good sources of information on market share data.

Free Cash Flow

In this mature sector, the name of the game is tons of free cash flow—cash flow from operations minus capital expenditures. Unlike a young company that must invest most of its cash flow back into its business to expand and meet growing demand, many of these century-old consumer goods firms are in the enviable position of raking in cash. Additionally, because many of these firms enjoy wide economic moats, you can expect them to continue earning returns on capital in excess of their cost of capital for some time to come.

With so much cash remaining, these firms often dispense a portion of it to shareholders in the form of dividends and share buybacks. Checking on just how much of a firm's free cash flow is transferred to shareholders can be a good way to assess whether management really has the shareholder's interests at heart. For example, Coca-Cola's track record suggests the firm doesn't hoard cash and prefers to return it to shareholders. Of the immense $3.5 billion in free cash flow generated in 2002, Coca-Cola paid out nearly $2 billion in dividends. You can look through the statement of cash flows to find out how much a firm has paid out in dividends to shareholders.

Belief in Brand Building

The strength of management's belief in brand building provides the foundation for the birth and cultivation of powerful brands. Firms that consistently invest in their brands through advertising and other non-sales-oriented communication will build up a brand's perceived value. For instance, Anheuser-Busch has consistently spent ad dollars to support its key brands in high profile (and expensive) media events such as the Superbowl. This helped lead to seven consecutive years of domestic market share gains between 1996 and 2002.

However, watch out for firms that cut corners by consistently putting their brands on sale. Although this may initially lead to increased volume and higher market share, it hurts profitability, and, in the end, constant discounting erodes even the most premium of brands. If a company is falling into a pattern of cutting its advertising spending every few quarters when sales aren't going so well, the firm may be more concerned with meeting earnings expectations for the next quarter than building a brand that will still be strong 5 or 10 years from now.

Innovation

Considering the degree to which consumer goods firms rely on a steady stream of new products to stay competitive, a firm's level of innovation is critical. Keep an eye on which companies consistently introduce new products that are successful in the marketplace and which ones always seem to come out first with a new product. Further, it's important to distinguish between whether a firm is simply introducing a new flavor of an existing product, such as Keebler launching another version of Pecan Sandies cookies, or if the company is rolling out a revolutionary product that didn't exist before but which meets some consumer demand, such as Procter & Gamble's Dryel home dry cleaning system or Listerine's PocketPak breath-freshening strips.

Companies often prefer the former type of new product because it's less risky and consumers are already familiar with the mother brand. However, innovation by line extension raises a greater possibility that consumers will substitute the new flavor for the flavor they usually buy, which reduces the opportunity for a larger boost in incremental sales. At a minimum, the product must offer some sort of substantial advantage over existing substitutes. In addition, the company must successfully educate consumers on the benefit of this product and familiarize the potential audience with the new brand. There are advantages to both approaches—neither one is wholly superior. The best bet is a company that does a good job of launching a string of single hits with line extensions and occasionally hitting a homerun with a revolutionary new product.

Conclusion

Though this mature sector is unlikely to grow much faster than the general economy, relatively static demand for food, beverage, household, and tobacco products can add up to fairly steady performance. Further, many of these companies enjoy the benefits of wide economic moats—sustainable competitive advantages that translate into pricing power and profitability. Though companies in this sector may seem staid and boring, without the thrills of more risky categories, we like the stability, relatively low risk, and, importantly, generous free cash flows.

Investor's Checklist: Consumer Goods

▶ Find companies that enjoy the cost advantages of manufacturing on a larger scale than most other competitors. One related issue is whether the firm holds dominant market share in its categories.

▶ Look for the firms that consistently launch successful new products—all the better if the firm is first to market with these innovations.

▶ Check to see if the company is supporting its brands with consistent advertising. If the firm constantly promotes its products with sale prices, it's depleting brand equity and just milking the brand for shorter-term gain.

▶ Examine how well the firm is handling operating costs. Occasional restructuring can help squeeze out efficiency gains and lower costs, but if the firm is regularly incurring restructuring costs and relying solely on this cost-cutting tactic to boost its business, tread carefully.

▶ Because these mature firms generate so much free cash flow, it's important to make sure management is using it wisely. How much of the cash is turned over to shareholders in the form of dividends or share repurchase agreements?

▶ Keep in mind that investors may bid up a consumer goods stock during economic downturns, making the shares pricey relative to its fair value. Look for buying opportunities when shares trade with a 20 percent to 30 percent margin of safety.

24

Industrial Materials

THE INDUSTRIAL MATERIALS sector includes a broad array of companies, which make everything from the fragrances used in soap to bulldozers and heat-seeking missiles. The general business model is simple: Industrial materials companies buy raw materials and facilities to produce the inputs and machinery that other firms use to meet their customers' expected demand for goods. This is a classic Old Economy sector, because it consists of companies that make tangible goods.

We divide industrial materials into two groups: (1) basic materials such as commodity steel, aluminum, and chemicals and (2) value-added goods such as electrical equipment, heavy machinery, and some specialty chemicals. The primary difference is that commodity producers have little or no influence on the price of the products they produce. Makers of value-added industrial materials, on the other hand, may be specialized enough or improve a customer's business enough for the manufacturer to share part of that benefit in the form of a premium price (the *value added*).

Nicolas Owens, Sanjay Ayer, Michael Hodel, and Brian Lund with Pat Dorsey.

From an investor's point of view, these companies are the classics. All the traditional rules apply, and textbook indicators such as asset turnover and debt ratios can reveal a great deal about the companies' performance and financial health. But, because most of these companies supply industry with inputs, they are closely tied to the economic cycle and most firms' shares tend to create little value for buy-and-hold investors between cycle peaks. To make matters worse, many segments of the industrial economy—particularly commodity producers—face destructive long-term price deflation. Low-cost competition and excess capacity can easily overwhelm any growth in demand, which is often in the low single digits at best.

The Problem with Cyclicality

The general idea of the business cycle is that economic growth is followed by an eventual slowdown or a recession, then a recovery, and then the cycle starts anew. When the economy is firing on all cylinders, profits and competition intensify, as does demand for economic inputs such as raw materials and labor, which in turn become more expensive. In this environment, interest rates often rise because capital is in demand. Increased operating expenses, interest payments, and competition erode businesses' margins and lead businesses to reduce capacity. As businesses cut costs by investing less and laying off employees, inventories and prices decline. Once the excesses are worked off, expansion can begin again.

Industrial materials producers often find themselves at the business end of the economic cycle bullwhip, where a small motion at the other end can cause great gyrations (see Figure 24.1). For example, when the economy is expanding, International Paper (IP) can harvest wood and run its mills at full capacity because demand for its lumber and bleach-board paper runs high. When the companies that use IP's products see consumer spending dry up, however, orders plunge. Thus, IP's sales magnify changes in GDP growth: When GDP growth rises, IP's revenue growth soars; when GDP growth contracts, IP's sales growth plummets.

Makers of big-ticket industrial items, such as Caterpillar, which manufactures off-road trucks and earthmoving equipment, or Deere & Co., a maker of agricultural equipment, can face another kind of cyclicality. These producers operate in mature industries, where demand is driven largely by replacement of

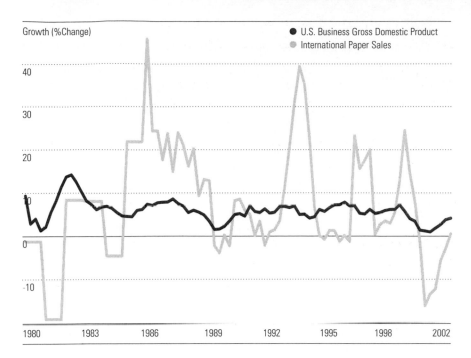

Growth (%Change)   ● U.S. Business Gross Domestic Product
                                          ● International Paper Sales

Figure 24.1   When the economy moves a little, cyclical firms such as International Paper move a great deal. *Source:* Morningstar, Inc.

older products. In times of economic uncertainty, builders and farmers can exercise some discretion in the timing of purchases. If their own prospects are uncertain, they can delay buying new equipment until better times.

Dealing with demand swings can be very difficult for industrial companies. Most of them manufacture commodity products with little pricing power, so profit margins tend to be very slim—around 5 percent on average. Companies compensate by dedicating themselves to achieving high production volumes, which often lead to high fixed costs for manufacturing facilities. When demand is strong, they can make a solid profit because incremental production beyond the breakeven point comes with a high margin (a concept known as *operating leverage*). But when demand falls, fixed costs become a burden that can threaten the very survival of a business. Only the most efficient producer, with the lowest fixed cost base in relation to sales volume, can remain profitable through a downturn.

Industrial materials companies also use product diversification to diminish the impact of cyclicality. Many, including Caterpillar and General Electric (GE), have large financing subsidiaries that make loans to their corporate customers as well as consumers. In many cases, these subsidiaries account for a large proportion of the corporation's value. To temper their overall cyclicality, companies can also diversify among products tied to longer and shorter cycles within the economy. For example, to complement its long-cycle businesses such as power generating equipment, GE has also diversified into short-cycle businesses, such as the NBC television network. General Electric also generates recurring revenue and profits from specialized servicing contracts for complex equipment that is already in use, such as jet engines used by airlines.

Economic Moats in Basic Materials

Economic moats in the basic materials industries tend to be very few and far between. The main reason is that many of these companies produce commodities; thus, they would create a sustainable competitive advantage only by becoming the low-cost producer.

Some commodity-producing companies achieve the low-cost position by increasing their size and attaining economies of scale. Consequently, their production cost per unit is less than the competition's. In the aluminum industry, Alcoa has this economic moat; in steel, it's mini-mill producer Nucor. In the low-cost position, a company can charge less than its competitors and still remain profitable. Ideally, this should drive inefficient producers from the market and strengthen the industry over the long term.

The reality is, however, much more complicated on several fronts. In many industries, such as steel, domestic firms have come under increasing pressure from foreign producers with much lower cost structures. Their cost advantage usually comes from some combination of three sources: the sheer benefit of geography, government subsidies and tariffs, or low labor costs.

After a long decline, culminating in the 1990s, America's steel industry experienced strong competition from foreign firms with much lower costs that churned out more steel than demand warranted, thus driving U.S. steel prices to bargain-basement levels. In recent years, more than 30 domestic producers, with relatively costly labor contracts and crushing pension and retirement obligations, could not operate profitably with steel prices at such low levels and filed for bankruptcy protection. Though the specifics and intensity of these problems vary from industry to industry, other commodity industries are dealing with similar issues.

Although basic materials industries do have significant barriers to entry—the cost of constructing a new steel, aluminum, or paper processing plant is steep—stiff price competition makes for mediocre profits at best. As mentioned previously, basic materials producers are highly susceptible to performance swings tied to the overall economic environment. The high cost of equipment and low profit margins mean these industries typically have poor returns on capital, so there's little to attract investment capital and even less to attract investors.

Economic Moats in Industrial Materials

A handful of industrial materials firms meet the definition of what Peter Lynch called "great companies in lousy industries" and boast sustainable or growing competitive advantages.[1] Such advantages can counteract the problems identified in this chapter—cyclicality, fierce price competition, slim profit margins, pernicious replacement cycles—because they provide companies with a more stable customer base, more predictable sales and profits, and the ability to reinvest their capital more efficiently.

Some wide-moat companies in the industrial materials sector include specialty chemical manufacturer 3M, mail meter maker Pitney Bowes, auto parts supplier Gentex, defense contractor General Dynamics (GD), and manufacturing powerhouse United Technologies Corp (UTX), which makes everything from Otis elevators and Carrier air conditioners to jet engines and the Black Hawk helicopter. Gentex and 3M have numerous patents that protect their markets from some competition. General Dynamics and UTX operate in very concentrated industries, and their customers would have a difficult time switching to another product even if there were more choices. Pitney Bowes enjoys both types of advantages: patented technology and high customer switching costs.

---

[1] Peter Lynch with John Rothchild, *Beating the Street* (New York: Fireside, 1994).

Technology and Competitive Advantage

Because industrial materials markets are mature, there's often fierce competition on price and little room for top-line growth. Thus, the only way to improve the bottom line and reward investors is to develop a differentiated product or to find ways to spend less making the same product. By definition, a commodity product cannot be differentiated, so for many industrial materials producers, investments in efficiency are the only way they can improve the bottom line. In the industrial materials sector, about as much technology spending is devoted to improving manufacturing efficiency as it is to developing new products.

Investments in technology can lead to lower-cost production methods. In the steel industry, for instance, the electric arc furnace allows Nucor to recycle scrap steel and produce finished steel products at a much lower cost than the big integrated producers, such as U.S. Steel, whose operations rely on an expensive, capital-intensive blast furnace to make steel. Nucor's technology provides the most important competitive advantage available in a mature commodity industry: the low-cost position. The proof is in the pudding: Between 1999 and 2001, Nucor's average gross margin was nearly double that of U.S. Steel (11.8 percent compared with 6.5 percent). Nucor is also working on developing a processing technique that will lower the costs of producing thin-rolled products. If the production technique is commercially feasible on a large scale, it will provide Nucor with yet another cost advantage over its rivals. Those rivals must spend on efficiency improvements just to keep the competitive gap with Nucor from widening, although they have little hope of attaining its level of efficiency.

While companies funnel a great deal of the money they spend on technology into efficiency improvements, product innovation can still play a crucial role in the industry. For chemical companies, new products represent one of the only available sources of internal sales growth. Chemicals giant DuPont earned its stripes by developing a series of groundbreaking chemical fibers between 1930 and 1960, including Nylon, Polyester, and Lycra. Diversified powerhouse 3M has excelled at incremental innovation, using slow-growth products such as tapes and adhesives in the production of high-tech applications such as mobile phones.

Some companies have found ways to take a raw commodity and alter it so it adds value for their customers. Such value-added products command a premium to what a basic commodity would fetch. For example, between 1993 and 2002, Alcoa spent more than $1.5 billion on R&D to develop new processes that make aluminum stronger, lighter, and better suited to more applications. These producers occupy a valuable niche within the basic materials sector.

Innovation is hardly an easy task, though. A whopping 80 percent of R&D projects result in economic failure. DuPont, for example, has maintained its industry-leading research and development budget, but blockbuster products have been noticeably absent in recent years. Furthermore, its former flagship products have become commoditized as low-cost Asian producers entered the market, stole share, and crimped the profitability of DuPont's textile business.

DuPont's experience highlights the problem with innovation in a slow-growth industry. Companies can pour millions of dollars into new product research, only for competitors to copy their technology without bearing the same development costs. This reduces the incentive for companies to innovate, and they have responded by focusing their R&D spending on process technology and manufacturing efficiency—to improve what they already do—rather than invent new products.

Another problem with innovation presents companies with a tricky balancing act. In the appliance industry, for example, companies must spruce up their products with new and convenient features to induce customers to buy new appliances before their existing ones wear out. Companies also need to create reliable, long-lasting products to maintain their brand image and customer loyalty. Better, innovative products can lengthen the replacement cycle and reduce product turnover and raise the hurdle rate of innovation. The better the product, the more difficult it becomes to get customers to replace that product.

Because of intense competition, especially in the basic materials sector, the main beneficiaries of research in industrial materials are the users of the new and cheaper products that result, not necessarily the investors who financed their development.

Hallmarks of Success in Industrial Materials

Efficiency is what it's all about in the industrial sector. Firms that can squeeze more from their assets than their competitors can are the ones that tend to make great long-term investments. As mentioned previously, competition only increases the pressure to lower costs, so the ideal situation is for a company to produce goods at the lowest cost in its industry.

Why? In general, there are two paths to strong profitability (as measured by return on invested capital, our favorite measure): high profit margins or high asset utilization. In the industrial sector, stiff competition often results in limited pricing power and, consequently, relatively meager profit margins. Thus, the firms with the best share performance are often those that generate the most revenue from their assets:

▶ Total asset turnover (TATO), one of the more commonly used measures of efficiency, is an easy ratio to calculate: annual sales divided by total assets (either average or year-end assets; just be consistent). To calculate average total assets, add the current year's total asset balance and the previous year's balance, and divide the sum by two. A general rule of thumb is that a TATO ratio above 1.0 is pretty good for an industrial firm. Such a ratio means that for every dollar that the company has invested in assets, it, in turn, generates at least one dollar in revenue every year.

Two wide-moat companies in this sector, United Technologies and General Dynamics, are also two of the most efficient operators. UTX managed a TATO of 1.0 in 2002, while GD's ratio was even higher at 1.2.

▶ Another popular efficiency metric is fixed asset turnover (FATO), which corresponds to total annual sales divided by net fixed assets. Net fixed assets are listed on the balance sheet, usually as "property, plant, & equipment, net of accumulated depreciation" or "net PP&E," for short. The FATO ratio is even more telling than TATO for industrial firms because industrials are so dependent on tangible assets such as factories and equipment to produce goods and generate revenue. Importantly, the FATO ratio excludes the impact of goodwill, which often weighs on the TATO of highly acquisitive industrial concerns.

Again, our wide-moat companies, UTX and GD, are standouts. UTX's FATO in 2002 came in at 6.2, while GD's was 7.7. Not surprisingly,

some of the no-moat commodity businesses that we cover are less successful when it comes to this metric—Dow's FATO ratio is regularly around
2.0, while DuPont's is even lower, typically below 2.0.

We mentioned that those industrials that are the most efficient tend
to have the best performance. Looking at just the four companies discussed in this section, we see that UTX and GD experienced the best
performance between 1992 and 2002, with total annualized returns (including reinvested dividends) of 17.2 percent and 31.5 percent, respectively. The total annualized returns of the less efficient firms, Dow and
DuPont, are not nearly as good, 9 percent and 8.7 percent, respectively.
Granted, there are numerous factors affecting long-run share performance, but we'd argue that efficiency is one of the most important factors
for industrial firms.

▶ Besides fixed assets, an industrial company needs to manage working capital efficiently. Looking at trends in how many days' worth of inventory
are sitting in warehouses or how many days its takes to collect customer
receivables can reveal a great deal about a firm's operations. If, for example, inventories are rising rapidly, a company may be producing more
than it can sell merely to keep its factories busy. This could sock the company with goods that will have to be sold at rock-bottom prices down the
road. Similarly, a jump in the number of days' sales outstanding (measured as accounts receivable divided by sales revenue and multiplied by
365 days per year) could indicate that the firm is pushing inventory on its
customers to mask a slowdown in demand.

▶ Most industrial firms have high operating leverage, which means that
most of their costs are fixed regardless of volume and sales levels. If they
can move more volume through the system by selling more of their
products, profit margins should increase because sales should rise while
costs stay about the same. However, operating leverage can cut both
ways. For example, truck maker Navistar saw operating margins climb
steadily to nearly 10 percent during the late 1990s as sales built to a cyclical peak. But in 2001, as demand for new trucks waned and Navistar's
revenue dropped by about 20 percent, operating margins plunged to 2
percent. With sales weak again the following year, Navistar found itself
deeply in the red.

▶ Another indicator of success is a regular and growing dividend payment to shareholders. In the industrial materials sector, dividends never really went out of style. Dividends not only represent a strong indicator of a company's financial health (its ability to make profits and pay them to investors), but also temper the volatility associated with these cyclical stocks. Regular cash payments in the form of dividends reward investors for holding stocks whose prices fluctuate depending on the pace of the overall economy.

Highly efficient operations are key to sustainable long-term profitability in the industrial sector. Look for firms that excel in getting more from their assets than competitors do, and you'll be on your way to finding the best industrial firms in which to invest.

Red Flags

Because industrial companies typically operate very traditional business models, spotting trouble often requires the use of only a few basic accounting measures. That's not to say there aren't complex companies in the sector—you need look no further than GE's opaque financials to see how complex an industrial firm can become. By and large, though, industrials are pretty straightforward, and looking at a few key measures can keep investors out of trouble. Keep an eye on three areas: too much debt, excessive pension obligations, and poorly planned acquisitions.

Debt

Because sales and profits can swing wildly, a heavily indebted firm may not be able to meet its obligations during a downturn. A useful indicator of a firm's debt level is the debt-to-capital ratio. This ratio expresses the amount of the company's obligations to creditors as a fraction of the firm's book value. The higher the ratio, the more risky the firm's financial position. Debt to capital can be calculated simply by dividing the company's total debt (long term and short term) in the liabilities section of the balance sheet by total assets, also on the balance sheet. Some companies adjust the denominator by excluding current liabilities, which gives a better long-term measure of the company's leverage. In general, a ratio above 40 percent adds some risk to the company, and we consider a ratio above 70 percent a bad sign.

Deere illustrates the importance of keeping debt levels reasonable. The maker of agricultural equipment survived the severe farm recession of the early 1980s, whereas financially weaker rivals, such as International Harvester (the predecessor of Navistar), weren't so lucky. Deere's debt-to-capital ratio (excluding current liabilities in the denominator) rose from 30 percent in 1979 to 53 percent at its peak in 1982, whereas International Harvester's ratio rose from 41 percent to 86 percent in the same period. International Harvester's ensuing bankruptcy and reorganization was one of the most spectacular business failures in history, and by 1985, Harvester had exited the farm equipment business altogether. Today, Deere enjoys a strong brand reputation while most of its competitors are amalgamations of restructured firms pulled out of bankruptcy.

Pensions

Pension and other postretirement benefit obligations also bear watching because many of the companies in this sector have been around for decades and have offered defined benefits to employees for years. (For a refresher on how pension plans affect a company, see Chapter 8.)

Let's use Deere as an example again. Because of increasing health care costs and revised actuarial assumptions, at the end of 2002, Deere's projected pension benefit obligation stood at $6.8 billion, up from $6.4 billion in 2001, while negative returns in its pension portfolio left the value of its plan assets at $5 billion, down from $5.9 billion at the end of 2001. The plan was thus underfunded by $1.8 billion. Accounting guidelines required Deere to increase the pension and postretirement benefit liability on its books at the end of 2002, which decreased shareholders' equity by about $1 billion.

Because a company can spread out the payments it will make to prop up a pension plan, an underfunded pension plan is not necessarily a red flag in and of itself. However, investors should use their judgment when evaluating how big a drain the deficit could be on a company when its pension plan is underfunded by a large amount, as in Deere's case.

Acquisitions

Industrial firms tend to grow slowly, so some are tempted to use acquisitions as a means to expand. Acquisitions give companies a great opportunity to destroy shareholder value, as well as an opportunity to take big upfront integration charges that can serve to inflate future margins.

For example, in early 2001, Dow Chemical acquired commodity chemical producer Union Carbide, adding $2 billion to the firm's debt load and increasing the number of its shares outstanding by one-third to close the deal. Subsequent events proved that the increased risk from the additional debt load and the dilution of shareholders' interests was not worth the trouble of integrating another firm's operations. Union Carbide's commodity product lines increased Dow's vulnerability to the economic cycle while the merger distracted management during a prolonged downturn.

The U.S. and global economies remained sluggish after the merger, but instead of focusing on positioning Dow for an eventual recovery, management was distracted by merging the companies and tackling Union Carbide's massive asbestos liability, which culminated in the CEO's removal by Dow's board in late 2002. Three years after the merger was announced, the company's stock price languished 38 percent below its level at the time of the announcement, about the same performance as the S&P 500 in the same time frame.

Chasing Market Share

Many firms benefit from positive operating leverage and then chase market share by cutting prices sharply, but we're wary of investing in industrial firms that are more focused on market share than profitability because they often confuse market share gains with efficiency. Many firms highlight their market share gains because the increased volume from these gains can lead to higher profit margins, but unless their TATO and FATO actually improve, market share itself is not an indicator of efficiency.

Freightliner, a unit of DaimlerChrysler, serves as a classic example. In the mid-1990s, as the maker of big-rig trucks was facing strong competition from rivals Volvo, Navistar, and Paccar, it began to guarantee the resale values of the trucks it sold. Although Freightliner's market share increased sharply in 1999, the strategy had a disastrous effect on the company's finances. At the end of 2001, the commercial vehicle division of DaimlerChrysler reported an operating loss in the billions, thanks in part to the guaranteed payments. At the end of the day, companies should be focused on chasing sustainable profits, not market share.

Finding Opportunities in Industrial Materials

To identify industries in the industrial materials sector with the best long-term fundamentals, figure out which industries have already undergone significant consolidation. Then, look for the low-cost producer relative to domestic and foreign competitors, and check that it is in excellent financial health and has additional revenue streams from value-added products or services that supply a variety of industries. Finally, determine what you think the company's stock is worth, subtract a fair margin of safety, and wait for a good buying opportunity.

Investor's Checklist: Industrial Materials

▶ This is a very traditional Old Economy sector, with many hard assets and high fixed costs.

▶ Industrial materials are divided into commodity producers (steel, chemicals) and producers of noncommodity value-added goods and services (machinery, some specialty chemicals).

▶ Buyers of commodities choose their product on price—otherwise, commodities are the same product, regardless of who makes them.

▶ The sales and profits of companies in this sector are very sensitive to the business cycle.

▶ Very few industrial materials companies have any competitive advantages; the exceptions are those in concentrated industries (e.g., defense), those with a specialized niche product (e.g., Alcoa, some chemicals makers), and, above all, those that can produce their goods at the lowest cost (e.g., Nucor).

▶ Only the most efficient producers will survive a downturn: The best bet is to be the low-cost producer and owe little debt.

▶ Asset turnover (total asset turnover [TATO] and fixed asset turnover [FATO]) measure a manufacturing firm's efficiency.

▶ Watch out for industrial firms with too much debt, large underfunded pension plans, and big acquisitions that distract management.

25

Energy

ALTHOUGH ENERGY CAN be harvested from myriad sources—coal, nuclear, hydroelectric, wind, solar—nothing can come close to challenging the dominance of oil and gas as a source of energy. Roughly two-thirds of the world's energy needs are supplied by oil and gas—not only to propel our cars and heat our homes, but also to fuel a large and growing number of electric power plants. It's no coincidence that the biggest companies in the energy sector are oil companies, such as ExxonMobil and BP.

From the Ground

Most of the energy we use starts out under the ground, locked up in the hydrocarbons of dead plants and animals. Finding and mining this oil and gas, known as exploration and production, is how energy companies create a great deal of value.

In oil and gas, a large percentage of the world's resources are under countries that are members of the Organization of Petroleum Exporting Countries (OPEC) cartel, primarily in the Middle East. While this creates plenty of

---

Paul Larson with Pat Dorsey.

political issues, OPEC's existence is also a large benefit to the companies digging up the oil. OPEC's goal is to maintain industrywide profitability by keeping commodity prices artificially high, achieved by coordinating and limiting supply. Though OPEC's members often cheat on their quotas, the cartel is extremely successful at manipulating commodity markets for the industry's benefit.

While the BPs and ExxonMobils of the world (the so-called *major integrated* energy companies) are involved in pumping oil and gas from the ground, some companies focus specifically on this activity, which is usually called *exploration and production* or the *upstream* portion of the industry. Although OPEC's production limits help these firms as well, they don't have the diverse assets of the major integrated firms. As a result, the volatility of commodity prices against the backdrop of a largely fixed cost structure makes profits wildly variable from one year to the next for firms that focus on exploration and production.

One question that inevitably pops into every energy investor's head is, "Will we run out?" Although there is indeed a finite amount of oil and gas on the planet, it will not be depleted in our lifetimes and probably not the lifetimes of our grandchildren, either. Technology has done an excellent job of making oil available that was previously thought to be inaccessible, such as deep under the ocean. Though some established areas, such as the Alaskan North Slope and the North Sea, are today starting to see diminished production, new finds and improved technologies continue to add to proven reserves at a faster rate than production is depleting them.

To the Pipelines

Once petroleum is lifted from the ground, it must be transported to refineries and then again to the end users. Although ships play an important role, pipelines are an often-overlooked method of transportation. In the United States, pipelines and the rates they can charge are regulated by the Federal Energy Regulatory Commission and various state agencies. Though revenue from a pipeline tends not to grow much from year to year, the vast majority of pipelines generate positive cash flow and provide services that are difficult to duplicate.

Pipelines also tend to be one of the energy businesses that are least sensitive to commodity prices. As long as commodity prices stay away from their extremes and volumes stay relatively consistent, pipelines are typically very profitable assets for a company to own. Major integrated oil companies generally own portions of many of the pipelines they use, but there are also several large independent pipeline companies in existence, such as Kinder Morgan.

To the Refineries

Once oil and gas makes it to the refineries, it is said to be *downstream*. Refineries break apart crude oil into its component parts and refine it into end products, such as gasoline, jet fuel, and heavy lubricants. Although there are a handful of independent refiners, most refineries are part of major integrated oil companies. For instance, ExxonMobil, which has some of the largest reserves in the ground, is also the largest refiner in the industry.

Over the long term, refining is typically a less profitable business than getting oil out of the ground because there is no refining cartel maintaining profits. Refining profit margins also tend to be cyclical, though the cycles do not necessarily happen with the same frequency as commodity prices.

To the Consumers

The other portion of *downstream* operations is called *marketing,* which includes operating convenience stations, as well as marketing fuels for industrial uses and electricity production. Sometimes service stations are owned by small independent marketers who franchise brands from the big oil companies, and other times the major integrated oil companies own and operate the stations themselves. ExxonMobil and Royal Dutch/Shell are some of the largest marketers of fuel, each with nearly 50,000 stations around the globe selling their brands.

Providing the Services

Oil and gas is such a big business that there is an entire industry focused on providing products and services to the oil companies. Typical services that the oil companies tend to outsource include seismic studies to find the oil as well as services related to drilling and maintaining wells. Halliburton, Schlumberger, and Baker Hughes are some of the giants of oil services.

While the oil companies themselves have long histories of high profitability, most oil services firms have had a much tougher time creating value for shareholders. This is because the services industry tends to be highly competitive, and economic moats are difficult to come by. Unlike the oil producers, the oil services companies do not reap the benefits created by the OPEC cartel.

The financials show what a tough industry oil services can be. Of the top four oil services firms we covered at this writing, none had earned above their cost of capital over the past five-year period. Profitability tends to be only mediocre in the boom years when oil prices are high, but bottom lines have tended to dip into the red when prices were low. The net effect has been an industry that has struggled to create any value for its shareholders.

In addition, the health of the industry tends to be extremely cyclical, with short-term demand for drilling services and equipment highly volatile and dependent on commodity oil and gas prices. When oil prices are high—as they were in 2000—Baker Hughes' phones are ringing off the hook with oil producers scrambling to drill more wells so they can get more oil to market while profits are high. But when oil prices tank to near $10 a barrel—as they did in 1998—demand can quickly evaporate and come to a grinding halt. Budgets for new drilling are often the first to be cut when oil companies are operating with lean cash flow. This makes the stocks volatile in the short term as the markets try to guess the next cyclical movement, while long-term investors are hampered by the red ink typically created in the cyclical lows.

Luckily, there are some bright spots in the industry because long-run demand for advanced oil services should increase as oil companies have to dig in more far-flung places and at deeper depths to find and produce from fresh oil fields. There are also significant opportunities today in newly opened markets such as Russia and Iraq, where the reserves are large but the production technology is outdated. Although there will inevitably be some bumps along the road when oil prices are low, we expect modest long-term sales growth for the overall oil services field. But it will continue to be difficult for companies in the services industry to parlay this growth into higher profitability because profits will likely continue to be competed away.

The Impact of Commodity Prices

As you might guess, commodity prices have a huge influence on the industry's health and how it operates. For oil companies, the amount of oil pumped from the ground in any given day is largely fixed, but the value of that black gold is highly variable. In addition, with a large percentage of operating costs also fixed, the oil business carries a large degree of inherent operating leverage.

Consider an oil company that can get oil from the ground to a refiner at an average cost of $15 a barrel. This cost is largely fixed, regardless of the price of crude. If crude is at $18 a barrel, the oil company makes $3 a barrel in profits. However, if oil takes off to $30 a barrel, the company makes $15 per barrel, or five times as much as it did at $18 a barrel, even though its revenue has less than doubled.

Figure 25.1 summarizes how commodity oil prices impact profits. Although other factors can come into play, the fact remains that commodity prices are the biggest influence on the sector's financial health at any given moment.

Not all oil, and not all oil companies, are created equal. For example, some crude in the Middle East can be brought to market for well under $10 a barrel. Meanwhile, some Canadian oil extracted from oil sands costs twice as

Profitability Levels for Different Segments of Oil Industry

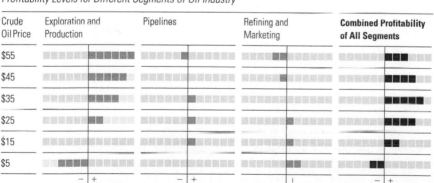

Figure 25.1   How crude oil prices affect the profitability of an oil company's different segments.
Source: Morningstar, Inc.

much to produce. When oil prices are high, oil companies can afford to produce in areas that might otherwise be uneconomical. Beyond dramatically impacting the oil company's financial statements, commodity prices also greatly influence how and where oil is produced.

Refining profit margins are much less dependent on commodity prices. High crude prices raise the cost of the refiners' raw goods, but some of this can be passed along to consumers. How much can be passed along is a function of the health of the global economy, as well as how much or little excess refining capacity there is at any given moment.

Though such a heavy reliance on commodity prices can make profits of energy firms highly variable from one quarter to the next, the average long-term profitability is very handsome. It's no coincidence that of the seven global companies that made more than $8 billion in profits in 2001, three were oil companies. If the long-term economics of the business were not attractive, the industry would not be as huge as it is today.

Economic Moats in Energy

It's not easy to create a lasting economic moat in an industry that's so strongly affected by commodity prices, but a few energy firms have managed to do so. Here's how.

Common Investing Pitfall: Being Faked Out by the Cycle

The energy sector is prone to intense cyclicality. Small changes in available supply and market demand tend to have an oversized effect on commodity prices and profits. However, neither cyclical peaks nor valleys tend to last very long. It is important to realize this before investing in the sector. Otherwise, you might be tempted to sell when the sector is doing relatively poorly (when things are about to begin looking up again) or buy at the peak when the companies are reaping a windfall (when growth is about to go into reverse). For example, ExxonMobil might have looked expensive in 1999 when it traded at more than 30 times trailing earnings that were depressed by the cyclical lows. However, earnings rebounded sharply, and the stock has outperformed the market since then. In general, crude above $30 a barrel represents a cyclical peak, near $10, a trough.

Organization of Petroleum Exporting Countries (OPEC)

By far, the most significant factor today that helps the companies that produce oil is the OPEC cartel. Though the cartel controls only a bit over a third of the world's oil output, the energy markets tend to be highly sensitive to small disruptions and spikes in supply. This gives OPEC more than enough power to manipulate commodity prices for the entire industry's benefit, keeping long-term commodity prices above the long-term costs to produce the commodities.

In addition, with reserves in OPEC's member countries far outstripping current production, it looks as though the cartel's influence will not be diminished soon, even with its member countries tending to slightly cheat on their quotas. If anything, OPEC's influence will strengthen over time as non-OPEC reserves continue to be depleted at a faster rate than OPEC reserves.

OPEC's goal, at this writing, is to keep oil prices in the $20 to $28 a barrel range. Below this range, profitability starts to suffer. Above $30, volumes suffer as consumers start to conserve and global economies start to sputter. To understand just how beneficial it is for energy investors to have OPEC influencing commodity prices, take the cartel's $20 to $28 target range and consider that most oil companies are profitable as long as oil prices stay above the mid-teens. The bottom line is that OPEC is highly beneficial to the industry's profitability and is one of the primary reasons the oil companies have been very solid investments.

Though OPEC has been successful at boosting commodity prices, its power over the market is not absolute. After all, OPEC's members can each cut only so much, and cuts don't always make an immediate impact. Moreover, when oil companies operate in OPEC-member nations, they are occasionally required to limit what they pump to maintain quotas. Still, this is a small inconvenience relative to the benefits the industry receives from the cartel's existence.

Economies of Scale

As in any other commodity industry, economies of scale play a major role in the profitability of energy companies. While costs upstream (finding and drilling oil) are largely a function of geology and geography of a company's reserves, keeping costs down can still provide a competitive advantage here. Downstream (refining and marketing), however, economies of scale are critically important because it is just about the only meaningful economic moat a company can build.

The fact that economies of scale play a major role in the industry can plainly be seen in the financial statements of the oil companies. Profitability and returns on invested capital are highly correlated to a firm's size. Larger companies have greater sway with suppliers, can spread overhead costs over a bigger base, and can generally ride out cyclical lows better.

Hallmarks of Success for Energy Companies

Oil companies have typically been successful at adding value for their shareholders. Here are some characteristics we look for in the industry.

Strong Financial Track Record

Over a complete cycle (e.g., five years), has a company been able to profit? For an integrated oil company such as ExxonMobil or BP, we want to see profits even during years when oil prices sag. The year 1998, when crude neared $10 a barrel, is a good barometer here. For a company that does only exploration and production and has no refining, dipping into the red during lean years is not disastrous as long as it can generate oversized profits during the boom years, such as 2000. The higher the profitability and the longer the track record, the better.

Clean Balance Sheet

Because they operate in a cyclical sector, it's important that companies have the financial wherewithal to make it through the lean times that periodically hit. This is especially true for companies focused on exploration and production. Growing while staying away from debt can be done, as ExxonMobil and Shell's essentially debt-free balance sheets prove. A debt-to-equity ratio below 1.0 is preferable.

Reserve Replacement Ratio Greater than 1.0

The reserve replacement ratio is the amount of new oil a company has found in a period divided by the amount of oil it has produced during that same period. If a company is pumping more than it's finding, reserves (which represent future production) will shrink. It may then need to spend more on exploration or acquisitions of existing fields to maintain revenues.

Shareholder-Friendly Uses of Cash Flow

The energy sector is mature, so steady firms such as the major integrated companies generate far more cash flow than can economically be reinvested in the business. Most good oil companies should pay a stout dividend and/or be repurchasing their shares while still spending on growth opportunities.

Risks in the Energy Sector

As with any sector, investors in energy face a number of risks. Perhaps the largest risk is the OPEC cartel losing its influence over the commodity markets. If that happened, long-term profitability would suffer greatly because commodity prices would float down to a level much closer to production costs. This could happen if one of OPEC's larger members, such as Saudi Arabia or Iran, decided to break rank and sell into the market at will. We do not see this as likely, however, because all the members of OPEC benefit from the cartel's existence, and their financial interests are aligned with OPEC's continued success.

Russia also is a threat to OPEC because it is the country with the largest reserves outside the cartel. Russia's output suffered in the 1990s because of the economic and political upheaval in the country, but its output has been on the rise in recent years. In 2002, Russia produced more than 8 million barrels a day, in the same ballpark as Saudi Arabia's output. While Russia's increased role as a key oil exporter lessens OPEC's influence, Russia's economy is also tied closely to the fortunes of the oil industry, and the country has shown a willingness to trim supply when prices are low.

There is also significant political risk in the energy industry. With many operations in numerous politically unstable countries, there is always the risk that a company will get kicked out, have its taxes raised exponentially, or otherwise have its assets impaired.

Finally, there is the chance that some technology will be developed in the future that could alter how the world gets its energy. The dream for cleaner and cheaper sources of energy will never die, and it will probably be realized at some point. Luckily for investors in the sector, there is nothing yet on the horizon that will change the world's addiction to oil and gas.

Conclusion

Even though there are certainly risks to be considered in the energy industry, those same risks have existed for decades and have not stopped the industry from creating hundreds of billions of dollars of value for their shareholders. Energy stocks have generally been outstanding investments for more than a century, and we think that this positive environment will persist for the foreseeable future. Over the long term, energy stocks should provide investors with continued strong returns, and it is an industry worth getting to know a little better.

Investor's Checklist: Energy

▶ The profitability of the energy sector is highly dependent on commodity prices. Commodity prices are cyclical, as are the sector's profits. It's better to buy when prices are at a cyclical low than when they're high and hitting the headlines.

▶ Even though the sector is largely cyclical, many energy companies keep their bottom lines black during the troughs. Look for this characteristic in your energy sector investments.

▶ OPEC is a highly beneficial force in the energy sector because it keeps commodity prices above its costs. It is worth keeping tabs on the cartel's strength.

▶ Because of OPEC, we view exploration and production as a much more attractive area than refining and marketing.

▶ Working in a commodity market, economies of scale are just about the only way to achieve a competitive advantage. As such, bigger is generally better because firms with greater heft tend to be more profitable.

▶ Keep an eye on reserves and reserve growth because these are the hard assets the company will mine for future revenue.

▶ Companies with strong balance sheets will weather cyclical lows better than those burdened with debt. Look for companies that don't need to take on additional debt to invest in new projects while also paying dividends or repurchasing shares.

26

Utilities

UTILITIES WERE ONCE considered to be conservative investments. They were the preferred investments for "widows and orphans" because they were thought to be a safe way to generate income via dividends. That is no longer the case today.

Deregulation has changed everything for this former safe haven. Many utility companies have gone from operating regulated monopolies with guaranteed returns to operating in a highly competitive and volatile commodity market with high fixed costs. Competition in the industry will only increase as deregulation continues to expand. The rules have changed, and the investment attractiveness of the entire sector has diminished as a result.

Electricity Primer

Though there are a handful of pure gas and water companies—Nicor and Philadelphia Suburban are two examples—utilities that provide electric service dominate the ranks of the publicly traded companies in the utilities sector.

———
Paul Larson with Pat Dorsey.

The electric utility business can be divided into essentially three parts: generation, transmission, and distribution. For most of the twentieth century, utilities operated as regulated monopolies, and most had all three parts of the business integrated into one entity. But because of today's regulatory environment, many utilities have been forced to separate their operations into more focused components. Some utilities operating in states that have not deregulated still operate as essentially integrated entities, while other utilities are focused on only one or two of the main functional areas.

Generation

These are the operations that run the power plants themselves: coal/natural gas/uranium in; electricity out. A 1992 federal law forced utilities to split their generating assets from the rest of their businesses, which set the stage for deregulation at the state level. Some states have full competition in electrical generation with rates set by the free market, while others still have fully regulated wholesale rates. In states with full deregulation, the distribution arm of the utilities often buys power from third-party providers who are in competition with their generation arm. In addition, some states such as Pennsylvania allow customers to choose their generators. A customer could, for instance, choose to pay a premium and get power purely generated from wind and solar.

Generation is perhaps the area that has the greatest competition today because electricity is a pure commodity, and the barriers to entry are comparatively low and falling. It is also the area that is furthest along in the deregulation process, opening the door for independent power producers. With competition heating up and profitability falling, it's becoming increasingly difficult to make a profit.

Transmission

Transmission is the business of transporting electricity over long distances— think tall high-tension/high-voltage wires. Some states have forced the utilities to sell their transmission assets to third-party operators who operate regional grids, but often the utilities keep their equity stakes in the transmission companies. Regardless of who operates or owns the grid, rates are regulated, and there is open access for generators. There was not always open access to the grid, and this is a cornerstone of deregulation creating more competition.

Transmission operations typically have fairly wide economic moats because there are huge barriers to entry due to large upfront costs as well as the NIMBY (not in my back yard) effect. However, with rates and returns regulated, companies have a difficult time creating excess value.

Distribution

Distribution-related companies own and service the *final mile* of cable that brings power to the individual homes and businesses. Even in states where customers can choose their generator, the operators of the final mile still handle the customer service and billing, in addition to charging for use of their systems.

Distribution is where utilities have their widest economic moat because they tend to own monopolies with essentially no alternatives, even in deregulated states. But the natural monopolies here also lend this area to the most government control. This means the rates customers are charged are regulated and returns on investment capped, making it difficult for utilities to parlay their economic moat into excess returns. Without excess returns, creating shareholder value is an uphill battle.

Regulation, Regulation, Regulation

Just as location is the primary driver of value in real estate, regulation is perhaps the single most important factor shaping the utility sector. Companies in the sector face heavy regulation on multiple levels, and the changing regulatory structure has dramatically altered the competitive dynamics of the industry.

From an investment perspective, the most important regulation is done at the state level because the states decide how utilities are structured, what degree of competition will be allowed, and what rates will be charged. Today, the structures are all over the board—some states still have regulated monopolies at essentially all levels, while others have portions that operate in totally free market conditions. Each state has a different structure, and those structures are in the process of changing.

The next most important level of regulation comes at the federal level. Through the Department of Energy (DOE) and Federal Energy Regulatory Commission (FERC), the basic ground rules for state regulation are set. It is largely the FERC's rule makings that got the deregulation ball rolling following 1992.

Finally, most utilities also face operating regulations at the federal level. The Environmental Protection Agency (EPA) wields a great deal of power because it regulates the levels of emissions power plants are allowed to release to the atmosphere. This is important because coal-fired plants still represent the majority of the generating capacity in the country. Those with nuclear-powered plants also must operate under the watchful eye of the Nuclear Regulatory Commission (NRC).

The point to remember is that legislators and regulators have enormous influence in the sector. No fundamental analysis of a utility company would be complete without understanding the basics of regulation and how that regulation affects the company's operations and its competitive positioning. It's not an easy task, making utilities much more complex to analyze than it might seem on the surface.

Financial Characteristics of Utilities

Most utilities carry a great deal of leverage, both operationally and financially. On the operations side, most of the costs are fixed, with fuel being the only significant variable cost. This operational leverage is not very important because, beyond normal seasonal patterns, demand for power does not change much one way or the other over time.

The financial component of their leverage is much more important today. It is easy to understand why utilities formerly welcomed taking on massive debt. With regulators capping rates, companies found that their profit margins and the allowed return on assets were kept positive but comparatively low. An easy way to increase the return on equity (as well as earnings and dividends per share) was to crank up the financial leverage.

From the lender's perspective, the utilities operated stable businesses with largely predictable cash flows, making servicing the interest easy. They were also eager to lend because the loans were backed by hard assets such as power plants and real estate that made for excellent collateral.

Unfortunately, many utilities are today struggling with their legacy of high debt. Though debt was not so important when the sector was more regulated,

Common Investing Pitfall: The Unsafe Dividend

Many investors are drawn to the utilities sector because of the generous dividend yields many of the stocks in the sector pay. However, dividends are only as safe as the financial health of the companies that pay them. With the utilities sector as a whole paying out roughly three-quarters of its earnings as dividends, the high payout ratio does raise the risk of dividends being cut when times are tough. Watch out if the payout ratio creeps above 90 percent or so or if the debt-to-total-capital ratio rises above 50 percent.

The saying "If it seems too good to be true, it probably is" applies to high dividend yields. If a stock's yield seems ridiculously high—for example, 15 percent when comparable investments are yielding only 5 percent—it's probably a sign the company has run into some sort of trouble. After all, when companies run into trouble, their stocks tend to fall, which pushes up their yields. In addition, an easy way for a struggling firm to conserve cash is by cutting dividend payments.

the landscape has changed. Instead of operating stable businesses, deregulation has greatly increased competition, making debt a dangerous drain on cash flow instead of a mere booster of returns.

Hallmarks of Success for Utility Companies

Though most investors should treat utilities with caution given the changing regulatory structure, there are solid companies in the industry that could make for good investments if bought at the right price. Look for the following characteristics.

Stable, Favorable Regulatory Structure

Utilities that operate in states where competition is minimal are positioned much better than those operating in states where deregulation has opened markets. In general, this means the Southeast and the Plains states are the most attractive because they are the furthest behind in deregulating and are in no hurry to do so. On the other hand, the Northeast and Southwest are the least regulated and least stable for utilities. For example, Southern Company, which operates primarily in the Southeast and has good relationships with its regulators, is much more attractive to us than a company such as Southern California Edison, which must deal with the volatile California regulatory and political environment that already bankrupted it once.

Strong Balance Sheet

Having large amounts of cash and comparatively lower debt levels is always attractive, but it is of great importance when going through turbulent change as the utility sector is. The average utility has a debt-to-total capital ratio of 60 percent, and we'd prefer to own companies with less debt.

Sticking to the Basics

We've noticed that companies that have attempted to enter industries outside their core businesses have tended to do much worse than companies that stayed focused. Ventures into areas such as building international power plants, speculative energy trading, and telecommunications services have nearly bankrupted several utility and energy companies. Utility companies that were comfortable with their identities as utility companies and stayed focused on what they did best have tended to do much better.

Risks in the Utilities Sector

As we mentioned at the beginning of this chapter, what was once one of the most stable and risk-free sectors became a sector fraught with risk. Unfortunately, the main driver of the increased risk for utilities—changing regulation—is still alive and well today.

For companies that operate in areas that have not deregulated yet, deregulation getting back on track is a looming risk. Increased competition is never a good thing for a company or its finances. In the utilities sector, the federal framework is already in place for states to deregulate should they so choose. Though California's energy crisis created by its poorly designed regulatory scheme caused deregulation to stall in many states, other states such as Pennsylvania have seen much more success in their deregulation efforts. As other states meet with success, the pressure will increase on those regulated states to finally take the deregulation plunge.

Another risk all utilities face—deregulated or not—is environmental risk. There is no getting around the fact that most power plants generate pollution of one sort or another. Should environmental regulations tighten, those operating power plants could be forced to spend on expensive upgrades to reduce their emissions.

Finally, there is significant liquidity risk in the entire sector: If firms have problems rolling over their debts when they come due, they could face a liquidity crunch that would cause them to take value-destroying measures. Whether it's taking on high-interest debt, selling assets on the cheap, or participating in dilutive secondary offerings, once a company has lost the confidence of the debt markets, it is a very difficult and expensive hole to get out of.

The Big Picture

The importance of deregulation in shaping the industry is paramount. The days of peace and stability in the utility sector are history, and companies are going to be forced to sink or swim in the competitive waters. A handful of companies are likely to do well for their shareholders, but we encourage investors to be extremely picky when it comes to buying utilities.

Investor's Checklist: Utilities

▶ Utilities are no longer the safe havens they once were. Treat them with an appropriate amount of caution.

▶ The competitive structure utilities must operate under is largely set at the state level. Some states have gone far along the deregulation path; others have utilities that are fully regulated. Keeping track of changing regulations in different states can be maddening, but it is necessary to understand the sector.

▶ Regulated utilities tend to have wide economic moats because they operate as monopolies, but it's important to keep in mind regulation does not allow these firms to parlay this advantage into excess returns. In addition, regulation can (and often does) change.

▶ Another risk all utilities face—deregulated or not—is environmental risk. Most power plants generate pollution of some kind. Should environmental regulations tighten, costs could go up.

► Utilities have a great deal of leverage, both operational and financial. This is not so important for regulated firms, but it exponentially raises risk for companies facing increasing competition.

► If you buy a utility for its dividend, make sure the firm has the financial wherewithal to keep paying it.

► Utilities that operate in stable regulatory environments with relatively strong balance sheets while staying focused on their core businesses are the best bets in the sector.

Appendix

At Morningstar, we're huge advocates of low-cost investing, which means trading infrequently. One of the best ways to find companies that can stay in your portfolio for a long time is to look for firms with strong competitive advantages, or wide economic moats. The list that follows contains all of the companies in Morningstar's coverage universe that we think fit this description—ones that are likely to keep competitors at bay for years to come. It's not an exhaustive list, of course, but it's a great starting point if you're looking for high-quality companies to put on your watchlist.

Sector	Wide Moat Company	TTM Sales ($Millions)
Health Care	Abbott Laboratories (ABT)	18,076
	Alcon (ACL)	3,009
	Amgen (AMGN)	5,523
	AstraZeneca PLC ADR (AZN)	17,841
	Biomet (BMET)	1,290
	Boston Scientific (BSX)	3,051
	Bristol-Myers Squibb (BMY)	18,169
	Eli Lilly & Company (LLY)	11,406
	Genentech (DNA)	2,901

(continued)

(Continued)

Sector	Wide Moat Company	TTM Sales ($Millions)
Health Care (cont.)	GlaxoSmithKline PLC ADR (GSK)	29,541
	Guidant (GDT)	3,415
	Biogen IDEC	442
	Johnson & Johnson (JNJ)	37,376
	Medtronic (MDT)	7,309
	Merck (MRK)	53,009
	Novartis AG ADR (NVS)	18,933
	Pfizer (PFE)	33,151
	Sanofi-Synthelabo ADR (SNY)	5,785
	Schering-Plough (SGP)	10,381
	Stryker (SYK)	3,156
	UnitedHealth Group (UNH)	25,982
	Zimmer Holdings (ZMH)	1,443
Consumer Services	H&R Block (HRB)	3,742
	Home Depot (HD)	58,247
	Lowe's Companies (LOW)	26,491
	Sysco (SYY)	25,479
	Wal-Mart Stores (WMT)	246,525
	Walgreen (WAG)	30,564
	eBay (EBAY)	1,445
Business Services	Automatic Data Processing (ADP)	7,081
	Cintas (CTAS)	2,614
	Equifax (EFX)	1,152
	Expeditors International of WA (EXPD)	2,404
	First Data (FDC)	7,905
	Fiserv (FISV)	2,644
	Getty Images (GYI)	479
	IMS Health (RX)	1,452
	Moody's (MCO)	1,070
	Paychex (PAYX)	1,054
	Total System Services (TSS)	955
	United Parcel Service B (UPS)	31,708
Financial Services, Insurance/Asset Management	AFLAC (AFL)	10,693
	Alliance Capital Management Holding LP (AC)	167
	American Express (AXP)	24,071
	Berkshire Hathaway (BRK.B)	44,255
	Blackrock (BLK)	574
	Eaton Vance (EV)	512

(Continued)

Sector	Wide Moat Company	TTM Sales ($Millions)
Financial Services, Insurance/Asset Management (cont.)	Marsh & McLennan Companies (MMC)	10,440
	Progressive (PGR)	9,946
	SLM (SLM)	3,119
Financial Services, Banks/Finance	Bank of New York (BK)	5,697
	Capital One Financial (COF)	9,883
	Citigroup (C)	93,101
	Fannie Mae (FNM)	53,470
	Fifth Third Bancorp (FITB)	6,937
	Freddie Mac (FRE)	8,986
	Northern Trust (NTRS)	2,709
	State Street (STT)	5,383
	Wells Fargo (WFC)	28,881
Software	Adobe Systems (ADBE)	1,194
	Autodesk (ADSK)	825
	Intuit (INTU)	1,495
	Microsoft (MSFT)	31,375
Hardware	Applied Materials (AMAT)	5,116
	Cisco Systems (CSCO)	19,005
	Dell Computers (DELL)	35,404
	IBM (IBM)	83,221
	Intel (INTC)	26,734
	Linear Technology (LLTC)	582
	Maxim Integrated Products (MXIM)	1,138
	Qualcomm (QCOM)	3,785
Media	Comcast A (CMCSA)	12,460
	Dow Jones & Company (DJ)	1,525
	John Wiley & Sons A (JW.A)	840
	McGraw-Hill Companies (MHP)	4,804
	Washington Post (WPO)	2,584
Telecommunications	None	
Consumer Goods	Altria Group (MO)	79,224
	Anheuser-Busch Companies (BUD)	13,710
	Avon Products (AVP)	6,326
	Cedar Fair LP (FUN)	503
	Coca-Cola (KO)	19,983
	Colgate-Palmolive (CL)	9,448

(continued)

(Continued)

Sector	Wide Moat Company	TTM Sales ($Millions)
Consumer Goods (cont.)	Gillette (G)	8,692
	Harley-Davidson (HDI)	4,517
	Hershey Foods (HSY)	4,085
	International Speedway A (ISCA)	556
	PepsiCo (PEP)	25,331
	Procter & Gamble (PG)	42,626
	Wm. Wrigley Jr. (WWY)	2,820
Industrial Materials	3M Company (MMM)	16,760
	General Dynamics (GD)	14,148
	Gentex (GNTX)	422
	Pitney Bowes (PBI)	4,451
	United Technologies (UTX)	28,540
Energy	Kinder Morgan (KMI)	1,081
	Kinder Morgan Energy Partners (KMP)	5,796
Utilities	None	

Wide moat companies within each sector. *Source:* Morningstar, Inc.

Recommended Readings

The Essays of Warren Buffett: Lessons for Corporate America by Warren E. Buffett and Lawrence A. Cunningham, 2001. Published by Lawrence A. Cunningham. Composed of excerpts from Buffett's writings over the years and nicely organized by topic, this book is endlessly provoking.

Finance & Accounting for Nonfinancial Managers by Steven A. Finkler, 2002. Published by Prentice Hall Trade. An easy-to-read introduction to accounting.

Common Stocks and Uncommon Profits and Other Writings by Philip A. Fisher, 1996. Published by John Wiley & Sons. The classic text—one that was a big influence on Warren Buffett—on how to spot great companies.

The Intelligent Investor: A Book of Practical Counsel by Benjamin Graham, 1985. Published by HarperCollins. A timeless book on risk and investments, with advice for both the defensive investor and the "enterprising" investor.

Value Investing: From Graham to Buffett and Beyond by Bruce C. N. Greenwald, Judd Kahn, Paul D. Sonkin, and Michael van Biema, 2001. Published by John Wiley & Sons. A fresh look at the mechanics of valuing companies, with plenty of concrete examples.

Analysis for Financial Management by Robert C. Higgins, 2000. Published by McGraw-Hill/Irwin. We haven't found a better introduction to financial statements and profitability analysis.

Buffett: The Making of an American Capitalist by Roger Lowenstein, 1996. Published by Doubleday. A great biography by a wonderful writer. You can't call yourself a serious investor and not be a student of Buffett.

Advances in Behavioral Finance edited by Richard H. Thaler, 1993. Published by Russell Sage Foundation. This collection of academic papers and essays covers the major topics in behavioral finance—a branch of finance that considers how people actually behave, quirks and all.

How to Buy Stocks by Brendan C. Boyd and Louis Engel, 1991. Published by Bantam Books. If you're new to stock investing, this is a good place to start. A useful overview of how the market works.

Financial Shenanigans by Howard M. Schilit, 2002. Published by McGraw-Hill Professional Publishing. The definitive guide to avoiding accounting fraud and detecting questionable reporting practices.

Letters to Shareholders, Berkshire Hathaway Annual Reports www.berkshirehathaway.com; www.berkshirehathaway.com/letters/letters.html

Decision Traps: The Ten Barriers to Brilliant Decision-Making and How to Overcome Them by J. Edward Russo and Paul J. H. Schoemaker, 1989. Published by Doubleday. This book sets the stage for behavioral finance.

Why Smart People Make Big Money Mistakes and How to Correct Them: Lessons From the New Science of Behavioral Economics by Gary Belsky and Thomas Gilovich, 2000. Published by Simon & Schuster. An easy read that introduces the basics of behavioral finance.

A Random Walk Down Wall Street by Burton G. Malkiel, 2003. Published by W. W. Norton & Company. This comprehensive and lucid look at what makes markets tick is a must for any well-read investor.

Stocks for the Long Run: The Definitive Guide to Financial Market Returns and Long-Term Investment Strategies by Jeremy J. Siegel, 1998. Published by McGraw-Hill Professional Publishing. The classic case for equities as a long-term investment. Full of authoritative data and historical perspective.

Devil Take the Hindmost: A History of Financial Speculation by Edward Chancellor, 2000. Published by Plume. A fascinating history of financial manias.

When Genius Failed: The Rise and Fall of Long-Term Capital Management by Roger Lowenstein, 2001. Published by Random House Trade Paperbacks. This story of the rise and fall of Long-Term Capital Management reads like a thriller. A fantastic read.

The Money Masters by John Train, 1994. Published by HarperBusiness. An interesting collection of short biographies that gives a brief look at the strategies of nine great investors.

Damn Right: Behind the Scenes with Berkshire Hathaway Billionaire Charlie Munger by Janet Lowe, 2003. Published by John Wiley & Sons. Warren Buffett sidekick Charlie Munger stays in the shadow of his better-known partner, but his insights about investing are just as penetrating.

Morningstar Resources

IN ADDITION TO this book, Morningstar publishes a number of products for stock enthusiasts. There's something for everyone, from newsletters to sourcebooks. Most can be found at your local library, or you can call Morningstar to start your own subscriptions (866-608-9570).

Morningstar® StockInvestor™
Monthly newsletter offers 32 pages of stock investing help—including two Morningstar stock portfolios for different investment styles, comprehensive analysis of selected portfolio stocks, as well as the best thinking of Morningstar's 30 stock analysts on additional stock prospects, including what to buy or sell.

Morningstar® Buy/Sell Report
Morningstar's new eight-page newsletter tells readers which stocks to buy and which ones to sell—and most importantly, why. In addition, each month the editors recap their previous picks and any changes in their opinions or our analyses that investors need to know about.

Morningstar.com
Morningstar's Web site features investing information on stocks, funds, bonds, retirement planning, and more. In addition to powerful portfolio tools, investors will find daily articles by Morningstar analysts and editors, including Pat Dorsey. Much

information on the site is free, and there's a reasonably priced Premium Membership service for investors requiring more in-depth information and sophisticated analytical tools. (A free trial for Premium Membership is available.)

Morningstar® Stocks 500™
Annual book of full-page reports on 500 of the best and most popular stocks. The new edition appears in January of each year and includes complete year-end results of stocks covered, comprehensive financial data, and key data on industry performance.

Index